AGING AND DIVERSITY

AGING AND DIVERSITY

An Active Learning Experience

By

Stephen B. Fried
Park College

Chandra M. Mehrotra
The College of St. Scholastica

Taylor & Francis
Publishers since 1798

USA	Publishing Office:	Taylor & Francis 1101 Vermont Avenue, N.W., Suite 200 Washington, D.C. 20005-3521 Tel: (202) 289-2174 Fax: (202) 289-3665
	Distribution Center:	Taylor & Francis 1900 Frost Road, Suite 101 Bristol, PA 19007-1598 Tel: (215) 785-5800 Fax: (215) 785-5515
UK		Taylor & Francis Ltd. 1 Gunpowder Square London EC4A 3DE Tel: 171 583 0490 Fax: 171 583 0581

AGING AND DIVERSITY: An Active Learning Experience

2 3 4 5 6 7 8 9   EBEB   05 04 03 02

This book was set in Times Roman. The editors were Laura Haefner and Greg Edmondson. Cover design by Curtis Tow, Curtis Tow Graphics.

A CIP catalog record for this book is available from the British Library.
∞ The paper in this publication meets the requirements of the ANSI Standard Z39.48-1984 (Permanence of Paper)

Library of Congress Cataloging-in-Publication Data

Fried, Stephen.
   Aging and diversity: an active learning experience/Stephen B.
Fried, Chandra M. Mehrotra.
      p.   cm.
   Includes bibliographical references and index.

      1. Aged—United States.   2. Minority aged—United States.
3. Pluralism (Social sciences)   4. Intercultural communication.
I. Mehrotra, Chandra M.   II. Title.
HQ1061.F725   1994
305.26—dc21   97-30921
                                                                          CIP

ISBN 1-56032-475-9 (case)
ISBN 1-56032-476-7 (paper)

Dedication

To eight diverse elders: Janice Boswell, Surajo Devi, Dr. Humphrey Doermann, Carolyn Goodstein, Frances Lavine, Dr. M. Powell Lawton, Dr. C. Kermit Phelps, and Dorothy Rosenwald.

Contents

Foreword

I have read *Aging and Diversity: An Active Learning Experience* from multiple perspectives: as a teacher of college teachers, as a researcher in the area of student learning and college teaching, and as a former teacher of a course on the psychology of aging. From each of these perspectives I found that the authors, Stephen Fried and Chandra Mehrotra, provide exciting and worthwhile reading material.

As a teacher and as a researcher on learning and teaching, I was greatly impressed by the creative approaches the authors have used to ensure that students will learn, remember, and be able to use what is presented. The active learning exercises are among the most extensive of any book I have seen. They are both memorable and interesting. Any student who uses the opportunities provided will be helped to learn, understand, and retrieve what they need, whether for further learning or for applications in work dealing with diverse elders. The diversity theme illuminates the importance of culture and context in the behavior and experience of individuals as they grow older.

But I do not want my foreword to further delay your entry into the world of *Aging and Diversity*. Enjoy and learn!

W. J. McKeachie
Professor Emeritus
Department of Psychology
University of Michigan

Preface: Introduction for Instructors

As America continues to diversify, it is essential that gerontology students develop an understanding of how factors such as ethnicity, gender, social class, and religion affect aging. In order to better address the health and human service needs of a rapidly growing and more diversified segment of the population, education in gerontology needs to be provided from a multicultural perspective. An important factor complicating this need is the fact that there is a lack of research on the effects of diversity on a range of factors important to the study of aging. For example, with the exception of Black and Mexican American elders, the research data for ethnic elders are quite limited (Yeo, 1991). While this may, to some extent, be due to the limited support available for research in this area of inquiry, it may also be due to the special challenges faced by investigators interested in conducting research in ethnic communities. As Bengtson (1979) and Henderson (1994) remind us, this research is fraught with problems requiring special considerations, issues not usually treated in textbooks or courses in research methodology. For example, the perspective of the middle-class, White, Christian, nonimmigrant researcher or practitioner may be quite irrelevant to the life circumstances of ethnic elders, particularly those from minority racial backgrounds.

While in recent years we have witnessed increasing levels of interest in the topic of diversity, many college professors and in-service instructors teaching aging-related courses have had little or no formal preparation in diversity and aging. In addition, most educators have limited access to the instructional materials they can use to enhance the knowledge, attitudes, and skills of students and service providers on aging and diversity issues. Even when they are able to locate a relevant journal article or book, such sources seldom provide them with the guidance and support they need in designing classes that will engage students in developing the knowledge and attitudes essential for working with diverse elders. We have prepared this book to address these unmet needs.

Aging and Diversity: An Active Learning Experience can be used as a course text in gerontology, adult development and aging, gerontological nursing, social work, health education, public health, allied health, family studies, and other subjects dealing with the aging process and older adults. The book may also be useful as a resource for instructors of undergraduate or graduate courses, for in-service staff in preparing classes and workshops, for instructors' professional development, or for students' self-development. Each chapter of the book presents the content in a focus area and provides activities to engage the student in active learning. Text chapters cover the following topics: an overview of diversity and aging, psychological aging, issues in health and sexuality, caregiving, work and retirement, religion and spirituality, and death, dying, and grieving. The book is not intended as a synthesis of all relevant research, nor does it cover all of the possible relevant topics. Instead, our intent is to present material appropriate for providing undergraduates and service providers with concepts to guide them in developing a broad comprehension of elements of diversity and their impact on the lives of older adults in the United States.

The following are some guidelines, assumptions, and principles that we use and that you may find helpful in teaching about diversity and aging:

1. *Increase students' awareness of elements of their own diversity*. Diverse factors, like gender, ethnicity, religion, and social class, apply to each of us. Therefore, it is essential for students to have a good understanding of their own cultural traditions. Increasing this understanding will assist them in developing greater awareness of the ways in which their values and behaviors could enhance or impede their work with the diverse population of older adults.

2. *Broaden students' world view*. Students should be encouraged to identify and become knowledgeable about the cultures that surround the geographical area where they work or the cultures of other students attending their college or university. Since some students may have grown up in relatively homogeneous environments, college provides them their first experience in dealing with persons from a variety of ethnic groups, religions, or income levels. Clearly, it is to their advantage to learn more about psychological concerns, health beliefs and practices, caregiving preferences, work and retirement behaviors, religious and spiritual perspectives, and death, dying, and grieving issues germane to diverse American elders.

3. *Enhance culturally relevant skills and programs*. While the services available for older persons have increased dramatically in the past 20 years, little consideration is typically given to approaches that would be particularly effective for ethnic and minority elders. Therefore, students in academic and continuing education programs should be taught culturally relevant skills in order to develop competencies essential for designing, implementing, and evaluating effective programs for a diverse array of older adults.

4. *Promote an understanding of the life course perspective*. A life course perspective is essential for developing an understanding of the process of aging. Students need to learn that cohort, class, gender, ethnicity, and other elements of diversity influence an individual's life course. As an example, because of the influence of the group on the individual, the salience of the ethnicity variable is

evident in the many ways in which it impinges on life course components, whether physiological, social, or cultural (Barresi, 1987). In short, both college students and service providers should be aware of the necessity of approaching the unique world of diverse elders from a perspective that provides them a broad level of understanding of these factors and their interaction with each other.

5. *Foster a multiethnic perspective*. While it is important to present an in-depth examination of a specific ethnic group, such an approach ignores the reality of a pluralistic society. Providing instruction in diversity and aging that crosses racial and ethnic groups has a better chance of achieving its objective because it allows participants to develop an understanding of both commonalities and differences among diverse groups. A major emphasis of educational programs should be to help students discover the varied coping mechanisms that grow out of different traditions and learn how to mobilize them in service to older adults (Giordano, 1992). Participants need to be aware of how positive ethnic identity can contribute to higher self-esteem. It is critical that these positive aspects not be romanticized or neglected in discussion of the special problems of each diverse group. Instead, it is helpful to create an appropriate climate and to guide the participants to be more conscious of aspects of diversity that help older adults view themselves positively and enable them to cope effectively with the problems they face.

6. *Provide activity-based learning experiences*. Students engaging in learning about diversity and aging are themselves from diverse groups in terms of ethnicity, age, language, and so forth. Since different "people learn in different ways" (Meyers & Jones, 1993, p. 10), active learning strategies may prove to be extremely helpful in strengthening their education in diversity and aging. The following are among the salient characteristics of active learning: (a) More emphasis is placed on developing learners' skills than on simply transmitting information (Meyers & Jones, 1993); (b) students engage in higher order thinking (analysis, synthesis, and evaluation) (Meyers & Jones, 1993); (c) students participate in activities such as case studies, simulations, and small-group problem-solving discussions (Fried, 1988; Fried & Mehrotra, 1994; Fried, Van Booven, & MacQuarrie, 1993); and (d) increased focus is placed on students' exploration of personal values and attitudes (Bonwell & Eison, 1991).

In order to encourage active learning, we have included a number of individual and small-group exercises and assignments as well as comprehension tests throughout the book. Each chapter includes (a) a preview with orienting questions, (b) a narrative that includes an introduction and summary, (c) a number of learning activities and a quiz, and (d) suggested readings. For each of the active learning vehicles, we include the following: (a) purpose and desired learning outcomes; (b) approximate time required to complete the activity, which will vary from student to student; (c) procedure; and (d) the actual learning activity. Forms of experiential learning activities include interviews, role plays, case studies, and an assortment of other exercises to be completed in class or as homework assignments. Also, we include, as an Appendix, an evaluation form that can be used with any of the learning experiences. Some instructors may wish to have their students complete all of the activities, while others may decide to choose those activities that most particularly fit with their own teaching style and learning objectives. All of the experiences can be completed as part of a program of independent study or as self-development for instructors, practitioners, or students.

Instructors may find that certain active learning experiences are not suitable for some classes or for particular students, and they need to be sensitive to the fact that some students may be uncomfortable engaging in activities related to various topics (e.g., death and dying, family customs, sexuality, and so forth). Students' values and need for privacy should be respected. Also, some of the activities involve students in interviewing community or family members. Principles of confidentiality and informed consent should be shared with students before they initiate these activities. Instructors may wish to submit learning activities to their institutional review boards if doing so conforms with institutional policy.

We wish you great success in designing and implementing educational experiences for students, service providers, and others interested in learning about diversity and aging. We are interested in receiving your feedback about your experiences in using this book. The subject of diversity and aging is most exciting, and we hope that you and your students find it as stimulating, engaging, and enjoyable as we do!

Acknowledgments

This book could not have been completed without the assistance and support of many persons. Nancy Bois typed the entire manuscript through its various phases. Her insights, patience, and hard work made our long-distance collaboration manageable. Nancy has our utmost respect. The library staffs at Park College, The College of St. Scholastica, and Central Michigan University demonstrated exceptional competence in providing us with a wide variety of reference material in a timely fashion. We want to thank the following colleagues: Dr. Joseph Blount and Dr. G. Mack Winholtz of Park College, Dr. Theodore Albrecht of Kent State University, Dr. Steven Zarit of Pennsylvania State University, Dr. Margaret Gatz of the University of Southern California, and Dr. Daniel Pilon and Dr. Larry Goodwin of The College of St. Scholastica. Megumi Kondo designed the two learning activities concerning Japanese Americans. Dorothy Fried conducted interviews, which formed the basis for a case on a Filipino American family. Debra Venerable provided insights for the activity on an African American Baptist funeral. We offer our appreciation to Dr. Wilbert McKeachie for his kind foreword to our book. Elaine Pirrone, Bernadette Capelle, and Laura Haefner of Taylor & Francis gave us many valuable suggestions regarding the content and style of the book.

We wish to acknowledge the support we received through a Lilly Grant to Park College. We are grateful to the Blandin Foundation for the continuing opportunities it has provided Chandra Mehrotra for his work with the Native American communities of Minnesota. We are particularly indebted to the National Science Foundation for funding Summer Institutes on Teaching the Psychology of Aging. In 1992 and 1993, we became acquainted at the institutes directed by Chandra Mehrotra. The administrators of Park College and The College of St. Scholastica have encouraged and supported our scholarship in this endeavor. Through their feedback, our undergraduate students helped us to fine-tune the active learning experiences contained in this book.

Our families offered us encouragement and assistance in so many ways. Stephen Fried wishes to acknowledge Connie Boswell, his wife and best friend.

Connie provided the extra effort that made this project possible. Steve also wishes to acknowledge his three children, Katy, Kim, and Kurt, as well as his brother and sister-in-law, Michael and Dorothy Fried. Chandra Mehrotra expresses deep appreciation to Indra Mehrotra, his wife and best friend, for her enduring support. He also thanks their two children, Vijay and Gita, for their ongoing interest in his work.

We dedicate this book to eight diverse elders who have shown us, through the ways in which they conduct their lives, how to age successfully.

Chapter 1

An Introduction to Aging and Diversity

OVERVIEW

Demographics of American Elders

- What is the demographic composition of American elders?
- What percentage of the older population is composed of women and minorities?
- What will be the composition of the older population in the future?

The Elements of Diversity

- How can elements of diversity have physical, psychological, and social consequences?
- What are some important elements of diversity?
- Why are race and ethnicity primarily social constructs?
- What is the interactional nature between elements of diversity and aging?

Why Should We Focus on Diversity and Aging?

- Why will the number of minority elders continue to increase?
- Why does the relationship between ethnicity and aging vary across different groups and within the same group?
- What are some implications of the fact that older people from different groups may have different needs?
- Why is ethnicity not a fixed entity?
- How do elements of diversity affect life course and role transitions?

Diversity and Acculturation

- What is the acculturation continuum?
- What effect does English-language proficiency have on the acculturation of ethnic minorities?
- How is acculturation influenced by the cohort effect?

Ageism and Diversity
- What is ageism?
- Why is ageism sometimes observed among health care and social service professionals?
- What are some examples of how sexism and ageism combine in the use of language?

Summary

Diversity and Aging Quiz

Glossary

Suggested Readings

Key: Diversity and Aging Quiz

A BRIEF OVERVIEW OF SUBSEQUENT CHAPTERS

In the next six chapters of *Aging and Diversity: An Active Learning Experience,* we will devote attention to the following chapter topics: Psychological Aging, Issues in Health and Sexuality, Work and Retirement, Caregiving, Religion and Spirituality, and Death, Dying, and Grieving.

Through the use of narrative and a wide variety of active learning strategies, such as quizzes, case studies, and interviews, you will examine topics in gerontology from the vantage point of human diversity. Chapter 2, "Psychological Aging," focuses on the relationships among culture, behavior, aging, research methods, personality, life satisfaction, coping with major life stressors, and mental health and aging. Chapter 3, "Issues in Health and Sexuality," centers on mortality and diversity, health beliefs and behaviors, socio-economic class, poverty, Medicare and Medicaid, rural issues, physical illness, and issues in diversity, sexuality, and aging. The focus of Chapter 4, "Caregiving," is on both informal caregiving and formal care. We begin by reviewing how caregivers' gender and racial/ethnic group membership affect informal caregiving and then proceed to discuss the various sources of formal care and the barriers that hinder their use. In Chapter 5, "Work and Retirement," we examine the issues of ethnic diversity as they affect older adults in their approaches to work, retirement, and choice of leisure pursuits. The thrust of Chapter 6, "Religion and Spirituality," is on the religious practices of older adults from different cultural groups. Chapter 7, "Death, Dying, and Grieving," explores Western conceptions of death and bereavement, the comprehensive study conducted by Kalish and Reynolds, and emphasizes beliefs and practices of a number of cultural groups.

Older adults evidence a wide diversity of behaviors, physical and mental health, sexual interests, caregiving styles and systems, work and retirement patterns, spiritual and religious systems, and customs and attitudes regarding death, dying, and grieving. The following vignettes[1] (brief narratives) provide examples of the wide-ranging possibilities surrounding the American aging experience.

Vignette 1: Martha Cosgrove has lived in a box under a bridge in Cleveland for close to 7 years. While she still hears those "awful little voices" now and again, it is not as bad as it was when she was in the state hospital. She does not take those silly little pills that they gave her over at the city health clinic because they make her feel like "snakes are crawling all over." Her stomach hurts a great deal of the time, and sometimes her feet swell up. At 66 years of age, Martha has endured many difficulties. Her father was lynched right in front of her eyes when she was 10 years old simply because he was Black, and her first husband loved drugs at least as much as he cared about her. But now it's winter and Martha is very cold.

Vignette 2: A 70-year-old retired automobile factory worker, Juan Herriera, is enjoying retirement. Rosa, his wife of 50 years, devotes her life to taking care of his every need. When they were growing up in Colombia, their families lived next door to each other. It has been a great marriage for Juan, but Rosa has been less content. Sure Juan made a decent living, but what was there for Rosa? After their children grew up, there seemed little for her to do except take care of Juan. She never worked; Juan just wouldn't allow it. Over the years, she thought of leaving the marriage but never did. Now Rosa is 68 years old and in good physical health, but she is just "going through the motions" in her marriage, much as she has done for the last 50 years.

Vignette 3: Samuel Goldstein is sitting on the deck of his condominium in Los Angeles. While he is 77 years old, he jokes that he doesn't look a day over 75! His wife, Pearl, died 2 years ago after a long bout with cancer. At the urging of his son, Sam began to mingle socially last year. It seemed awkward at first, but now Sam likes all the attention that he is receiving from several widows. His latest love interest is Irma, whom he met at a social function over at the synagogue. Next weekend, Sam and Irma are going to San Diego. At this point, Sam is not interested in remarriage, just in having some fun and in the companionship that his relationship with Irma provides.

Vignette 4: Mei-kum Chan celebrated her 80th birthday in a nursing home. Last year, she fractured a hip, and her son and daughter-in-law felt that they could no longer care for her at home. Mei-kum's son, David, and his wife, Jan, run their own small business. The business has been a struggle, but they are starting to make a little money. The cost of the nursing home is putting a great strain on family finances, but what could they do? She needs the care, and since David is an only child, it is his responsibility! Mei-kum, David, and Jan all regret Mei-kum's placement in the nursing home. While growing up in China, Mei-kum lived with her parents, siblings,

---

[1]All of the vignettes and cases contained in this book are fictitious. All the names of persons included in these activities are pseudonyms.

and, for many years, a frail grandfather. Mei-kum expects to one day die at home among her loved ones.

Discussion Questions

1 The older adults described in these brief vignettes find themselves in quite different circumstances. What part might social class play in each of the four examples?
2 What role does gender play in each situation?
3 How might the ethnicity of each of these older adults influence their physical and mental health?

As you begin this first chapter of *Aging and Diversity: An Active Learning Experience*, the book asks you, the reader, to participate fully in the experience of learning. Through reading and discussing the contents of this book and through completing a variety of learning activities, you will become more aware of how differences in factors such as gender, ethnicity, social class, and language affect Americans as they age. Throughout each of the book's chapters, you will be provided with activities to be completed as part of a classroom experience or as self-study. You will be completing quizzes, analyzing case studies, conducting interviews, and evaluating research studies.

DEMOGRAPHICS OF AMERICAN ELDERS

This is the age of aging. As of 1992, there were more than 32 million older Americans (i.e., those 65 years old or older). Older adults constitute almost 12% of the total U.S. population. There are more than 19 million older women, providing a ratio of almost 1.5 older women for every older man. During the 20th century, the proportion of Americans over the age of 65 has more than tripled (American Association of Retired Persons [AARP], 1993). The older population is itself aging at dramatic rates. By the year 2000, 45% of the older population will be 75 and older (Soldo & Agree, 1988). In addition, the size of the 85+ population is expected to more than triple between 1980 and 2030 and to be nearly seven times larger in 2050 than in 1980 (U.S. Senate Special Committee on Aging, 1991).

Until now, the study of the aging of America has been a study of older Whites, who, in 1990, made up 89.9% of America's older population. But this situation is changing rapidly. The number of ethnic minority elderly persons will grow much more rapidly than the number of White elderly people over the next 50 years. As a consequence, the percentage of older adults in the United States that is made up of Blacks and other non-White minorities would increase from 10.2% in 1990 to 15.3% in 2020 and 21.3% in 2050 (Angel & Hogan, 1994). As shown in Figure 1.1, the number of older Blacks would climb from 2.6 million in 1990 to 9.6 million in 2050, the Hispanic elderly of any race would

Minorities Aged 65 and Older

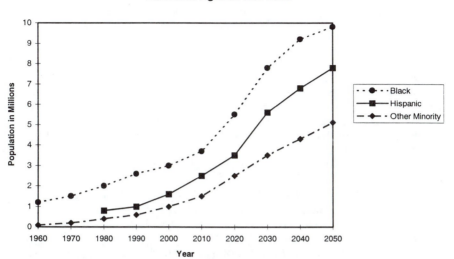

Figure 1.1 Minorities aged 65 and older. (From Angel & Hogan, 1994. Used with permission.)

grow from 1.1 million to 7.9 million, and elders of races other than White or Black would grow from 600,000 to 5 million (Taeuber, 1990). Ethnic groups in this last category include Native Americans and Asian Americans. In short, Blacks, Hispanics, and other minority groups will become an even larger and more important segment of America's older population.

THE ELEMENTS OF DIVERSITY

Since diversity is the central focus of our discussion, it is important to begin by identifying the variables that produce this diversity. When we consider diversity, we generally think about ethnic groups distinguished by race, religion, national origin, or some combination of these factors. However, this book is not restricted to an examination of "minority groups." Instead, we also include a discussion of diversity based on a full range of variables such as gender, language, religion, work status, and community size. Given the large number of older adults who live in small towns and rural communities and have special needs, we think it is important to include them as well. In short, we believe that casting our net widely allows us to capture a more realistic and interactive view of the mosaic represented by the diverse older population in the United States.

The diversity of older adults encompasses a great many factors; aspects of diversity have physical, psychological, and social consequences. While gender is biologically determined, it has psychological and social implications as well as physiological ones. For example, the fact that women live longer than men affects marriage, widowhood, levels of poverty, and even the recreational activities provided in nursing homes. Elements of diversity characterizing older adults are many and varied. Among the most prominent of these factors are:

- *cohort* (persons born at about the same time)
- *income* (size and sources of personal finances)
- *social roles* (parent, widow, retiree)
- *gender* (based on gender, people may learn to perceive the world differently and be perceived differently)
- *sexual orientation* (heterosexual, bisexual, homosexual)
- *ethnicity* (a shared sense of identity that includes a set of cultural meanings based on national origin, religion, language, and/or race)
- *race* (a social construct that people may use to categorize themselves or others)
- *cultural identification* (values or behaviors shared with a group based on national origin, language, religion, or occupation)
- *friendship patterns* (persons with whom people choose to socialize and the frequency of the interactions)
- *religion, spirituality* (practice of an organized religion; a personal set of spiritual values)
- *value system* (belief system regarding behavior and life goals)
- *language* (spoken at home and in the community)
- *community* (size, region)
- *work status* (employed full time or part time, volunteer, unemployed)
- *occupation* (present or former)
- *family composition* (marital status, children)
- *formal education* (years of schooling, diplomas, degrees)
- *living arrangements* (live alone, with adult children, congregate housing)
- *health status* (healthy, frail, disabilities, chronic illnesses)
- *functional independence* (degree of ability to take care of personal needs, presence of cognitive or physical disabilities)
- *generation as American* (first generation, etc.)
- *degree of acculturation* (traditional, bicultural, assimilated)
- *personal interests* (preferred activities, hobbies, attitudes)
- *personality* (temperament, characteristic style of adaptation, patterns of relating to others)
- *dietary practices* (preferred foods)
- *time* (historical time, time in one's life)

Race and Ethnicity as Social Constructs

The 26 elements just delineated represent only a partial listing of the possible ways in which human beings may reflect differing physical, psychological, and social characteristics. It is important to note that an element of diversity can be a social construct, in other words, a convenient way to characterize how some persons may define themselves or others. Race is such a social construct. Contemporary anthropology has discarded the concept of race as a method for effectively categorizing human populations (Ferraro, Trevathan, & Levy, 1994). While race continues to be used for social demarcation on U.S. census forms (O'Hare, 1992), on employment applications, and in research throughout much of the social and health sciences, race as a biological concept is incorrect.

Ferraro, Trevathan, and Levy (1994) suggest that "to understand the demise of the concept of race, we need to examine the history of scientific and popular thinking about race. First, how is race defined?" (p. 142). These anthropologists go on to describe how most persons use skin color as a marker of race; however, as they point out:

> Because skin color is caused by several genes, there are many limitations to its usefulness. It is quite possible, for example, for three people who are siblings to be placed in three different races, if skin color is the criterion used. (Ferraro, Trevathan, & Levy, 1994, p. 142)

Skin pigmentation, while often used to distinguish one race from another, varies dramatically among those considered to be Caucasoid, Mongoloid, or Negroid. In addition, there is much overlap in skin color among what are often considered to be distinct racial groups (e.g., light-skinned Blacks and dark-skinned Whites) (Schaefer, 1990).

Regardless of the inadequacies of the concept of race, typically, human beings are characterized as belonging to one race or another or of being of mixed race. Frequently, these categorizations are based on social or political factors. Individuals may identify with a "racial" group based on family and community or may be categorized as belonging to a "lesser" group and afforded fewer opportunities, greater restrictions, or even extermination. Those of mixed race may choose to view themselves as belonging to one race over another depending on the parent or grandparent with whom they identify. For example, if one has a Japanese father and a Black mother, one may identify more closely with one's father and see oneself as a Japanese American, identify more with one's mother and label oneself as a Black American, or view oneself as of mixed race and not select either "racial" label (O'Hare, 1992).

Another element of diversity, one that is defined socially, is ethnicity. Typically, religion and/or language determine an individual's ethnicity (O'Hare, 1992). In some categorizations (e.g., U.S. Census Bureau forms), ethnic and racial definitions overlap. For example, persons viewing themselves as Hispanic may classify themselves as White, Black, American Indian, or Asian. "In the 1990 Census . . . 43% of Hispanics classified their race as 'other race,' that is, not White, Black, Asian, or American Indian. And most people (96%) in the 'other race' category were also of Hispanic origin" (O'Hare, 1992, p. 6).

Interactional Nature of Elements of Diversity and Aging

Figure 1.2 depicts the interactional nature of several elements of diversity and aging. Physical, psychological, and social aspects of diversity influence one another. For example, an individual's gender and biological age affect his or her marital status, but the influences can also be seen in the other direction. Older men are much more likely to be married than are women of a similar age, since women, on average, live longer than men, and men of the oldest cohorts tended to marry women younger than themselves. Older men and women who wish to marry or remarry have very different possibilities if they choose to marry persons of similar ages, since there are significantly fewer unattached older men.

The interaction of several elements of diversity and aging can be seen in research conducted by Thanh Tran (1990), who, in an effort to understand English-language acculturation, analyzed data from a national survey of more than 2,000 Vietnamese immigrants. As a result of problems with skills in English, many older Vietnamese individuals experience language problems so serious that these persons are not able "to shop for food, to apply for aid, and to contact the police or fire department when needed" (Tran, 1990, p. 99). Degree of language proficiency was associated with age, gender, health, education, and length of time in the United States. The most significant findings involved age and gender. Younger refugees appeared to experience fewer problems in acquiring a second language, and older Vietnamese women experienced more difficulties with learning and using English than did men. Perhaps the latter finding is due to the fact that, in traditional Vietnamese society, women occupy roles affording them lower status and education than their male peers. Those respon-

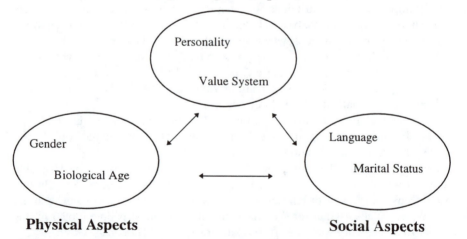

Figure 1.2 Interactional nature of elements of diversity and aging.

dents with more education, better health, and longer American residence demonstrated better language skills.

The following activity, "The Case of Sergei Korsakov," illustrates further
the interaction of several elements of diversity in the life of an older adult.

ACTIVE LEARNING EXPERIENCE: THE CASE OF SERGEI KORSAKOV

Purpose

The purpose of this activity is to illustrate the interaction of elements of diversity
and aging. Upon completion of this activity, you will be able to:

1 List and discuss several elements pertaining to the diversity of older
adults.
2 Understand how these elements interact.
3 Apply this knowledge in conducting a case analysis.

Time Required

30 minutes (15 minutes to answer the questions in groups and 15 minutes for
class discussion).

Procedure

1 Your instructor divides the class into groups of three to five.
2 Each group answers the questions following the case.
3 Each group selects one person to record and present the group's findings
to the entire class.
4 After the groups have answered the questions, the group recorders share
responses with the entire class.
5 The instructor leads a class discussion on group responses.

The Case of Sergei Korsakov

Read the following case study. With your group, read and analyze the case and
answer the questions that follow it.

Sergei Korsakov is an 80-year-old widowed great-grandfather who lives with one of
his adult grandsons, the grandson's wife, and their two teenage daughters in Boston.
Mr. Korsakov speaks Russian, English, and German fluently and practices the Russian Orthodox faith. He is retired from a very successful law practice and is a second-
generation immigrant from Russia. Mr. Korsakov is physically healthy except for a

manageable arthritic condition. An avid stamp collector, reader of detective fiction, and fan of professional hockey, Sergei especially enjoys dining on Lithuanian foods similar to the ones his Lithuanian mother used to cook when he was a child. In Sergei Korsakov's case, elements of diversity come to interact with one another to help form a unique individual. His marital status, living arrangement, work and occupational status, health status, personality, preferred foods, and interests, along with the size and location of his community, combine to help form the person known as Sergei Korsakov. If even one of these elements were different, the combination of elements would also be different. Such changes would make the complex config-uration of diverse elements that help to compose Sergei Korsakov entirely different.

Discussion Questions

1 With what groups (e.g., attorneys, Russian Americans) might Sergei identify?

2 What are some ways in which the following elements of Sergei Kor-sakov's diversity could interact with one another: personality, language, religion, leisure interests, health status, living arrangements, food preferences, and size and location of community?

3 List three elements of diversity of one of your older adult family members.

WHY SHOULD WE FOCUS ON DIVERSITY AND AGING?

Older adults, like all human beings, are unique and diverse. Consider the follow-ing factors that promote this diversity.

First, the number of older adults from present-day minority ethnic groups will continue to increase, and in some parts of the country they will be the majority population. There are several reasons for this increase. For example, in recent years a substantial number of refugees have come to the United States from Cambodia, Laos, and Vietnam. Their ethnic backgrounds are substantially different from that of the host society. In addition, we have witnessed significant changes in the immigration policies of the United States. The most visible impact of these changes is the increasing diversity of the population. For example, the number of Muslims, Hindus, and Buddhists emigrating to the United States has been markedly increasing (Waugh, Abu-Laban, & Qureshi, 1983; Williams, 1988). This means that basic knowledge of the values preserved and transmitted by these formerly "foreign" traditions has immediate relevance for both students and service providers. While statistics continue to show decreasing differences in life expectancy among White and minority elders, research also indicates that members of many minority groups who live into their 70s have a longer life expectancy than their White peers (Soldo & Agree, 1988).

Second, the relationship between ethnicity and aging varies a great deal across different groups and within the same group. For example, the Hispanic population represents a variety of cultures and nationalities. One finds important differences within the older population from this group. In addition, there are significant differences among Asian American, American Indian, and African American older adults. As indicated earlier for the Hispanic population, we find important differences within each of these groups as well.

Third, older people from different groups may have specific needs. Understanding these needs is essential for developing effective programs and services. For example, transportation and health care needs of older adults living in geographically isolated communities are very different from those living in metropolitan areas. A systematic assessment of their unmet needs should precede the development of new programs and services.

Fourth, ethnicity is not a fixed entity. It changes in response to the experiences and interactions in the life of the individual or the group. Older adults who have come to the United States in the latter part of their lives are affected by their ethnicity much differently than their children who were either born in America or came to the United States prior to entering school. These differences across cohorts, within the same ethnic groups, should be taken into consideration by those responsible for designing innovative programs for older adults at different points in time.

Finally, elements of diversity, such as gender, social class, cohort, and ethnicity, affect life course and role transitions. For example, the grandparental role is more significant in Native American, African American, and Asian Indian families than in most families of the White middle class. Widowhood provides another example. In view of reduced life expectancy for low-income adults or for members of certain ethnic groups, there are a large number of widows whose husbands died at earlier ages. Their experience of widowhood is affected by the degree of integration of older adults within the group. In groups that provide for a closer and protective role for family members, widows find solace and comfort. However, they may also experience restrictions on the activities they may undertake.

DIVERSITY AND ACCULTURATION

As we have indicated, differences make a difference. It is important to develop an understanding of differences across groups and within groups. However, it is also important to pay attention to the process of acculturation, which occurs as a result of ongoing interaction of ethnic group members with the host society. Acculturation occurs along a continuum (Valle, 1989). On one end is a traditional position reflecting allegiance to the culture of one's origins. If elders have partial allegiance to both their culture of origin and the dominant American culture, they can be said to be bicultural. On the other end of the continuum are assimilated elders whose behaviors demonstrate their identification with and integration into mainstream American culture (Henderson, 1994; Valle, 1989). Henderson (1994) alerts us not to make the mistake of assuming that assimilated and bicultural elders "do not appear 'ethnic enough' to warrant special attention. In reality, such people have not lost their ethnic-minority heritage; they have simply added to it a great facility for using the cultural system of the majority population" (p. 37).

One important measure of acculturation to American values and norms is the English-speaking ability of older adults. In a research study with Mexican American elders, Lubben and Becerra (1987) found that English-speaking Mexicans exhibited patterns of behaviors and relationships falling between those of Whites and Mexican Americans who spoke Spanish only. These patterns reflected the bicultural nature of many of the Mexican Americans who spoke English. For example, the investigators observed that the more assimilated the individual, the less extensive the family interaction. In addition, cultural differences with respect to social networks appeared to diminish as an individual became more assimilated into American society. Thus, the diversity that we find within Mexican American elderly people may be due to differences in degree of acculturation. Some members of the group have developed fluency in the English language and have adopted mainstream American values and norms, and those who speak Spanish only adhere to traditional cultural patterns and are less acculturated to American values.

When visiting Chinatown sections in large metropolitan areas, one finds that Chinese elders also span the acculturation continuum. We will find substantial differences between age groups. Why? As indicated earlier in this section, acculturation is facilitated by developing language skills and by interacting with members of the host society. Because of accumulated effects of acculturation, the influence of the wider society will be greater on younger members of the ethnic group, who will live longer in the host society, than on the older members who grew up in another environment and emigrated to the United States as adults. Thus, if we examine the language skills of 50-year-old immigrants and their 20-year-old sons and daughters, the differences will be a result of the different experiences of these two groups rather than the result of aging 30 years. Attributing these differences to aging would be like concluding that people are more likely to speak Italian (or some other foreign language) when they are 50 years old than when they are 20. In short, it is important to distinguish between age effects and cohort effects. Age effects reflect differences due to underlying processes (biological, social, or psychological changes), whereas cohort effects are differences due to experiences and circumstances unique to the particular generation to which an individual belongs.

AGEISM AND DIVERSITY

Elders are frequently stereotyped. Stereotyping of older adults is an outgrowth of ageism, just as generalities based on race reflect racism. Geriatrician Robert Butler and his associates describe ageism as "the prejudices and stereotypes that are applied to older people sheerly on the basis of their age" (Butler, Lewis, &

Sunderland, 1991, p. 243). One of the particularly strange aspects of ageism is that it may reflect a degree of self-hatred or at least be based on fears of aging, disability, dependence, and death. After all, isn't becoming old a goal shared by most persons?

Interestingly, ageism is not simply a reflection of ignorance about the variability of older persons. Sometimes we find high levels of ageism among those whose professional responsibilities involve contacts with elders. Perhaps this is somewhat understandable, since these same professionals (nurses, social workers, and rehabilitation specialists, among others) are likely to work with the most frail, dependent older adults. If we characterize all older adults as senile, we generalize our experiences with a demented aunt, father, or grandparent as if they were normative for all elders. Certainly senility is not a consequence of aging but, rather, a result of pathology that affects only a minority of older persons. An Alzheimer's patient is demented not because she or he is 80 years old but as a consequence of the disease.

Older persons from various racial groups may experience both racism and ageism (Crandall, 1980). This concept, called double ethnic jeopardy, has not received much research support. The notion is difficult to measure; more longitudinal studies are needed to evaluate whether variables other than race or ethnicity may be responsible for such differing outcomes as poverty, health status, and longevity (Cavanaugh, 1993).

Gender stereotyping, or sexism, may combine with ageism to limit the opportunities and resources of older women. For example, the poverty rate for older women is almost twice that for older men (AARP, 1993). Sexism may combine with ageism regarding the terms used to describe older adults. In his study of the use of ageist terminology in the English language, Herbert Covey (1988) found that women have traditionally been described as ''old'' at younger ages than their male counterparts. According to Covey:

> Terms for old men tend to be focused on their being old-fashioned, uncouth, conservative, feeble, stingy, incompetent, narrow-minded, eccentric, or stupid. Terms for old women are focused on mysticism, bad temper, disagreeableness, spinsterhood, bossiness, unattractiveness, spitefulness, and repulsiveness. Terms for old men are sometimes defined in positive tones connoting wisdom and respect. Old women have not been so fortunate. (p. 291)

Ageism joins with sexism in contemporary language in some ''women's magazines.'' In an examination *of Lear's*, a magazine aimed at women over 40, Wang (1988) uncovered advertisements incorporating ageist language, and DeRenzo and Malley (1992) found a significant increase from 1969 to 1988 in the use of such language in skin-care product advertisements in *Vogue*.

As we have noted, older adults may possess a host of diverse characteristics and be stereotyped on a variety of dimensions. For example, we may hear that ''all widows are alike.'' Or we may hear a joke implying that ''all old men are sexless'' or that, if they demonstrate sexuality, ''they are dirty old men.'' In this way, the element of gender can become a part of a stereotyped view, both ageist and sexist.

The next learning activity is devoted to common ageist stereotypes.

ACTIVE LEARNING EXPERIENCE: THE AGING STEREOTYPE GAME[2]

Purpose

The purpose of this activity is to prompt you to think about common stereotypes involving older adults. By working through this activity, you will be able to examine some of your own personal biases. Upon completion of the activity, you will be able to:

1 List common stereotypes associated with aging.
2 Discuss how ageism affects attitudes toward older adults.

Time Required

45 minutes (25 minutes to complete the activity sheet and 20 minutes to discuss the activity in class).

Procedure

1 The class is divided into groups of four to seven.
2 Each group develops lists of at least 15 negative and 15 positive beliefs concerning older people.
3 Each group chooses one person to record the stereotypes generated through group discussion.
4 After all groups have completed their lists, each group shares its lists with the entire class.
5 The instructor leads a class discussion that identifies themes emerging from the lists.

The Aging Stereotype Game

1 List 15–20 negative stereotypes about older adults.
2 List 15–20 positive stereotypes about older adults.

[2]This activity appeared previously in S. B. Fried, D. Van Booven, & C. MacQuarrie (1993). *Older adulthood: Learning activities for understanding aging*. Baltimore: Health Professions Press.

SUMMARY

This chapter has provided a general overview of diversity and aging. We devoted a section to the demographics of America's elderly population in which we emphasized the growth of this population as well as the increasing numbers of female and minority elders. Following this discussion, we turned our attention to the elements of diversity. In this section, we delineated 26 elements and discussed the limitations of the terms *race* and *ethnicity*. Race, which is not a useful biological term, continues to function as a social construct. Also, we highlighted the interactional nature of the elements of diversity and aging. In answering the question "Why should we focus on diversity and aging?" we presented five key points: (a) The number of older adults from present-day minority groups will continue to increase, and in some parts of the country they will be the majority population; (b) the relationship between ethnicity and aging varies a great deal across different groups and within the same group; (c) older people from different groups can have specific needs; (d) ethnicity is not a fixed entity; and (e) elements of diversity, such as gender, social class, cohort, and religion, affect life course and role transitions. In another section of the chapter devoted to diversity and acculturation, we described the continuum of acculturation and discussed the roles of English-language proficiency and generation in the acculturation process. The final section contained material on the definition of ageism, the appearance of ageistic attitudes among health care and social service professionals, and the combination of sexism and ageism in the use of language.

The following quiz addresses some of the key points of Chapter 1.

ACTIVE LEARNING EXPERIENCE: DIVERSITY AND AGING QUIZ

Purpose

The purpose of this activity is to assess your knowledge of diversity and aging. Upon completion of this activity, you will be able to:

1   Assess your knowledge of diversity and aging.
2   Receive feedback regarding your knowledge of diversity and aging.

Time Required

30 minutes (10 minutes to complete the quiz and 20 minutes to discuss the answers with another person or your class).

Procedure

    1 Complete the quiz.
    2 Your instructor reviews the answers to the quiz in class.

Diversity and Aging Quiz

Indicate whether each of the following statements is true or false.

		True	False
1	In the year 2030, 25% of older Americans are expected to be members of minority groups.	_____	_____
2	The stereotyping of older adults is called racism.	_____	_____
3	A relatively organized system of shared meanings is called a culture.	_____	_____
4	Diversity includes a number of factors such as religion, language, social class, and gender.	_____	_____
5	Race is primarily a social construct.	_____	_____
6	The degree of acculturation may be different for foreign-born persons than for their second- or third-generation children and grandchildren.	_____	_____
7	Between 1900 and 2030, the older Hispanic population is projected to show an increase of almost 400%.	_____	_____
8	Differences among people decrease with age.	_____	_____
9	Ethnicity is a fixed entity.	_____	_____
10	Acculturation occurs as two or more cultures interact.	_____	_____
11	In the United States, there are 147 older men for every 100 older women.	_____	_____
12	Expressing the desire to ''take care'' of older adults when they are capable of self-care may be a form of ageism.	_____	_____
13	Cohort effects are due to experiences unique to a particular generation.	_____	_____

                                                                    True   False

14 An individual's language skills have a significant effect on her
       or his degree of acculturation.   _____ _____

15 The relationship between ethnicity and aging varies within the
       same ethnic group.   _____ _____

GLOSSARY

Acculturation   The process of learning a culture, which is promoted by ongoing inter-
     action between members of an ethnic group and those from the host society.

Ageism   Practice of stereotyping and discriminating against people because they are
     older.

Cohort   An aggregation of people having a common characteristic. The term generally
     refers to the time period in which persons were born.

Cohort Effect   Sociocultural influences specific to a group of persons sharing a common
     set of experiences.

Culture   A relatively organized system of shared meanings, including beliefs and sym-
     bols, that guide but do not determine individual behaviors.

Double-Jeopardy Hypothesis   The idea that minority group elders experience a double
     disadvantage relative to White elders regarding key aspects of life, including health.
     While many minority elders do experience disadvantages, this hypothesis has re-
     ceived little support from gerontological research.

Ethnic Group   Persons who share a sense of identity based on national origin and/or
     cultural factors such as language, religion, or dietary practices.

Ethnicity   A shared sense of identity that includes a set of cultural meanings.

Ethnogerontology   The study of causes, processes, and consequences of ethnic group
     membership and identification for the aging of individuals and populations.

Host Society   The larger culture of the country in which people reside. The norms and
     values of the dominant group or groups in the host country affect members of other
     ethnic groups.

Life Expectancy   The average length of time a group of individuals of the same age
     will live, given current mortality rates. While life expectancy can be reported for
     any age, life expectancy at birth is most commonly used.

Race   A social distinction based in part on observable physical differences such as skin
     color. A social construct used to classify and separate people.

SUGGESTED READINGS

Bull, C. N. (Ed.). (1993). *Aging in rural America*. Newbury Park, CA: Sage.

This volume contains essays addressing numerous topics concerning rural elders.
Subjects include demographics, housing, transportation, physical and mental health care
needs and services, and both formal and informal social support. Two highly useful
chapters are Novella Perrin's "Elder Abuse: A Rural Perspective" and Vira Kivett's
"Informal Supports Among Older Rural Minorities."

Gelfand, D. E. (1994). *Aging and ethnicity: Knowledge and services.* New York: Springer.

One of the leading researchers in the area of ethnicity and aging discusses popular theories of aging, immigration, the history of American ethnic elders, security, family assistance, church, and available and needed services. Gelfand draws on his many years as an active applied and theoretical researcher. References at the end of each chapter lead the reader to some excellent source material.

Gelfand, D. E., & Barresi, C. M. (1987). *Ethnic dimensions of aging.* New York: Springer.

This volume examines many of the critical interrelationships between ethnicity and aging based on the critical thinking of a large number of researchers and practitioners. The book is composed of three sections: "Theory and Ethnic Dimensions of Aging," "Research and Ethnic Dimensions of Aging," and "Practice, Policy, and Ethnic Dimensions of Aging." Each section includes five to six chapters written by authors representing a variety of disciplines.

Jackson, J. S., Chatters, L. M., & Taylor, R. T. (Eds.). (1993). *Aging in Black America.* Newbury Park, CA: Sage.

This book includes chapters prepared by leading researchers on topics related to African American elders. Readings cover community, family, friends, religion, health, group identity, political participation, retirement, work, and the life course.

Minority elders: Five goals toward building a public policy base. (1994). Washington, DC: Gerontological Society of America.

Prepared by the GSA Task Force on Minority Issues in Gerontology, this publication includes a discussion of specific policy goals; background papers on demography, economic security, longevity and health status, family support systems, and Native American elders; and an annotated bibliography of recent articles appearing in the *Journal of Gerontology* and *The Gerontologist.* The articles and annotations make for fairly difficult reading because they are intended primarily for gerontology scholars, faculty, and graduate students.

Palmore, E. B. (1990). *Ageism: Negative and positive.* New York: Springer.

The author argues that attitudes toward older adults have become more positive over the last several decades. Palmore views negative stereotypes toward the elderly as reflecting ugliness, psychopathology, illness, mental decline, uselessness, poverty, isolation, and impotence.

Sokolovsky, J. (Ed.). (1990). *The cultural context of aging: Worldwide perspectives.* New York: Bergin & Garvey.

Although this book endeavors to take a global perspective, several chapters are devoted to ethnicity in the American context. Especially insightful are Sokolovsky's chapter on aging, ethnicity, and family support; Peterson's chapter on African American women; and Henderson's contribution on Alzheimer's disease as viewed through a cultural context.

Stanford, E. P., & Torres-Gil, F. M. (Eds.). (1992, Fall/Winter). Diversity: New approaches to ethnic minority aging [Special issue]. *Generations, 15*(4).

The American Society on Aging addresses diversity with a special issue of its journal, *Generations*, devoted to minority elderly populations. Among the issues raised are the use of ethnicity as an indicator of need in targeting and means testing, creation of culturally relevant paradigms in minority aging, and the impact of immigration trends on population distribution.

Stoller, E. P., & Gibson, R. C. (Eds.). (1994). *Worlds of difference: Inequality in the aging experience*. Thousand Oaks, CA: Pine Forge Press.

This book examines social inequality, variations in cultural meanings, and the life course. The major issues of the text are explored in an introductory chapter written by the editors. The 38 readings cover numerous groups based on ethnicity, gender, sexual orientation, and socioeconomic class. The richness of our diverse culture and the impact of inequality are highlighted.

Takaki, R. (1993). *A different mirror: A history of multicultural America*. Boston: Little, Brown.

This well-written book tells the history of America from the vantage point of the following ethnic groups: American Indians, African Americans, Irish Americans, and Jewish American immigrants from Eastern Europe. The author, a leading scholar in multicultural history, writes of the struggles of these diverse groups. On the last page of the book, Takaki proclaims: "Our diversity has been at the center of the making of America" (p. 428).

KEY: DIVERSITY AND AGING QUIZ

1 **True.**   According to projections made by staff members of the United States Administration on Aging, about 25% of the total U.S. older adult population will be made up of minorities in the year 2030 (U.S. Senate Special Committee on Aging, 1991).

2 **False.**   Robert Butler and associates refer to ageism as "the prejudices and stereotypes that are applied to older people sheerly on the basis of their age" (Butler, Lewis, & Sunderland, 1991, p. 243).

3 **True.**   Culture does refer to an organized system of meanings regarding prescribed values and roles (Birren, 1988, p. 159).

4 **True.**   Among the many elements of human diversity are age, ethnicity, language, health status, religion, gender, sexual orientation, and social class (Kavanaugh & Kennedy, 1992, p. 1).

5   **True.**   Biologically, race has been defined as a group that shares a number of physical traits based on gene frequencies. As a result of migration and invasion, ''pure gene frequencies have not existed for some time, if they ever did'' (Schaefer, 1990, p. 13). According to Ferraro, Trevathan, and Levy, ''although they [races] remain pervasive social concepts, they no longer have validity as biological concepts'' (1994, p. 142).

6   **True.**   People who come to America later in life are less likely to become as fully acculturated as their children and grandchildren, who have spent all or most of their lives in the United States (Barresi, 1987, p. 21).

7   **True.**   The older Hispanic population is expected to increase by 395% between 1990 and 2030 (U.S. Senate Special Committee on Aging, 1991).

8   **False.**   Research tends to provide support for the idea that variability increases with age, since the possibility of differing experiences grows with each passing day and year (Dannefer, 1988, p. 361).

9   **False.**   Ethnicity is not a fixed entity. An individual's ethnicity is affected by changes in his or her life and by alterations in the experiences of the ethnic group to which he or she belongs (Gelfand & Barresi, 1987, p. 8).

10   **True.**   As different cultural groups interact with one another, a gradual process of acculturation occurs (Cavanaugh, 1993, p. 58).

11   **False.**   As of 1992, there were 147 older women for every 100 older men (AARP, 1993, p. 1).

12   **True.**   Younger adults expressing an interest in ''taking care'' of older adults who are able to take care of themselves may be demonstrating a subtle form of paternalistic ageism (Fried, Van Booven, & MacQuarrie, 1993, pp. 29–30).

13   **True.**   Cohort effects result from similar historical events and experiences common to a group of people born during a specific time period (Barrow, 1992, p. 59).

14   **True.**   If members of an ethnic group are unable to communicate in the language of the host society, they will be unlikely to become fully acculturated (Barresi, 1987, pp. 30–31).

15   **True.**   Each ethnic group may represent a number of smaller diverse groups, and there are significant differences among individuals from the same group (Gelfand & Barresi, 1987, pp. 5–17).

Chapter 2

Psychological Aging

OVERVIEW

Culture, Behavior, and Aging

- What are some distinctive aspects of culture?
- What are social clocks?
- In what ways can gender and ethnicity influence social clock patterns?
- How do social class and minority group membership affect age norms?

Research Methods for Examining Diversity and Psychological Aging

- What research methods do gerontologists employ?
- What are some problems facing the gerontologist who wishes to conduct research with ethnic minorities, including persons not proficient in the English language?
- Describe Myerhoff's participant observation study of elderly Jews.
- What are some ethical issues involved in conducting research with diverse elders?

Models of Personality and Adulthood

- What are the types of models of personality and adulthood?
- How do these models account for individual differences based on diversity?
- Is there stability in personality across adulthood?
- How is ethnic identity related to an individual's life stage?
- What is the role of gender in determining the aging personality?
- How does gender affect personality at differing life stages?

Life Satisfaction

- What are the determinants of life satisfaction in later life?
- What did Andrews and associates find when they compared the life satisfaction of Hispanic elders with that of other older Americans?

Coping With Major Life Stressors Among Diverse Elders

- Describe a model of the possible relationships between stress and coping among vulnerable elders.
- How can social support serve as a resource for older women in dealing with stress while causing them additional stress as well?
- What did Krause and Goldenhar find in studying psychological distress and environmental factors among immigrants from Cuba, Mexico, and Puerto Rico?

Diversity, Mental Health, and Aging

- What attitudes toward mental health and mental health services are held by diverse elders?
- Why don't more elders, especially ethnic ones, use mental health services?
- What are some of the barriers faced by elderly clients, particularly those from minority populations, when they do seek care from mental health professionals?
- What are some of the prevalent attitudes toward elders and mental health held by health care providers?
- What is a cultural broker?
- How did Taussig and associates demonstrate the utility of Spanish-language neuropsychological tests?
- Why is there an increasing need for Hispanic and Spanish-speaking mental health professionals?
- What may be the relationship between depression and acculturation among Mexican American elders?
- Which group of depressed elders is at the greatest risk for suicide?
- What are common criteria used to diagnose Alzheimer's disease?
- By what process did Braun and associates develop ethnic-specific outreach materials for subgroups of Asian/Pacific Islanders in Hawaii?
- Describe the partnership model developed by Vissing and associates for providing Alzheimer's disease services in rural New Hampshire.

Summary

Diversity in Psychological Aging Quiz

Glossary

Suggested Readings

Key: Diversity in Psychological Aging Quiz

Key: Example of a Research Critique

This chapter centers on the psychological realm of the aging individual as affected by aspects of diversity. Elements such as ethnicity, class, gender, cohort, and religion affect behavior and emotion across the life span. What is considered appropriate or "normal" behavior as a member of a particular group may be deemed inappropriate or maladaptive if one ascribes to a different religion or lives in a certain neighborhood. In this chapter, we consider the following topics: (a) the relationships among culture, behavior, and aging; (b) research methodologies for examining diversity in psychological aging; (c) personality and aging; (d) life satisfaction; (e) coping with major life stressors; and (f) mental health and aging. As a way of introducing our discussion of psychological factors, consider the following vignettes.

Vignette 1: Ralph Rodriguez feels stressed much of the time. A 72-year-old widower, Ralph is in moderately good health (his arthritis is sometimes painful but manageable). His main concerns revolve around his finances and the fact that three of his four children live in distant communities. Living in the home in San Antonio where he and his wife raised their children, Ralph misses his kids, two of whom live in Los Angeles and the third in Baltimore; the one daughter who lives within a 15-minute drive is going through a divorce. His nearby daughter is, in Ralph's words, a "basket case." Ralph worries about the grandkids, but being around them makes him really nervous. He has several good friends, but all of them have both money and health problems. If Ralph had more money, he would jump on a plane and visit his kids and their families.

Vignette 2: Walter Wainright is very sad. Last year, Don Barker, his companion of 30 years, died after a long bout with lung cancer. Walter has shut himself off from most of his friends, eats very little, and has difficulty sleeping. Except for a sister who lives a thousand miles away, he has no contact with his family. Thirty years ago, when he informed family members of his sexual orientation, his family, with the exception of his older sister, Ida, cut off all contact with him. Walter has battled episodes of depression for most of his life. In the past, he coped with the recurring sadness by immersing himself in his work as an electrical engineer. The work and his relationship with Don provided a structure enabling him to somewhat manage the episodes of depression. Last month, Walter retired from his corporate job. He is reluctant to seek help from a mental health professional because, when he sought such assistance 30 years ago, the psychologist seemed judgmental toward Walter and his lifestyle.

Vignette 3: Wanda Wallace is beginning to plan research for her master's degree. She would like to investigate issues related to life satisfaction among Southeast Asian American elders living in a metropolitan area near her university. Over the last several years, Wanda has been doing a great deal of reading about immigrants from Southeast Asia, but she lacks contacts within these communities, as well as skills in the relevant languages. As part of her graduate studies, her course work has included classes in gerontology, survey research, and statistics. While she is very interested in pursuing this general area of research, she feels overwhelmed by the problems of studying persons from cultures so different from her own. Wanda is wondering how her interests in diversity and aging can be integrated with the requirement of completing a thesis and what she needs to do to ensure the quality of her research project.

Discussion Questions

1   In the first vignette, Ralph is experiencing a great deal of stress based on financial difficulties and isolation from much of his family. His daughter's marital difficulties only exacerbate the situation. What personal or community resources might Ralph be able to draw upon in coping with his distress?

2   Walter Wainright resists the idea of going to a professional psychotherapist because he does not want to be judged or stereotyped. Given these concerns, what kinds of mental health services might be most effective for him? Why?

3   What practical problems might Wanda face if she decides to conduct a survey of elderly Southeast Asian immigrants?

CULTURE, BEHAVIOR, AND AGING

In Chapter 1, culture was defined as a relatively organized system of shared meanings, including beliefs and symbols, that guides but do not determine individual behaviors. According to Triandis (1994), culture displays three distinctive aspects: (a) the social rules members use, (b) shared elements such as specialized customs or language, and (c) transmission to others through education, media, examples set by family members, and so forth. In a broad view of culture, the term can be applied to differing social classes, genders, religions, and even occupations, implying that every individual is involved with numerous cultures simultaneously.

Every culture and subculture reinforce a set of approved behaviors. For example, the larger American society encourages all of its members to follow a social clock (Hagestad & Neugarten, 1985; Neugarten & Hagestad, 1976). Societal members are told both explicitly and implicitly when it is "appropriate" to begin to drive and date and when it is appropriate to marry, graduate from high school or college, and retire. Sanctions may be placed on persons who are "off-time," while reinforcements are in store for those who are "on-time." For example, a prospective student who applies to medical school at 50 years of age may well find strong resistance to her or his entry, while a 62-year-old executive may be strongly encouraged by financial incentives to retire from the business organization in which he or she works.

The particular social clock that an individual follows may be dictated by elements of diversity. For example, Helson and associates (Helson & McCabe, 1994; Helson, Mitchell, & Moane, 1984; Helson & Moane, 1987; Helson & Wink, 1992; Mitchell & Helson, 1990) suggest that how one's personality changes in adulthood is linked with whether one goes along with or departs from prescribed social clocks. These researchers describe the following three social clock categories that they applied to their examination of women who were college seniors in 1958 or 1960: (a) a feminine clock based on initiating a family by 28 years of age, (b) a masculine occupational clock based on establishing a career by the age of 28, and (c) those women who were not adhering to either of the two previous schedules. The female subjects were studied again approximately 5 and 20 years later, and they were given personality inventories both at graduation and 20 years afterward. Helson and Moane (1987) studied possible changes on personality scales for women who were following varying social clock patterns over a time frame from 21 to 43 years of age. Generally, women who attempted to follow a social clock project demonstrated positive personality changes, including increased independence, self-control, and tolerance. Women in the same sample were asked to describe their life agendas and the expectations that other people had for them at age 52 (Helson & McCabe, 1994; Mitchell & Helson, 1990). These women demonstrated "little awareness of social clock pressures. They were functioning well, knew who they were, and most did not feel the need to prove themselves in new ways" (Helson & McCabe, 1994, p. 90).

The social clock revolves around age norms. Cultures encourage people to behave in ways that are consistent with their age, as defined by the social rules of the culture. For example, social class strongly influences the age at which people marry and, consequently, when they begin having children. In the United States, there is a strong tendency for members of the working class to marry long before their middle-, upper-middle-, and upper-class counterparts (Collins & Coltrane, 1991), and the age of marriage influences number of children, level of marital satisfaction, and likelihood of divorce (Gelles, 1995).

Behavioral expectations, including age norms, may vary according to ethnicity, minority status, and social class. Cool (1990) contends that "an individual may ignore and/or disguise ethnic membership at times when . . . occupied with other roles . . . and . . . revitalize the ethnic identity and/or membership at a later date" (p. 266). In this way, ethnic identity is somewhat fluid, occupying a more or less central place in a person's life, depending on circumstance and choice. Minority group status is related to ethnicity in that membership in a particular ethnic group may provide the basis on which members of majority groups discriminate. Socioeconomic class is related to both ethnicity and minority group membership. An individual's ethnic and/or minority group identification may be influenced by his or her class status. In American society, social class is associated with three primary factors: (a) occupational status, (b) income, and (c) education. As of the writing of this book, access to educational, occupational, and financial opportunities continues to at times be linked to ethnicity, minority group membership, and/or social class.

In the following activity, you are asked to analyze how elements of diversity affect the behavior of one of your parents or grandparents or another older family member.

ACTIVE LEARNING EXPERIENCE: EFFECTS OF ELEMENTS OF DIVERSITY ON THE BEHAVIOR OF YOUR PARENT/GRANDPARENT

Purpose

The purpose of this activity is to provide an opportunity for you to evaluate the potential effects of various elements of diversity on the behavior of your parents or grandparents. Upon completing this activity, you will be able to:

   1   Describe some of the possible influences of religion, ethnicity, minority status, occupation, and education on adult behavior.
   2   Analyze possible effects of elements of diversity on your parent or grandparent.

Time Required

45 minutes (30 minutes to complete the questions and 15 minutes to discuss the answers with another person).

Procedure

   1   Either as a homework assignment or in a class setting, complete the questions included in this activity. If this activity is completed as homework or in self-study, you may wish, if it is possible or feasible, to contact the relative whom you are describing.
   2   Discuss your responses with another person.
   3   Your instructor leads a class discussion of student responses to the activity.

Effects of Elements of Diversity on the Behavior of Your Parent/Grandparent

In this learning activity, you are to focus on *one* of your parents *or* grandparents. If you would feel more comfortable analyzing the behavior of another relative, you may do so. Prepare written responses to the following questions. After completing your responses, discuss them with another person.

1 Who is the person being described (your parent, grandparent, other relative)?

2 How old is this person?

3 Does this person belong to a specific ethnic group and/or religion, and, if so, which one(s)?

4 If the person belongs to such a group (or groups), give specific examples of how your relative's association with the group affects his or her behavior (e.g., attitudes, dietary practices, self-concept).

5 Does this individual belong to a minority group?

6 If so, in what ways does being a member of that specific minority influence his or her behavior?

7 What is or was your relative's occupation? Give specific examples of how your relative's occupational status has affected his or her behavior.

8 What is the individual's educational background, and how has it affected his or her behavior (e.g., attitudes, interests, goals)?

RESEARCH METHODS FOR EXAMINING DIVERSITY AND PSYCHOLOGICAL AGING

In this section of the chapter, we turn our attention to research methods used by gerontologists to establish facts and develop theories relevant to diversity and psychological aging. Some gerontologists conduct basic research aimed at answering theoretical questions about older persons or the aging process (e.g., analyzing the validity of the double-jeopardy hypothesis), while others engage in research with the solution of a practical problem as the immediate goal (e.g., evaluating mental health services for aging persons at a rural facility).

Cozby (1993) describes a variety of research methods useful to gerontological researchers, including survey research, case study, observation, archival research, and experimentation. Survey research, which includes questionnaires, interviews, or both, uses self-report measures to identify demographic information (e.g., religious identification or gender), attitudes (e.g., perceptions of Korean American elders), or behaviors (e.g., quality and number of social interactions with neighbors). The efficacy of survey methodology depends on the quality of sampling procedures, the wording of questions, and possible biases of the respondents and the researcher (Gelfand, 1994; Henderson, 1994). One problem facing researchers desiring to examine ethnic minorities is the high cost often involved in locating subjects and training interviewers (Markides, Liang, & Jackson, 1990). A significant issue in studies of subjects literate in languages other than English "is that of linguistic and cultural equivalence of our instruments" (Markides & Mindel, 1987, p. 41). Frequently researchers use back-translation, which involves a survey instrument being translated from English into the target language by one person and then translated back into English by a second individual. The efficacy of this process is complicated by cultural equivalence in that a term or phrase may connote entirely different meanings for subjects from different language and cultural groups (Markides & Mindel, 1987).

Also, there is a body of literature indicating that the gender or ethnicity/race of an interviewer may affect subject responses (Markides, Liang, & Jackson, 1990). Such responses may also be affected by the researcher's social class, even if the respondent and the interviewer share a similar ethnic background (Gelfand, 1994).

Another research strategy, the case study, may be particularly useful when dealing with clinical issues such as the development of depressive symptomatology in an ethnic elder. A case approach can give life to many of the nuances involved in the etiology and treatment of a psychological disorder in the context of diversity. By centering on one individual, the investigator can obtain detailed information; however, a key drawback of this approach is the limited generalizability of results to others.

Gerontologists may use field research to understand complexities in the lives of diverse elders. Conducted in natural settings, field studies are used so that researchers may comprehend "the subjective meanings of the people being studied" (Frankfort-Nachmias & Nachmias, 1992, p. 272). Social scientists, including anthropologists, psychologists, and sociologists, use participant observation to study older adults in existing natural environments. In order to perform this type of research, the investigator selects the role of either complete participant or participant-as-observer. In the former, researchers conceal their personal identity so as to minimize the effect of their presence on those being studied. Typically, when this approach is taken, the investigator attempts to maintain a "low-key" posture (Frankfort-Nachmias & Nachmias, 1992). There are some problems with such concealment. If subjects are not informed of the social scientist's presence as a researcher and of the goals of the study, the social scientist's behavior is suspect on ethical grounds. Also, researchers are placed under great strain in that they must play the part of participant whenever any of the subjects are present. Some researchers may overidentify with subjects and lose objectivity. Note-taking during periods of observation is severely limited, since such behavior could give away the investigator's true identity (Frankfort-Nachmias & Nachmias, 1992).

Because of ethical and methodological considerations, gerontologists may wish to function in the role of participant-observer. In this form of participant observation, investigators gain access to the subjects in their natural setting and develop relationships with them by communicating their actual identity as well as the goals of the research project. In this way, the social scientist studies subjects in their environment but not by pretending to be another member. Some researchers choose to get involved, to varying degrees, in certain functions of the subject group. Jennie Keith (1988), a prominent anthropologist who has conducted participant observation studies of diverse elders, suggests that "the observer's personal involvement in a research setting is always a central means to understanding it. Rather than using a research instrument, the participant observer becomes one" (p. 213).

Barbara Myerhoff (1979) contributed a fascinating example of participant observation with a study of a Los Angeles community center serving elderly

Jews. She spent 2 entire years, as well as periods of 2 additional years, studying older adults who frequented the Aliyah Center. The center serves a great many more individuals than the over 300 who pay dues. The existence of the Aliyah Center makes it possible for hundreds of elderly Jews to live in the community. Without the hot meals and social support, they would most likely have to live with adult children or in a geriatric facility. Emphasizing a secular Judaism, the center offers social and religious celebrations, discussion groups, and a multitude of classes. Most of the center's participants, having come from backgrounds of poverty, emigrated from Eastern Europe. Having avoided the almost certain extinction of the concentration camps of the Holocaust and by outliving many of their peers, the center Jews had become "survivors twice over" (Myerhoff, 1979, p. 23). While survivors' guilt can be emotionally disabling, many of these elders coped extremely well. Their relationships, ceremonies, and classes helped them create meaning in their present existence.

Many of these Jewish elders had emigrated to the United States in their youth or as young adults, married others from similar backgrounds, and raised children, many of whom were to become professionals and executives. Their children's educational and financial accomplishments often served to strain the ties between the "Old World" elders and their American offspring.

Myerhoff, a middle-aged PhD in anthropology and a Jew, interviewed more than half of the 300 center members and, in the course of the study, observed the entire membership. She spent much of her time with 38 subjects, tape recording from 2 to 16 hours of interviews with each of them. As part of the research, Myerhoff conducted a center class on "living history" in which she was able to begin the process of her subjects sharing their life narratives. In addition, Myerhoff interviewed other significant persons, such as volunteers, rabbis, and politicians. She visited center participants in their homes, accompanying many on shopping and medical visits; visited members as they moved to hospitals and convalescent centers; and attended numerous funerals.

Other popular research methods used in the study of diversity and psychological aging include archival research and experimentation. When using information that already exists to answer scientific questions, an investigator is applying the archival method. Archival research may include an analysis of written (e.g., personal letters or themes in popular magazines) or statistical (e.g., census data) records. For example, Arluke, Levin, and Suchwalko (1984) analyzed attitudes on elder sexuality and love as depicted in popular advice books. Experimentation on diversity and aging, which may be conducted in a laboratory or field setting, attempts to isolate the cause or causes of a phenomenon. This method is marked by careful attention to the elements of control and random assignment of subjects to experimental and control groups (Leedy, 1993).

Whatever the research method used, the gerontologist must be cognizant of the ethical implications of her or his work. Such concerns as informed consent, privacy, and confidentiality are central to the practice of a humane gerontology. When the rights of subjects are violated, individual subjects and the discipline of gerontology are apt to suffer. Also, the common resistance to research found in ethnic communities may be lessened through researchers displaying high ethical standards, constructing high-quality research instruments, communicating through both formal and informal channels about the intent of the research, and effectively selecting and training interviewers (Bengtson, Grigsby, Corry, & Hruby, 1977; Henderson, 1994).

As the next active learning experience, you will read and evaluate a research article on diversity and aging from a gerontological journal.

ACTIVE LEARNING EXPERIENCE: RESEARCH CRITIQUE

Purpose

This activity creates an opportunity for you to read and evaluate examples of research in diversity and aging. Upon completion of this activity, you will be able to:

1   Analyze an empirical article from the literature on diversity and aging.
2   Describe the research methodology used in the article.
3   Discuss possible ethical issues raised by the research.

Time Required

Approximately 3 to 3.5 hours (2.5 to 3 hours of learner preparation and 30 minutes of class discussion).

Procedure

1   You are to read an article describing research on diversity and aging. Pertinent articles appear in such journals as *The Gerontologist*, the *Journal of Gerontology, Psychology and Aging,* and *Research on Aging.*
2   Check with your instructor to make sure that the article you wish to evaluate meets the following criteria: (a) It is relevant to aging and diversity; (b) it comes from an appropriate academic journal; and (c) it contains original research (i.e., it is not simply a review of previous studies).
3   After reading the article, complete the six items listed below.
4   On the day it is due, turn in your completed critique to your instructor.
5   Your instructor will lead a discussion of student critiques.

Note: You should provide a complete citation of the article, the research method(s) used, a description of the subjects, the results, ethical issues, and personal reactions.

PERSONALITY, DIVERSITY, AND AGING

In this section, we turn our attention to the relationships among elements of diversity, individual personality, and aging. We place special emphasis on general models of personality and adulthood and on gender and personality.

Models of Personality and Adulthood

In order to address the possible ways in which elements of diversity may affect personality as a person progresses from middle to older adulthood, we must first discuss basic models of adult personality. An auspicious task confronting the investigator and the student is to define the term *personality*. According to Rybash, Roodin, and Santrock (1991), personality refers to "the distinctive patterns of behavior, thought, and emotion that characterize each person's adaptation to the situations of his/her life" (p. 544). The questions of how the aging process influences these distinctive patterns and how various elements of diversity interact with aging in modifying or maintaining adult personality need to be addressed by psychological researchers.

Psychologists and other behavioral scientists have generated several models to conceptualize the possible relationships between aging and personality. Most models of adult personality can be considered to be of two types: trait or developmental stage. McCrae and Costa (1984, 1988), having produced a great deal of data in support of a trait approach, find considerable stability in personality traits across adulthood. These researchers examined such factors as neuroticism, extroversion, and openness to experience and described those persons high in neuroticism as likely to engage in detrimental health habits (e.g., smoking), to complain of problems of a financial or sexual nature, and to express general dissatisfaction. In this approach, extroverts are perceived as those who seek contact with others through their occupational choices and social attachments and who display high levels of assertiveness and positive emotion. Persons with greater openness to experience demonstrate a high degree of spontaneity and rely more on their emotions than on a firm logic.

Trait approaches to personality make little effort to account for individual differences based on elements of diversity. Clearly, ethnicity and social class, as well as gender and other factors, affect traits such as extroversion and openness to experience. Depending on an individual's culture and her or his status within that culture, the expression of a particular trait may be reinforced or sanctioned. For example, an older woman may suppress her tendency toward assertion if she is punished for it by others.

Atchley (1989), in his continuity theory of older adult personality, suggests that older adults use their experiences and personal coping skills to manage the various changes in their physical, psychological, and social realms. In order to adjust to the changes that accompany aging, elders seek to maintain both internal and external continuity. For example, older adults who called upon their spiritual/

religious beliefs and practices in coping with losses and uncertainties earlier in their lives will most likely apply these strategies in their later years. Those ethnic elders who previously sought emotional support in their younger days will tend to continue that behavior. In a recent review of gender and the life course, Moen (1996) asserts that women are more likely than men to experience discontinuity in their lives as a result of "progressive declines in their child care responsibilities, and the intermittency of their labor-force participation concomitant with an increased likelihood of other family caregiving, with age" (p. 177).

A number of behavioral scientists have examined the adult and aging personality from a developmental stage framework. Consistent with this approach is the life course theory of psychoanalyst Erik Erikson (1982). Erikson postulates eight stages through which humans may progress from infancy through older adulthood. With each stage, the developing person experiences an ego crisis whose successful resolution is necessary if the individual is to progress to the next psychosocial stage. Erikson views adulthood as consisting of three such stages: (a) early adulthood, which involves the conflict of intimacy versus isolation; (b) middle adulthood, centered on the issue of generativity versus stagnation; and (c) older adulthood, focused on integrity versus despair. During the last stage, old age, those persons who have achieved wisdom have integrated the previous seven stages, perceive their life as having been worthwhile, and are able to accept the finality of their lives. In contrast, people who have not achieved such integration despair of death and question the very meaning of their lives. Over the course of his distinguished career, Erikson studied a variety of subjects, including Ogala Sioux children (Erikson, 1963), Martin Luther (Erikson, 1958), and Mahatma Gandhi (Erikson, 1969). However, the degree to which Erikson's approach to adult personality is applicable to persons from diverse social and cultural groups awaits further research.

Ethnic identity is related to the life stage of an individual (Luborsky & Rubinstein, 1987). The various stages of life call on a person to deal with differing tasks that may bring focus to or away from ethnic identity. How an individual develops psychologically can be profoundly affected, in several ways, by ethnicity (Luborsky & Rubinstein, 1987). Some of the more significant of such influences are as follows: (a) The way people see themselves (self-concept) is related to ethnicity; (b) in part, personal values and communication styles emanate from ethnicity; and (c) both ethnic values and communication styles affect interpersonal relationships. In an effort to better understand ethnic identity among male elders, Luborsky and Rubinstein studied a sample of Irish American, Italian American, and Jewish American subjects at the Philadelphia Geriatric Center. In conducting their research, the investigators used both a brief written instrument centering on aspects of ethnicity and a series of several-session in-depth interviews. In summarizing their findings, Luborsky and Rubinstein suggest that the particular meaning that elders place upon their ethnicity is related to their psychological development, their family history, the historical context of when and how they experienced key life events, a particular situation (for example, the death of a spouse, which may bring on a need to reintegrate oneself psychologically), and earlier ethnic experiences, which can be reinterpreted throughout the life course.

Gender and the Aging Personality

Most of the classical theories of personality, such as those of Freud, Jung, and Adler, while mentioning both genders, clearly view male emotions and behaviors as the norm against which all "humanity" is to be measured. As of the writing of this book, a typical text for a college course in personality (see, for example, Ryckman, 1996) may contain only one theory, that of Karen Horney, that devotes itself to the feminine personality.

Contemporary psychologists are examining the role of gender in determining the aging personality. However, the findings are difficult to interpret. Margaret Huyck (1990), in reviewing studies of gender differences and the aging personality, suggests that "the size, consistency, and meaning of gender differences in personality remain controversial matters. . . . Many personality measures do not reveal consistent sex differences" (pp. 127–128). In further summarizing the relevant research, Huyck (1990) asserts that the genders appear most different from late adolescence through young adulthood, becoming more alike in the latter part of middle age. During adolescence and young adulthood, issues surrounding sexuality come to the forefront for most individuals. Concerns about body image, sexual feelings, sexual relationships, and intimacy are a significant part of the individual human experience during these years. So it is in the context of these concerns that male and female adolescents and young adults attempt to demonstrate their "masculinity" and "femininity" through their clothing, music, social patterns, and so forth. But, of course, as we age, some things change.

According to David Gutmann (Fry, 1988; Gutmann, 1966, 1968, 1974, 1987, 1992), women tend to become more assertive in later life, while their male counterparts shift in the direction of passivity. On the basis of years of cross-cultural research, Gutmann has argued that as a result of parenting, most men have suppressed their dependency needs, whereas women have given up many of their tendencies toward aggression in order to raise their children. In many cultures that Gutmann analyzed, men were expected to compete and generate incomes, while women were assumed to occupy the nurturing role. But as their children grow and become fully functioning members of society, parents, particularly older adults, are able to "reclaim their powers" (Gutmann, 1987).

Changes in American culture affect relationships between gender and personality. Most women are called upon not only to provide much of the family's nurturance but also to develop marketable skills so that they can contribute significantly to the family income. Phyllis Moen and associates (cited in Moen, 1996) found that women who return to school after marrying and giving birth express a greater degree of mastery over their lives than women who do not. Those women who are able to manage the numerous roles typically expected of them and who make conscious and autonomous life choices appear to show increased self-esteem in their later years.

In the next activity, you will analyze gender similarities and differences among adolescents and young, middle-aged, and older adults whom you know.

ACTIVE LEARNING EXPERIENCE: GENDER SIMILARITIES AND DIFFERENCES ACROSS ADOLESCENCE AND ADULTHOOD

Purpose

In this learning experience, you will examine the behaviors of several adolescent, middle-aged, and older adult men and women whom you know. Upon completion of this activity, you will be able to:

    1 Describe several adolescent and adult behavioral patterns that may be related to gender roles.
    2 Analyze possible changes in contemporary gender roles as affected by aging.

Time Required

50 minutes (35 minutes to complete the questions and 15 minutes to discuss the answers with another person).

Procedure

    1 Either in a class setting or as a homework assignment, complete the questions included in this activity.
    2 Discuss your responses with another individual.
    3 Your instructor leads a discussion of responses to this activity.

Gender Similarities and Differences Across Adolescence and Adulthood

In this activity, you are to describe gender-role-related behaviors of (a) an adolescent female, (b) an adolescent male, (c) a young adult female, (d) a young adult male, (e) a middle-aged female, (f) a middle-aged male, (g) an older adult female, and (h) an older adult male. You are to describe the behavior of friends or family members. Answer the following questions. After completing your written responses, discuss them with another person.

Adolescent Female (13–18 Years of Age)

1 List two social behaviors in which she engages regularly that are consistent with what society expects of her as a female.

2 List any behaviors in which she engages that conflict with what is expected of her as a female adolescent.

Adolescent Male (13–18 Years of Age)

1 List two social behaviors in which he engages regularly that are consistent with what society expects of him as a male.

2 List any behaviors in which he engages that conflict with what is expected of him as a male adolescent.

Young Adult Female (19–30 Years of Age)

1 Describe two of her social behaviors that are consistent with societal expectations for her as a female.

2 List any behaviors in which she engages that are in conflict with what is expected of her as a young adult woman.

3 Does she get any messages from her family or friends regarding the appropriateness or inappropriateness of her goals or behaviors? If so, what are some of these messages?

Young Adult Male (19–30 Years of Age)

1 Describe two of his social behaviors that are consistent with societal expectations of him as a male.

2 List any behaviors in which he engages that are in conflict with what is expected of him as a young adult man.

3 Does he get messages from family or friends regarding the appropriateness or inappropriateness of his goals? If so, what are some of these messages?

Middle-Aged Female (31–55 Years of Age)

1 Describe two of her behaviors that you consider to be consistent with societal or family expectations of her as a middle-aged woman.

2 What are some of the messages that she receives from her family or friends regarding her behaviors?

3 In what key ways is her life similar to and/or different from the males in her family?

Middle-Aged Male (31–55 Years of Age)

1 Describe two of his behaviors that you consider to be consistent with societal or family expectations of him as a middle-aged man.

2 What are some of the messages that he receives from his family or friends regarding his behavior?

3 In what key ways is his life similar to and/or different from the females in his family?

Older Adult Female (56 Years of Age and Up)

1 What societal and family expectations influence her behavior as an older woman?

2 How does her role in the family or among her peers as an elderly woman differ from the role of middle-aged women?

3 In what ways is she similar to, and in what ways is she different from, male older adults you know?

Older Adult Male (56 Years of Age and Up)

1 What societal and family expectations influence his behavior as an older man?

2 How does his role as an elderly man in the family or among his peers differ from the roles of middle-aged men?

3 In what ways is he similar to, and in what ways is he different from, female older adults you know?

LIFE SATISFACTION

Life satisfaction, sometimes referred to as subjective well-being, concerns an "individual's perceptions of overall life quality" (George, 1990, p. 190). A person's degree of satisfaction is thought to be linked to the relationship between his or her goals and achievements and to be associated with socioeconomic position, attachments to family and community, and health (George, 1981; Krause, 1993). In reviewing 25 years of research, George (1990) concludes that the subjective well-being of older adults has improved slightly relative to that of younger persons. Studies conducted in the 1960s showed elders to be less satisfied than nonelders; by the 1970s, however, older adults indicated a little more life satisfaction than younger respondents. According to George, this pattern continues, with around 85% of older adults indicating overall life satisfaction. While most elders indicate a positive sense of well-being, some do not. Socioeconomic class is frequently linked directly or indirectly to perceptions of life satisfaction (George, 1990). Income affects level of health, ability to engage in various activities, and sense of security.

In addition, economics may play a crucial role in the various social exchanges in which older adults and younger people engage (Barresi, 1990; Dowd, 1975, 1978; Dowd & Bengtson, 1978). As applied to relationships between elders and younger persons, exchange theory suggests that the former lose power, and this situation may be intensified among ethnic elders (Barresi, 1990). Barresi contends that as younger ethnic individuals adopt dominant group values, traditional intergenerational relationships break down, leaving many older ethnic persons with little to exchange with their younger family members.

Jane Andrews and associates (1992) compared the life satisfaction of Hispanic elders with that of other older Americans. Andrews, Lyons, and Rowland (1992) conducted a telephone survey of about 2,300 Hispanic subjects. These researchers compared the findings of their survey (conducted in 1988) with data from a Louis Harris survey conducted in 1986. The Harris survey, which included more than 2,500 respondents, attempted to study a random sample of the American elderly population. Interestingly, only 48 Hispanic elders were included in the Harris survey.

Before reviewing the results of the study by Andrews, Lyons, and Rowland, it is important to note, as the authors do, that telephone surveys present some specific concerns. Such surveys, of course, fail to include households without phones, resulting in underestimations of individuals at the lowest income levels. Also, because the data are based solely on self-report, it is not possible to verify them.

The results of this study show major differences between Hispanics and other older adults. Fewer than half of the Hispanic subjects indicated that they were very satisfied, as compared with almost two thirds of the larger population of older adults. For Hispanic elders, life satisfaction scores were directly related to health and finances. In the general sample from the Harris survey, 14% reported insufficient income, as compared with 41% of the Hispanic elders contacted by Andrews and her associates. In summarizing their findings, Andrews, Lyons, and Rowland (1992) concluded:

> Compared to all elderly, elderly Hispanics are less likely to be very satisfied or achieve peace of mind or happiness. . . . The higher the level of health status, income, facility with English, educational attainment, and functional status, the better the overall subjective well-being of elderly Hispanics. (p. 37)

COPING WITH MAJOR LIFE STRESSORS AMONG DIVERSE ELDERS

In this section, we explore how diverse elders adapt and cope with major life stressors. Included is a discussion of a model of coping as well as material on the coping patterns of some diverse groups of older adults.

At this point, it is important to note that while many people associate old age with disability and decrements, most older adults function independently until they are very old (Kahana, Kahana, & Kinney, 1990). Furthermore, there are few data to support an association between advanced age and psychological distress (Feinson, 1991). While older adults may be faced with a number of recurring "distressors," such as chronic illness, aging in and of itself is not linked directly with an increased state of distress.

Figure 2.1, based on a model developed by Kahana, Kahana, and Kinney (1990), depicts some of the possible relationships between stress and coping among vulnerable elders, along with issues of diversity.

Methods of coping with life stressors depend on both internal and external resources. Included among internal resources are self-esteem, internal locus of control (viewing oneself as being able to effectively influence one's life), ability to find meaning in life, general personality style, and cognitive skills. Kahana and associates (1990) view external coping resources as involving social, environmental, and economic factors. Specifically, social elements could include ethnicity, gender, and cohort; environmental elements could involve regional considerations, living arrangements, and access to services; and economic elements would constitute issues of financial resources and social class.

Social support is a significant external resource for coping with stress. Apparently, older women are the recipients of more social support than are elderly men (Antonucci, 1985; Krause, 1988); however, they experience the same level of psychological disorder as their male peers. In attempting to explain this paradoxical finding, Krause (1988) argues that the relationships of elders are based on a norm of reciprocity in that older adults seek exchanges with others in an equitable fashion. In other words, high-quality relationships are characterized by doing things for one another as well as receiving from each other. Krause, drawing upon research by Antonucci (1985) and Kessler, Price, and Wortman (1985), writes "that elderly women, in addition to receiving more support than elderly men, also report providing more support to others . . . and . . . women's greater involvement in the lives of others can be a source of psychological disorder" (p. 178). Thus, while social support can help to serve as a buffer and a resource in dealing with life problems, it can cause additional distress as a result of concerns and worries about persons in an individual's social support network. Because of societal and family expectations, older women may be particularly vulnerable to this additional distress (Krause, 1988).

Relationships between some of the elements of diversity and psychological distress can be illustrated by research conducted by Krause and Goldenhar (1992), who investigated psychological distress and various environmental factors among elders who immigrated to the United States from Cuba, Mexico, and Puerto Rico. Using data gathered through the 1988 National Survey of Hispanic People, these investigators analyzed more than 1,339 cases from a telephone survey. Key variables measured included education, language acculturation, financial strain, social isolation, depressed affect, positive affect, age, gender, and years of residence in the United States. While Krause and Goldenhar view their findings as preliminary, the results do point to an association between financial strain among

The Role of Coping Strategies and Resources in Reducing Adverse Stress Conflicts

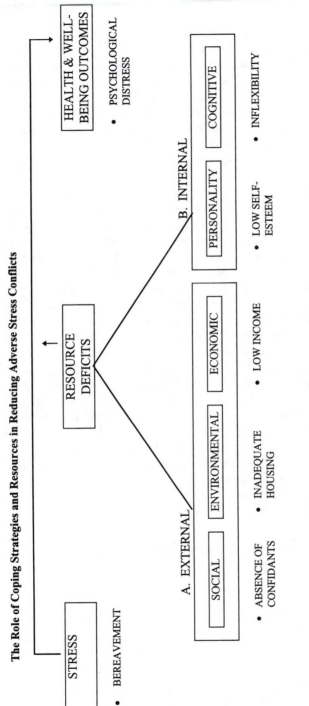

Figure 2.1 The role of coping strategies and resources in reducing adverse stress conflicts. (Kahana, Kahana, & Kinney, 1990. Copyright © 1990 Springer Publishing, Inc., New York 10012. Used by permission.)

Hispanic elders and level of acculturation. Data from this study support the notion that those Hispanics who are more acculturated experience a lower degree of social isolation as well as fewer financial problems, contributing, in part, to fewer symptoms of depressed mood. Furthermore, Krause and Goldenhar found that while there was not a statistically significant difference between elderly Puerto Rican Americans and their Mexican American and Cuban American peers regarding positive affect, Puerto Rican American subjects did experience significantly more depressive symptoms than Cuban American subjects. The researchers suggest that such "effects arise from the complex interplay between education, acculturation, and financial strain" (p. 287).

Stressors such as lack of formal education and social isolation can, of course, have a profound impact on the ability of diverse elders to cope. Carolyn Aldwin (1992) delineates three general ways in which aging can affect aspects of stress and coping. Aldwin considered the following categories: (a) biological processes, (b) cohort differences, and (c) processes of psychological development. Health concerns and chronic illness often associated with old age create distress for elders as they become more frail or as their loved ones become ill and/or die. The coping strategies available to many older adults may be a function of cohort. For example, depending on historical time and culture, elders may or may not be interested in obtaining professional assistance in dealing with concerns related to psychological discomfort. Also, as Aldwin notes, age can affect the styles that people employ in managing life's problems. It would be hoped that experience allows adults, particularly older adults, to use successful coping strategies. In earlier research, Aldwin (1990, 1991) found elders likely to refuse to accept personal responsibility for a significant stressor while, at the same time, handling the problems associated with it. In this way, their defensiveness conserves energy and saves face but does not preclude them from attempts at stress management. Further studies considering the effects of culture and ethnicity on aging and coping could prove illuminating.

In the next active learning experience, you will analyze two cases concerning distressors, resources, and coping strategies of diverse elders.

ACTIVE LEARNING EXPERIENCE: COPING WITH STRESS FOR DIVERSE ELDERS

Purpose

The purpose of this activity is to engage you in an examination of distressors, resources, and possible coping strategies for diverse elders. After completing this activity, you will be able to:

1 Describe the nature of some distressors affecting diverse elders.
2 Discuss possible resources for coping with the distress.
3 Formulate strategies for coping.

Time Required

40 minutes (25 minutes to complete the questions and 15 minutes to discuss the answers with another person).

Procedure

1 Complete the questions following each of the two cases included in this activity.
2 Discuss your responses with another person.
3 Your instructor will lead a discussion of student responses.

Coping with Stress for Diverse Elders

Read each of the following brief cases. After reading each case, prepare written responses to the accompanying questions. After completing the answers to the questions, discuss your responses with another person.

Case 1: Buzz Walker is a 77-year-old Black man living in Birmingham, Alabama. Three months ago, Maggie, his wife of 40 years, died of lung cancer. Buzz took care of her the best that he could, but it just wasn't enough. He misses her terribly; he's having trouble sleeping, and he doesn't have much of an appetite. Buzz's hands and arms hurt from the arthritis. He calls it his old friend, "Arthur" (some friend!). Buzz and Maggie belonged to the same church for more than 20 years. Every Wednesday and Friday they went to services, and Maggie sang in the choir. Most of their friends are from the church. Buzz worked off and on as a handyman, but Maggie was the one who always had the steady job. Money is real tight, but Buzz expects to manage. It's not money that occupies his mind, but how much he misses Maggie. They never had any children, but Maggie and Buzz used to joke that "they" were each other's kids.

Discussion Questions

1 Describe several of Buzz's distressors.
2 List any deficits in his resources.
3 What possible resources does Buzz have?
4 Develop a possible strategy for Buzz to use as he copes with the loss of his wife.

Case 2: Sylvia Weinstein, an 80-year-old retired teacher, lives in a small suburban community about an hour's drive from New York City. Sylvia's husband, Murray, died 10 years ago. Although Sylvia taught school for many years, she never learned to drive. Murray drove, took care of the finances, and pretty much managed their lives. Sylvia's pension income is adequate to meet her needs. She has few friends. Her closest friend, Ann, died last year from a heart attack. Sylvia's children are very concerned about her, but both of them are preoccupied with their own lives. Her son, Marvin, is in the middle of a bitterly contested divorce, and her daughter, Sheila, continues to battle chronic emotional problems. Marvin and Sheila and their respective children live in New York City. Sylvia enjoys her time with the grandchildren, particularly Marvin's youngest daughter, Tessie. Sylvia feels pretty good physically, but she's bored much of the time.

Discussion Questions

1 Describe several of Sylvia's distressors.
2 List any deficits in her resources.
3 What are Sylvia's possible resources?
4 Develop a possible coping strategy for Sylvia.

DIVERSITY, MENTAL HEALTH, AND AGING

The mental health of older adults can be related to numerous elements of diversity, including gender, class, place of residence, cohort, and ethnicity. In this section, we place emphasis on gender and ethnicity as we explore attitudes toward mental health and mental health services from the perspectives of older adults and service providers. We include a discussion of two significant types of psychological dysfunctions among minority elders: depression and dementia.

Attitudes Toward Mental Health and Mental Health Services

An individual's perceptions about her or his state of psychological well-being are influenced by a host of factors, some of which are elements of diversity such as gender, cohort, and ethnicity. Adults from older cohorts, including many ethnic elders, may view mental health services as representing treatment only for those who are "crazy" (Gelfand, 1994; Johnson, 1995; Rybarczyk, 1994). Some ethnic elders may wish to deny the severity of their psychological stress in order to avoid the stigma they associate with psychiatric problems. Others may blame such problems on personal or spiritual shortcomings (Gelfand, 1994). Older men may have learned to deny strong feelings as a problem-solving strategy, and instead of verbalizing personal or interpersonal concerns, they may experience a process of somatization in which psychological problems are converted into physical concerns (Rybarczyk, 1994). When an older man does accept that there is some psychological basis to his problems, it may be verbalized as a "problem with nerves." In this way, the individual continues to view the malady as physically based. Of course, many psychological disorders (e.g., dementias) do have a strong physiological basis, and all psychological problems affect the entire person.

Diverse elders may seek help for emotional issues, but that help often comes from sources other than social service agencies. For example, Ruth Greene and her colleagues found that, among older Blacks who sought professional assistance for psychological problems, only 4% visited a social service agency. In this same national sample, 18% visited a hospital, 17% went to a physician, and 7% sought the help of a minister (Greene, Jackson, & Neighbors, 1993).

Why don't more elders, particularly ethnic ones, avail themselves of mental health services? In addition to the aforementioned denial and somatization, elders, particularly those from ethnic backgrounds, may be thwarted by the very persons and institutions that are supposed to represent the "helping professions" (Johnson, 1995; Rybarczyk, 1994; Sue & Sue, 1990). Health professionals, because of a lack of specialized training in gerontology or ageistic sentiments, may perceive that counseling younger clients is more positive than counseling elderly ones and that older adults are not as likely to benefit from psychological counseling as are younger persons (Ford & Sbordone, 1980). Gaps in training and stereotypical attitudes may also help to explain why physicians may not be inclined to diagnose psychiatric disorders in elderly clients (German, Shapiro, Skinner, VonKorff, Klein, Turner, Teitelbaum, Burka, & Burns, 1987; Rabins, Lucas, Teitelbaum, Mark, & Folstein, 1983; Rybarczyk, 1994; Waxman & Carner, 1984). Frequently, physicians misperceive psychological problems as purely manifestations of physical illness (Rybarczyk, 1994).

Some of the barriers facing prospective clients who are elderly may relate to therapists' own psychological conflicts. Older clients, including minority ethnic clients, may unwittingly reinforce counselors' anxieties about their own aging, bring to counselors' awareness their own personal unresolved conflicts with their elderly parents, or demonstrate counselors' discomfort in dealing with clients who may have physical or cognitive disabilities (Butler, Lewis, & Sunderland, 1991).

In addition, service providers from the majority or dominant culture may be less inclined to work with ethnic minorities, or such staff may lack skills in cross-cultural interactions (Johnson, 1995; Sue & Sue, 1990). Ethnocentric values and behaviors may create significant obstacles for ethnic clients who could benefit from relevant psychological counseling. Professional therapists may discount the legitimacy and efficacy of the informal support networks so often used by minority clients. Even definitions of what constitutes mental health or psychological disturbance may be so different that a client from a minority ethnic perspective and a mainstream majority culture therapist may have great difficulties in communicating, even when they are both vocalizing in the same language (Johnson, 1995; Sue & Sue, 1990). Family norms and expectations may differ widely from American subculture to subculture; thus, the behavior of an elder or an adult child may appear pathological to a therapist but, in actuality, be normative in the context of a given ethnic group. In order to accommodate such differences, McGoldrick (1982) suggests that ethnic families could benefit from the use of a cultural broker, a counselor

> who validates their ethnic traditions, helps them make sense of the differences in assimilation levels between each of the members, validates the anxiety created by

reconciling ethnic traditions with the cultural mainstream, and helps them sort through what traditions they can productively maintain and which ones need modification. (Johnson, 1995, p. 185)

Counseling and clinical psychologists perform assessments of elderly clients in order to ascertain the nature and scope of emotional and behavioral dysfunctions. Because of cultural traditions, values, and/or level of English-language proficiency, older ethnic clients may have great difficulty obtaining accurate diagnoses of the existence, nature, and extent of their psychological problems. Clinicians are sometimes able to address language issues through the use of appropriately translated standardized psychometric instruments (Taussig, Henderson, & Mack, 1992). In order to help meet this need, I. Maribel Taussig and associates (1992) used Spanish-language translations of a series of psychological testing instruments including a structured interview, a scale for activities of daily living, a depression inventory, a checklist for memory and behavior, and an entire battery of neuropsychological tests. These clinicians wanted to ensure that the translations were consistent with the reality that specific words meaningful to one group of Spanish-speaking clients may be offensive or meaningless to those from another Spanish-speaking ethnic group. Five psychologists from Argentina, Colombia, Cuba, Mexico, and Puerto Rico back-translated an initial translation of the instruments. Using the Spanish-language neuropsychological tests, the researchers assessed four subject groups: 19 Spanish-speaking elders and 19 English-speaking elders meeting accepted criteria for "probable" Alzheimer's disease and 18 Spanish-speaking and 18 English-speaking elders of comparable ages with no known neurological disease. All of the Spanish-speaking subjects had Spanish as their only or primary language. The researchers demonstrated the utility of the Spanish-language neuropsychological tests in that the instruments "differentiated between elderly comparison subjects and mildly-to-moderately demented AD [Alzheimer's disease] patients" (p. 101).

Since ethnic elders, especially those who are first-generation immigrants, may not be fluent or comfortable in speaking or understanding English, it behooves the helping professions to insist that their graduates be conversant in another language. Since the largest growing minority cultures in America are Hispanic, Spanish-speaking therapists are most sorely needed. Sometimes service agencies employ language translators; this is often not an optimal strategy, however, since linguistic nuances may be missed or the presence of translators may be viewed as interfering with the privacy needs of clients (Gelfand, 1994). Certainly, there will continue to be a strong need for members of ethnic minorities to be trained as clinical and counseling psychologists, psychiatrists, social workers, psychiatric nurses, and so forth. These individuals, having been educated in the helping professions and mindful of ethnic values and practices, may be instrumental in improving the delivery of quality mental health services to ethnic minority elders and their families.

The next activity asks you to rate your attitudes regarding issues related to mental health and diverse older adults.

ACTIVE LEARNING EXPERIENCE: ATTITUDES TOWARD MENTAL HEALTH AND DIVERSE OLDER ADULTS

Purpose

The purpose of this activity is for you to gauge your attitudes toward diverse elders, their psychological disorders, and the treatment of their dysfunctions. Upon completion of this activity, you will be better able to:

1   Understand your personal attitudes concerning mental health issues and diverse elders.
2   Analyze how your attitudes could affect your working relationships with older adults.

Time Required

40 minutes (10 minutes to complete the answer sheet, 10 minutes to discuss responses with another person, and 20 minutes for class discussion).

Procedure

1   Complete the questionnaire.
2   Discuss your responses with another student.
3   Your instructor leads a discussion of student responses.

Attitudes Toward Mental Health and Diverse Older Adults

Indicate to what extent you agree or disagree with the statements to follow. Please respond accurately and indicate your true response, not how you think you "should" respond.

		Strongly agree	Agree	Disagree	Strongly disagree
1	Old age is the worst time of life.	_____	_____	_____	_____
2	I don't want to get old.	_____	_____	_____	_____
3	It is normal for older people to be depressed.	_____	_____	_____	_____

	Strongly agree	Agree	Disagree	Strongly disagree
4 It is normal for older people to be confused.	_____	_____	_____	_____
5 Older people resist change.	_____	_____	_____	_____
6 If I were a mental health specialist, I would prefer working with younger people rather than older ones.	_____	_____	_____	_____
7 Older adults have difficulty in being analytical about their feelings and behaviors.	_____	_____	_____	_____
8 Psychotherapy lacks usefulness for elders.	_____	_____	_____	_____
9 · Ethnic minority elders are suspicious of health care professionals from majority culture backgrounds.	_____	_____	_____	_____
10 Ethnic elders should learn English if they wish to benefit from mental health services.	_____	_____	_____	_____

After you have responded to the questionnaire items, share your responses with another person. Discuss the impact your attitudes may have on your effectiveness in working professionally with older adults.

Depression

One of the most common psychological disorders in older adulthood is depression (Butler, Lewis, & Sunderland, 1991). However, a majority of studies support the notion that depressive disorders are less common among older adults than among younger ones. In elderly persons, depression is often exhibited as a lessened experience of pleasure, apathy, problems with appetite and sleep, and negativity, while, in younger persons, it is manifested through a more conscious perception of sadness (Rybarczyk, 1994).

The concept of depression is rooted in the traditions of Western medicine. While symptoms and behaviors associated with depression (e.g., apathy and sleep problems) are universal, the concept of depression apparently has no linguistic equivalent in some non-Western cultures (Carr & Vitaliano, 1985).

When depression occurs in ethnic minorities, it may be linked to acculturation. For example, Kaveh Zamanian and associates (Zamanian, Thackery, Starrett, Brown, Lassman, & Banchard, 1992) surveyed a sample of 159 older Mexican Americans in order to determine possible relationships between depressive symptoms and acculturation. These researchers viewed acculturation as the process by which people from one culture adapt to a different culture.

Previous studies have suggested that depression among Mexican Americans is linked to acculturation in one of the following three ways: (a) less acculturated persons are more vulnerable; (b) less acculturated persons experience lower risk; or (c) those persons adapted to both the Mexican and the dominant culture are less vulnerable. Zamanian et al.'s subjects responded to demographic items, two depression scales, and the Acculturation Rating Scale for Mexican Americans (Cuellar, Harris, & Jasso, 1980). Interestingly, subjects who were low in acculturation level exhibited higher scores on the depression scales than either highly acculturated or bicultural subjects. Zamanian's research group concluded that "retention of aspects of Mexican culture without concomitant attempts to incorporate aspects of the dominant culture results in the most vulnerable position to depression" (p. 116).

Across adulthood, women are more likely to experience major depressive disorders than are men (Herzog, 1989). In elderly men, depression is characteristically related to physical illness, or it may appear after surgery (Rybarczyk, 1994).

There is a relationship between depression and suicide, and the rate of suicide among the elderly is the highest of any age group (the highest rate is found among White men in their 80s). Rates for women reach a peak in midlife; in non-White men, rates peak in young adulthood (Rybarczyk, 1994). Although women are more likely to attempt suicide, men are more likely to actually commit suicide, since they are apt to use more lethal means (Butler, Lewis, & Sunderland, 1991). According to Rybarczyk (1994), the best predictors of elderly male suicide are serious health problems, social isolation, and the death of a spouse. It is as yet unclear why elderly White men are at a greater risk for suicide. Perhaps White men experience even more "rolelessness" than women or minority men since, in general, they have farther to fall in terms of status (Rybarczyk, 1994).

Dementias

A number of mental disorders may give rise to the dementia syndrome in older adulthood, with the most common of these disorders being Alzheimer's disease (AD). AD may be seen in older adults who are experiencing progressive loss of short- and long-term memory as well as impaired judgment or abstract thinking, changes in personality, or additional problems with higher cortical functioning (Raskind & Peskind, 1992). Several criteria have been established by the National Institute of Neurological and Communicative Disorders and Stroke and the Alzheimer's Disease and Related Disorders Association to diagnose AD. The diagnosis is made on the basis of (a) clinical examination and neurological testing, (b) deficits in at least two areas of cognition, (c) a progressive worsening of memory, (d) lack of a disturbance of consciousness, (e) initial onset between 40 and 90 years of age (mostly after age 65), and (f) "the absence of systematic disorders or other brain diseases that could account for the progressive deficits in memory and cognition'' (cited in Raskind & Peskind, 1992, p. 479). Depressive symptoms are found among Alzheimer's patients, and it is not uncommon for patients who are suffering from depression to be labeled as demented or for those with dementia to be categorized as depressed. In fact, some studies have shown that a number of Alzheimer's disease patients are experiencing depression as well (Raskind & Peskind, 1992).

Many researchers assume that the prevalence of Alzheimer's and related disorders is similar for ethnic minorities and the American population as a whole (Braun, Takamura, Forman, Sasaki, & Meininger, 1995). However, there is evidence that the rates of Alzheimer's disease and other dementing illness vary among ethnic populations (Larson & Imai, 1996). Such differences may be due, in part, to the general lack of appropriate neuropsychological assessment tools for elders without English-language skills and variations in reporting an elder's confusion and memory loss. Symptoms of AD and related disorders may be interpreted differently in various cultural groups. For example, disorientation may be viewed as a natural component of aging or as a stigma for the family (Yeo, 1996).

Of great concern to health care providers is the fact that, in comparison with majority culture caregivers, minority caregivers are significantly less likely to use agencies offering services for the families of Alzheimer's patients. Kathryn Braun and her colleagues (Braun, Takamura, Forman, Sasaki, & Meininger, 1995) list the following strategies for increasing service use: (a) develop culturally sensitive outreach materials in the language of the targeted population and present them in an appropriate context; (b) disseminate the materials through minority-oriented public media; (c) work with community groups and leaders to encourage service use; and (d) evaluate services as to their accessibility and acceptability to minority persons.

In order to increase the knowledge base about dementias as well as awareness of available services, Braun and her associates developed and tested outreach materials on Alzheimer's disease for Asian/Pacific Islanders in Hawaii. The research team used focus groups for developing and understanding the ethnic-specific needs of Filipinos, Vietnamese, and Chinese. During the focus group sessions, subjects described their respect for elders and their use of both family and neighborhood for elder care. Also, focus group participants described symptoms of dementia in concepts and words from their language and culture. The cultural groups showed some clear differences, with Filipinos suspicious of public agencies, perhaps as a result of their fears about the immigration service. Braun's team used current service practice literature to draft culturally tailored materials for Hawaiians, Japanese, Koreans, and Samoans. All of the ethnic groups expressed the belief that educational literature on dementia should be communicated by an individual from their cultural group, one both knowledgeable and respected. The groups suggested that information on dementia should be given in ways consistent with cultures and languages. The investigators concluded that videos would be used to represent a family drama in a home setting.

By means of pretests, discussions, and posttests, outreach brochures and videos were reviewed by ethnic samples, the materials proving to be very helpful.

In addition to providing services tailored to ethnic elders, it is also important to develop Alzheimer's services for rural elders and their families. On the basis of their work in rural New Hampshire, Yvonne Vissing and associates (Vissing, Salloway, & Siress, 1994) described the North Country Alzheimer's Partnership, a 3-year demonstration project. These authors suggested the following possible models for organizing such services: (a) the imported model, which makes use of the expertise of agencies from outside a rural community; (b) the local initiative model, which relies on the services of existing local agencies and personnel; and (c) the partnership model, which combines "the best of both worlds: the placement of outside expertise within the structure of established community organization" (p. 310). Using the partnership model, the North Country Alzheimer's Partnership offered comprehensive assessments, case management, and referral services, as well as individual treatment and service planning.

The National Institute for Mental Health provided the funding for the project. Two state agencies provided the principal investigators and were administrators of the grant, and a regional tier of agencies offered expertise in case management. A county community action agency and six regional home health agencies provided nursing assessments. Persons with Alzheimer's disease, along with their primary caregivers, participated in the project.

Vissing and her colleagues provide evaluation data suggesting that the project was successful in addressing rural clients' needs. However, there were problems. These authors believe that the complex administrative organization and problems associated with integrating outside agencies with local ones were limiting factors. They suggest that a variation of the model, a limited-term partnership, be used in providing Alzheimer's-related services in rural settings. According to Vissing and associates, "In such a model, outside professionals can work in concert with local providers to construct care systems and to model professional practice with the understanding that the system will become the legitimate property of the local community" (p. 315).

SUMMARY

In this chapter, we have discussed relationships among aging, culture, and behavior. The initial section included material on the social clock, with an emphasis on the differing social clocks affecting women, as well as information on the relationships among age norms, social class, and minority ethnic status. The next unit of the chapter described possible research strategies for understanding diversity and psychological aging. Under this topic, we discussed special problems involved in research with ethnic elders, the process of back-translation, a description of Barbara Myerhoff's participant observation study of a Los Angeles community center serving Jewish elders, and research ethics. Next we investigated personality, diversity, and aging by looking at models of personality and aging, ethnic identity and older adult personality, and gender and the aging personality. A subsequent section, devoted to life satisfaction, included a discussion of a study by Jane Andrews and associates comparing the life satisfaction of Hispanic elders with that of other older adults. We then viewed the ways in which diverse elders cope with major life stressors by describing a model developed by Eva Kahana and associates, research on social support and older women, and Krause and Goldenhar's work demonstrating an association between acculturation and a lower degree of social isolation among Hispanic immigrant elders. The final part of the chapter was devoted to diversity, mental health, and aging. Material centered on attitudes of elders toward mental health, attitudes of mental health professionals toward diverse elders, assessment of clients, and suggestions for increasing the use and quality of relevant mental health services. A section on depression highlighted the notion of depression as culture bound and featured a discussion of a study by Kaveh Zamanian and associates on the relationship between acculturation and depression in a sample of Mexican Americans. A discussion of Alzheimer's disease featured a description of a project by Kathryn Braun and colleagues, who developed and tested culturally sensitive outreach materials on Alzheimer's disease for Asian/Pacific Islanders in Hawaii. In addition, we included a discussion of a project developed by Yvonne Vissing and associates aimed at providing Alzheimer's-disease-related services to rural New Hampshire elders and their families.

In order to review issues relevant to this chapter, complete the following quiz.

ACTIVE LEARNING EXPERIENCE: DIVERSITY IN PSYCHOLOGICAL AGING QUIZ

Purpose

The aim of this activity is to gauge your present knowledge of issues related to psychological aging and diversity. Upon completion of this activity, you will be able to:

1 Assess your knowledge of diversity and psychological aging.
2 Gain feedback on your knowledge of these issues.

Time Required

30 minutes (10 minutes to complete the quiz and 20 minutes to discuss your answers with another person or in a classroom setting).

Procedure

1 Complete the quiz.
2 Your instructor leads a review of the answers to the quiz in class.

Diversity in Psychological Aging Quiz

Indicate whether each of the following statements is true or false.

		True	False
1	Regardless of gender, class, or ethnicity, all Americans share the same ''social clock.''	_____	_____
2	Social class is related to both ethnicity and minority group membership.	_____	_____
3	In research on aging, the race and gender of an interviewer can influence subject responses.	_____	_____
4	The translation of research instruments can pose significant problems for researchers of aging and ethnicity.	_____	_____
5	Experimental methodology is the best form of research for those studying diversity in psychological aging.	_____	_____
6	Personality lacks stability across adulthood.	_____	_____
7	Ethnic identity can affect self-concept, values, communication styles, and interpersonal relationships.	_____	_____
8	Personality studies show consistent differences between adult men and women.	_____	_____
9	Life satisfaction is associated with socioeconomic class.	_____	_____
10	Social support can cause female elders additional distress.	_____	_____
11	Because of their own anxieties about aging, some mental health professionals have difficulties in treating older clients.	_____	_____
12	There are words to describe the concept of depression in every known language.	_____	_____
13	Alzheimer's disease is viewed in the same way by all ethnic groups.	_____	_____
14	A cultural broker is a therapist or family member who reinforces ethnic values and behaviors.	_____	_____

GLOSSARY

Alzheimer's Disease   A neurological disorder resulting in the gradual and progressive loss of brain cells. Causing progressive memory loss, this disease results eventually in an individual's inability to remember even simple tasks like eating and bathing.

Archival Research   This methodology involves the use of existing statistical or written data, such as health records or personal letters.

Back-Translation   A technique used in developing equivalent cultural and linguistic survey instruments. One individual translates the survey into the target language, and that translated instrument is then translated back into English (or whatever the original language of the survey) by another individual.

Case Study   The focus is on a particular individual subject. The strength of this technique involves the depth with which a particular subject is analyzed, but a key weakness is an inability to generalize results.

Cultural Broker   The role of a therapist or of a member of an ethnic family aimed at reinforcing ethnic values and behaviors as well as understanding and blending the level of assimilation of an individual or family with the host or majority culture.

Experimental Research   Characterized by precision and control and conducted either in a laboratory or field setting, this research strategy includes the random assignment of subjects to experimental and control groups. This type of research attempts to identify cause and effect relationships.

Life Satisfaction   This refers to a person's subjective sense of well-being. It is typically associated with the relationship between a person's goals and achievements and is also linked with socioeconomic status, health, and family and community attachments.

Observational Research and Field Study   These techniques allow the investigator to observe subjects in real-world settings. In field studies, subjects are aware that they are being studied, while in observational studies, subjects are often unaware. These methods are fraught with issues of ethics and objectivity.

Personality   This is among the most complicated of all constructs in the behavioral sciences. It refers to that which differentiates an individual's behaviors and thoughts as well as characteristic patterns of adaptation.

Psychometric Instrument   A standardized test, administered by a psychologist, that measures psychological factors such as elements of personality, intelligence, or psychopathology.

Social Clock   Cultures and subcultures define age norms for their members. Persons are reinforced for performing or accomplishing tasks "on-time" and sanctioned for engaging in these same behaviors "off-time."

Socioeconomic Class   Related to both ethnicity and minority group membership, social class is associated with income, education, and occupation.

Survey Research   Commonly used by ethnogerontologists, this technique involves self-reports through questionnaires and interviews to obtain demographic, behavioral, and attitudinal data. Research quality depends on sampling strategies, cost, survey language, and possible researcher or respondent bias.

SUGGESTED READINGS

Binstock, R. H., & George, L. K. (Eds.). (1996). *Handbook of aging and the social sciences* (4th ed.). San Diego, CA: Academic Press.

Included in this timely volume are chapters on quantitative research, qualitative research, aging and culture, and gender and aging, along with a useful synthesis of research on race, aging, and ethnicity by Kyriakos Markides and Sandra Black. The various chapters make for difficult reading.

Birren, J. E., & Schaie, K. W. (Eds.). (1996). *Handbook of the psychology of aging* (4th ed.). San Diego, CA: Academic Press.

This text includes a number of relevant chapters devoted to, for example, reviews of research on social cognition, motivation and emotion, and personality. This authoritative guide, while difficult to read, is an excellent source on methodologies for conducting research on the psychology of aging.

Brink, T. L. (Ed.). (1992). *Hispanic aged mental health.* New York: Haworth Press.

This book, also published as an issue of *Clinical Gerontologist* (Volume 11, Numbers 3 and 4, 1992), includes 16 articles, with discussions of the diversity of aging in Latin America and the Caribbean, caregiving for Alzheimer's patients in Hispanic families, translation and validation of psychometric scales, acculturation and depression, curses, and barriers to health care access.

Harel, Z., Erlich, P., & Hubbard, R. (Eds.). (1990). *The vulnerable aged: People, services, and policies.* New York: Springer.

This volume is devoted to an examination of vulnerable elders. Sections cover diversity and service needs, special populations, and policies and programs. Readers interested in coping and stress should consult the chapters by Kahana and associates and by George.

Helson, R., & McCabe, L. (1994). The social clock project in middle age. In B. F. Turner & L. E. Troll (Eds.), *Women growing older: Psychological perspectives* (pp. 68–93). Thousand Oaks, CA: Sage.

This chapter describes the authors' research on women's social clock projects involving work and family. The authors studied 142 mostly White, upper-middle-class women who had been examined in their late 20s, early 40s, and early 50s. Helson and McCabe focus the chapter on data collected when the participants were 43 and 52 years old.

Henderson, J. N. (1994). Ethnic and racial issues. In J. F. Gubrium & A. Sankar (Eds.), *Qualitative methods in aging research* (pp. 33–50). Thousand Oaks, CA: Sage.

Henderson's chapter informs the reader about the different cultural contexts of gerontological researchers and elders from diverse populations. Using his own research on ethnic minority Alzheimer's support groups, Henderson cautions researchers to be cognizant of ethnocultural variables. Included are discussions of the targeted ethnographic survey, fieldworker status and role variations, and ethnic, generational, and social status disparity as important factors in ethnogerontological research.

Sue, D. W., & Sue, D. (1990). *Counseling the culturally different: Theory and practice* (2nd ed.). New York: Wiley.

Anyone with an interest in counseling and psychotherapy can benefit from reading this text. The authors, a counseling psychologist and a clinical psychologist, present compelling material on the politics of counseling, barriers to effective cross-cultural counseling, the culturally skilled counselor, counseling specific ethnic populations, and other relevant topics. Included is a final chapter on critical incident cases that can be used in preparing students to become more adept in cross-cultural counseling.

Wykle, M. L., Kahana, E., & Kowal, J. (Eds.). (1992). *Stress and health among the elderly*. New York: Springer.

This excellent assortment of readings includes material on social support, coping, loss, widowhood, extreme stress, and minority elders. Especially recommended are chapters by Jackson and Antonucci, Aldwin, Boaz Kahana, and Hubbard.

Yeo, G., & Gallagher-Thompson, D. (Eds.). (1996). *Ethnicity and the dementias*. Bristol, PA: Taylor & Francis.

This volume contains five sections titled "Overview of Issues," "Assessment of Cognitive Status with Different Ethnic Populations," "Working with Families of Dementia Patients from Different Ethnic Populations," "Special Issues and Special Populations," and "Implications for the Future." Included among the contributors are leading experts in psychology, medicine, nursing, social work, and related helping professions. Some chapters reflect integration of empirical studies, while others describe practical strategies for working with ethnic elders and their families.

KEY: DIVERSITY IN PSYCHOLOGICAL AGING QUIZ

1 **False**. Gender, class, and ethnicity have an impact on an individual's life course, affecting the timing of important events (Barresi, 1990). Helson and associates (Helson, Mitchell, & Moane, 1984; Helson & Moane, 1987) have investigated feminine and masculine social clocks.

2 **True**. In American society, members of certain ethnic and minority groups are more likely to belong to a particular class or classes (Stoller & Gibson, 1994).

3 **True**. Respondents can be influenced by the gender, race, or class of an interviewer, and interviewers may be influenced by the characteristics of respondents (Gelfand, 1994).

4 **True**. It is difficult to translate research instruments so that they are both linguistically and culturally equivalent (Markides & Mindel, 1987).

5 **False**. The appropriate methodology depends on a variety of factors, including hypotheses, access to subjects, budgetary constraints, and research skills. There is no best or superior methodology (Leedy, 1993).

6 **False**.   Some researchers have found a great deal of stability in personality across adulthood (Costa et al., 1986).

7 **True**.   In their study of Irish American, Italian American, and Jewish American male elders, Luborsky and Rubinstein (1987) found that an individual's ethnic identity is related to self-concept, values, communication style, and relationships.

8 **False**.   The findings on gender differences in adult personality "do not reveal consistent sex differences" (Huyck, 1990, p. 128).

9 **True**.   Life satisfaction or subjective well-being is associated with socioeconomic class, relationships between goals and achievements, attachments to family and community, and health (George, 1981, 1990; Krause, 1993).

10 **True**.   Older women experience more social support, but they are also expected to reciprocate that support, which can bring about additional distress (Antonucci, 1985; Kessler, Price, & Wortman, 1985; Krause, 1988).

11 **True**.   As a result of personal anxieties about aging or unresolved conflicts with their own elderly parents, some therapists may experience difficulties in working with elderly clients (Butler, Lewis, & Sunderland, 1991).

12 **False**.   The concept of depression is rooted in Western medicine. While symptoms associated with depression appear to be universal, the concept of depression has no linguistic equivalent in some non-Western cultures (Carr & Vitaliano, 1985).

13 **False**.   Differing ethnic groups may view symptoms associated with Alzheimer's disease quite differently. In some cultures, symptoms of memory loss and confusion may be seen as "normal" consequences of aging. In some ethnic communities, dementias, such as Alzheimer's disease, may be associated with the stigma of having a "crazy" family member (Yeo, 1996).

14 **True**.   A cultural broker is a therapist or family member who reinforces ethnic values and behaviors and who assists in blending the individual or family with the majority or host culture (McGoldrick, 1982).

KEY: EXAMPLE OF A RESEARCH CRITIQUE

1 Complete citation of the article: Krause, N. (1993). Race differences in life satisfaction among aged men and women. *Journal of Gerontology: Social Sciences, 48,* 235–244.
2 Research method(s) used: The researcher constructed a conceptual model. Hypotheses from the model were tested via data from the Aging of the Eighties Survey, which had been conducted in 1981 by Louis Harris and Associates.

3 Description of subjects: A subsample of data from retired Black and White elders was analyzed.

4 Results: Older Blacks reported lower levels of life satisfaction. The differences in races seemed to be related to interactions among level of education, financial planning for retirement, concerns with current finances, and financial dependence on family.

5 Ethical issues: This use of the archival data complies with ethical practice in gerontological research.

6 Personal reactions: The author suggests that the model could be expanded to include other variables. Also, using current data gathered from Black and White elders during the mid- to late 1990s could add to the value of this research.

Chapter 3

Issues in Health and Sexuality

OVERVIEW

Mortality and Diversity

- What is the relationship between gender and mortality?
- What are some of the findings regarding minority group membership and mortality?
- What is the racial mortality crossover effect?
- Discuss some of the possible methodological problems with mortality studies of Asian Americans.

Health Beliefs and Behaviors

- How does culture affect health and illness beliefs and practices?
- Describe and apply Kleinman's explanatory model framework to distinguish health beliefs and practices of diverse elders and health professionals.
- What is *curanderismo*?
- Discuss Zborowski's findings regarding culture and the expression of pain.

Socioeconomic Class, Poverty, Medicare, and Medicaid

- What are some of the relationships between elements of diversity and poverty among older Americans?
- What is Medicaid?
- Describe Medicare, Part A and Part B.
- How does one interpret the notice called Explanation of Part B Benefits?

Rural Issues in Health and Illness

- How does the health of rural elders compare with that of urban elders?
- Discuss Thorson and Powell's findings on the health of metropolitan and nonmetropolitan Nebraska elders.

- What is the health status of older American Indians residing in rural and reservation settings?

Physical Illness

- What are the most frequently reported health conditions of older Americans?
- What are arthritis and osteoporosis, and why might these chronic disorders be more prevalent among older women than among older men?
- Why do older women report more instances of acute and chronic illness and use health services at different rates than do their male counterparts?
- Contrast the double-jeopardy hypothesis and the age-as-leveling theory.
- Describe Black-White differences in the health status of older adults.
- Why are Black elders more pessimistic about their health than are White elders?
- How do Hispanic elders compare with White elders in terms of health status?
- What are some differences between Hispanic groups when it comes to the health of older adults?
- Why might findings suggesting that Asian American elders are healthier than Whites misrepresent the relative health status of some ethnic groups?
- What are some findings from health studies that break down Asian/Pacific Islanders into specific ethnic subgroups?
- How does the health of Native American elders compare with that of elders in the general population?
- What is the relationship between socioeconomic class and health in later life?

Issues in Diversity, Sexuality, and Aging

- What is menopause, and what are its characteristics?
- What are several physical and psychological problems having a relationship to menopause?
- What changes in the physiology of sex do women experience with aging?
- What changes in the physiology of sex do men experience with aging?
- What are some examples of ageistic attitudes and behaviors that demean the sexuality of older adults?
- What are some of the ways in which older adults express their sexuality?
- What are some of the effects of American social institutions denying the reality of long-term, committed same-sex relationships?
- In general, do older gay men and lesbians cope with life problems similar to those of older heterosexuals?
- What are the family configurations within which older gay men and lesbians age?

Summary

Issues in Health and Sexuality Quiz

Glossary

Suggested Readings

Key: Issues in Health and Sexuality Quiz

This chapter addresses a variety of issues regarding health, diversity, and aging. We place emphasis on gender and ethnicity as we discuss such topics as mortality, health beliefs and behaviors, social class and health, rural issues, and sexuality. Representative examples of research are highlighted throughout the chapter. There have been numerous studies related to health and diversity, especially investigations on gender and mortality, gender and morbidity, and Black-White differences in mortality and morbidity. This chapter is designed as a discussion of what we believe to be among the most significant findings in this area. Interested readers are encouraged to continue their studies through sources described in the accompanying suggested readings and those listed in the reference section.

The following vignettes serve to introduce the present topic.

Vignette 1: Mavis Johnson lives in the small town in southern Iowa where she was born. A 90-year-old widow, Mrs. Johnson lives off a check from Social Security and a very modest annuity. Her health has declined gradually in the past five years. In addition to very painful arthritis affecting her hands, she has high blood pressure, other cardiovascular problems, and failing eyesight. Most of her family continues to live in this not very affluent farming community. A son and a daughter help with chores, grocery shopping, and the maintenance of her small house. Mrs. Johnson has monthly appointments with two physicians whose offices are 60 miles away. The county in which she resides maintains a health clinic that is open a few days a week and staffed with public health nurses. Mavis wants to see a doctor when she has health concerns, but that entails a trip to the city and the necessity that her son or daughter take off from work in order to drive her to her appointments.

Vignette 2: Luisa Garcia, a 70-year-old widow, suffers with chronic neck pain. Every week she visits a spiritual healer in order to gain protection from the evil spirits she believes are plaguing her. The healer, like Luisa, emigrated from Puerto Rico. The spiritual healing includes a form of diagnosis and *despojas* (cleansing ceremonies). After every visit to the healer, Luisa feels some relief from the pain. A devout Catholic, Luisa combines her belief in the power of evil spirits with daily prayers to God, the Virgin Mary, Jesus Christ, and a host of saints. Her parish priest, Father Estaban, is aware of her neck pain, and he encourages Luisa to visit the neighborhood health clinic, which is staffed by public health nurses and physicians.

Luisa sees no need to consult anyone but Maria, her spiritual healer. While she likes Father Estaban and believes that he is a good man, she resents his trying to tell her how to deal with her physical discomfort. After all, for generations, Luisa's family has dealt with physical and psychological pain through spiritual healing and prayer. She tells Father Estaban that, at 70 years of age, she is not about to change her practices.

Vignette 3: Jean Chang is devoted to her father, Robert, a 67-year-old widower. Three years ago, Jean left her position as a college professor in order to care for her father. Robert, who has a form of muscular dystrophy, emigrated from Taiwan to the United States 35 years ago. An only child, Jean was born in the United States. Robert expresses a great deal of anger toward Jean, as well as toward everyone else with whom he interacts. His bitterness spans the many years in which he has dealt with the dystrophy. He is not interested in counseling, since he doesn't believe that he has any psychological problems, just physical ones. Robert experiences a great deal of pain, has little feeling and strength in both his arms and legs, and has very limited mobility. Robert lives with Jean, her husband, David, and their two teenage daughters. Jean is Chinese American. David's grandparents emigrated from Germany in the 1930s to avoid persecution as Jews. Although Jean finds excuses for her father's inappropriate behavior (e.g., screaming at the family), David and the kids do not. David and the teenagers would like to see Robert placed in a nursing home, but Jean will not hear of that.

Discussion Questions

1 Mavis Johnson lives in a rural community where health care services are quite limited relative to those available in a metropolitan area. What health care services should be available for all older adults, regardless of where they live? How would these services be financed?

2 Why do Luisa Garcia and Father Estaban have such different views regarding appropriate health care?

3 What are some of the possible options available to Robert, Jean, and David?

MORTALITY AND DIVERSITY

Gender and Mortality

As we discussed in Chapter 1, the American population is aging and continuing to get older. According to the American Association of Retired Persons (AARP) (1994), those individuals reaching the age of 65 in 1992 would live, on average, another 17.5 years. While these statistics are encouraging because of an ever-increasing average life span, such averages do not adequately address significant differences due to gender and race/ethnicity.

Typically, American women live longer than men. Next to age as a demographic factor, gender accounts for "the largest differentials in mortality rates" (Verbrugge, 1989, p. 31). Verbrugge documents the significantly lower mortality rates of women throughout the 20th century but warns that the difference is getting smaller (Verbrugge, 1989). This narrowing may be due to several factors, including increased health awareness among middle-aged men.

Gender differences in longevity affect a multitude of life issues. For example, since, among the elderly cohort, women generally married men older than themselves, about half of all older women are widowed, and there are around five times as many older widows as older widowers (AARP, 1994). Children are more likely to know and interact with grandmothers and great-grandmothers, in part, because their female elders do, on average, live longer than the family's male elders.

Minorities and Mortality

Minority group membership may also affect mortality. Typically, members of minority groups (e.g., Blacks, Hispanics, and Native Americans) experience higher overall mortality rates than the majority population; however, some minorities (e.g., Japanese Americans) demonstrate lower rates (Angel & Hogan, 1994). The relationship between minority group membership and mortality may differ relative to age grouping. For example, Blacks demonstrate a shorter life expectancy than Whites up to the age of 85; after that age, however, there is "racial mortality crossover," meaning that the relationship between minority group membership and mortality changes in the other direction (Markides & Black, 1996). In other words, Blacks who live to be 85 have a greater life expectancy than their White counterparts (Gibson, 1994; Markides & Black, 1996). This mortality crossover may be due to several factors: (a) a significantly higher Black infant mortality rate, (b) Whites receiving better nutrition and medical services, (c) Whites who might have died at younger ages surviving to around the age of 85, and (d) hardier and more resilient Blacks living past 85 (Barresi, 1990). Those Blacks around the age of 85 most likely have experienced inadequate health care services at some point in their lives, but their resiliency, both physical and psychological, appears to propel them to, on average, outlive their White peers.

While a number of studies (Gardner, 1994; Tanjasiri, Wallace, & Shibata, 1995; Yu & Liu, 1992, 1994) indicate that older Asian Americans, as an aggregate, have the lowest mortality rates of all groups, such figures should be understood as preliminary. There are possible methodological problems with many mortality studies. For example, mortality research, as does most all health research on ethnicity, typically lumps a wide variety of Asian/Pacific Islanders into one ethnic category (Takeuchi & Young, 1994). Placing groups with higher rates of adult mortality (e.g., Cambodians and Laotians) with groups having lower rates (e.g., Japanese and Chinese Americans) distorts the actual mortality for each of the specific groups composing the Asian/Pacific Islander category.

Also, there are various concerns with the quality of the available data. For example, mortality researchers may rely on public health clinic records, which may include incorrect or missing information. Incorrect data may reflect problems with a client's ethnic identification based on an interviewer's faulty assessment. Highly significant data, such as educational level and income, may be missing from client records, and some significant variables such as primary language and generation may not be included on health forms (Takeuchi & Young, 1994). In addition, some large sets of data may contain incomplete or inappropriate categories of race/ethnicity. For example, the National Medical Expenditure Surveys of 1977 and 1987 included the following coding categories for race: (a) Black, (b) Hispanic, (c) White, and (d) other. The surveys did not provide a specific category for Asian/Pacific Islanders and confounded what demographic information was available by designating Hispanic as a race, which it is not (Yu & Liu, 1992).

Minority group membership may interact with other elements of diversity to affect mortality rates. For example, Native Americans in the general population live 9 years longer than Native Americans residing in New York City. This significant difference based on place of residency appears to be due to environmental factors, including inadequate housing (Gelfand, 1994).

HEALTH BELIEFS AND BEHAVIORS

Individual beliefs about the presence, meaning, cause, and treatment of physical illness result, in part, from the various elements of diversity. For example, culture plays a large role in determining how one views health and illness. Among a number of Asian cultures, health is based largely on integration and balance among oneself, nature, and other persons, and illness not only represents "the absence of negative states . . . but incorporate[s] the presence of positive as well" (Matsumoto, 1996, p. 222).

Kleinman (1980) developed an "explanatory model framework" (p. 104) to differentiate the health beliefs of individual patients and health practitioners. Explanatory models emphasize differing points of view regarding a particular illness as well as its treatment. It is Kleinman's contention that culture, ethnicity, social class, and experience influence the formation and use of these models, providing both patients and practitioners a means of interpreting specific episodes of sickness. For example, an elderly Chinese American woman who has emigrated recently from an inland Chinese province to San Francisco may employ quite a different explanatory model to make sense of her hypertension (high blood pressure) than her son who came to the United States 20 years earlier. The elderly woman may view the illness from the perspective of rural Chinese folk medicine, while her middle-aged son may appreciate the folk tradition but be more anchored in Western professional medicine. If the woman becomes a patient of an American medical practitioner, the physician may well bring a totally different meaning system to the possible causes and preferred treatment of the hypertension. All three models—those of the mother, son, and practitioner—are valid, since they bring meaning to the three individuals. However, different explanatory models can present difficulties by contributing to miscommunication, stereotyping, or other misunderstandings leading to problems such as misdiagnosis and lack of patient compliance to a treatment plan.

Elders from a variety of cultural backgrounds may possess health beliefs derived from folk medicine rather than from current professional medical practice. One such belief system is *curanderismo*, a type of folk medicine practiced by some Mexican Americans in America's southwestern region (Gafner & Duckett, 1992; Marsh & Hentges, 1988; Trotter, 1985). This belief system, extending back to the Spanish conquest of the Americas, involves a blend of Catholicism, medieval medicine, and the medicine of indigenous Indians (Gafner & Duckett, 1992). According to Gafner and Duckett (1992), *curanderismo* entails the following: (a) a belief that God heals the sick through persons, called *curanderos*, who are blessed with the don, a special gift; (b) the reality of a number of conditions that can be cured; (c) the belief in mystical diseases such as "susto, meaning loss of spirit of fright" (p. 148); (d) the belief that both illness and health exist on material, mental, and spiritual levels; and (e) the use of proscribed rituals and herbs for healing. Use of *curanderismo* ranges from partial to exclusive. Some Mexican American elders might visit a licensed physician and take recommended prescription medicine but, for additional assistance, also consult a nearby folk healer. This folk healer might suggest that the afflicted person also drink a particular kind of herbal tea, pass a raw egg over a painful area of the body, or give a massage while applying an aromatic oil. The particular treatment would depend on both the assumed nature of the problem and the special expertise of the healer.

There are several reasons why Mexican Americans may find *curanderos* to be an attractive alternative to "modern" medical practitioners. *Curanderos* are usually found right in the person's neighborhood, appointments are unnecessary, payment may not be required, there are no insurance or medical history forms, there are no laboratory tests, and, most important, the *curandero* and the patient share commonalities regarding language, beliefs about illness, and religious traditions (Gafner & Duckett, 1992).

The meaning of symptoms can be influenced by culture. For example, one important symptom of illness is pain, but the acknowledgment of the presence, severity, and expression of pain is mediated by culture. Zborowski (1969) studied physical pain among patients at the Veterans Administration hospital in Bronx, New York. Specifically, Zborowski was interested in the relationship between a patient's cultural background and response patterns to pain. The study included 146 patients identified as Irish, Jewish, Italian, or Old American. The category of Old American included persons of Anglo-Saxon origin, usually Protestant in religion, who were at least fourth-generation Americans. The observation and interview portions of the research project demonstrated a difference in the expression of pain for Italian and Jewish patients as compared with Irish and Old American ones. In general, Irish and Old American subjects "played down" their pain, while Italian and Jewish subjects "played up" the pain. The researchers attempted to control for the nature of the illness. Both observations and interviews pointed to consistent differences in the expression of pain. For example, according to Zborowski (1969):

> Thus while the Irish and American patients said that they prefer to hide their pain, the Jewish and Italian patients admitted freely that they show their pain. . . . Our observations suggested that anxiety and worry . . . are most frequently expressed by Jewish patients. (pp. 240–241)

Certainly, the differences within cultural groups regarding the expression of pain are great as well. In other words, an individual who is an Italian American or a Jewish American may be characteristically inexpressive regarding pain, while some fourth- or fifth-generation Anglo Americans may be very expressive and "play up" their pain on a consistent basis.

In the following learning activity, you will analyze conflicts between folk and "modern" medical practices affecting a Filipino American family.

ACTIVE LEARNING EXPERIENCE: CONFLICT BETWEEN FOLK AND "MODERN" MEDICINE IN A FILIPINO AMERICAN FAMILY

Purpose

This activity provides you with an opportunity to explore the practice of both folk and "modern" medicine by an elderly Filipino American couple and the resulting conflicts with their adult children. Upon completing this activity, you will be able to:

1 Describe folk healing techniques used by some older Filipino Americans.

2 Discuss intergenerational conflicts that may arise over differing explanatory models of health and illness.

Time Required

35 minutes (20 minutes to read the case and answer the questions and 15 minutes to discuss the answers with another person).

Procedure

1 Read the case and answer the questions that follow it.
2 Discuss your responses with another person.
3 Your instructor will lead a discussion of individual responses.

Conflict between Folk and "Modern" Medicine in a Filipino American Family

Read the following case and answer the questions that follow it.

Benigno and Patria Bulosan, who are both 85 years old, have been married for the past 65 years. Their marriage has been strong despite all of the political upheavals in the Philippines, their financial struggles, the deaths of two of their six children, and their emigration from their ancestral home in northern Luzon to Chicago. Mr. and Mrs. Bulosan have learned only a few words of English, continuing to converse with each other and with their family and friends in the Ilocano dialect spoken in the community where they were born, raised, and spent their lives until coming to the United States in 1983.

During the past 20 years, Patria has experienced great discomfort due to osteoarthritis. She deals with chronic pain in her fingers, hands, and arms. When she first felt the aching in her fingers, she attributed it to fatigue and worry and prayed that it would stop. When the pain continued and its intensity increased, Patria used a variety of oils and ointments, as well as various roots and herbs. These folk remedies failed to bring relief, so she sought out a local folk healer who attributed the pain to "bad air" and subsequently used a treatment with Mrs. Bulosan called *ventosa*, in which a coin is wrapped in cotton, its tip is dipped in alcohol, it is lit, placed on an inflamed joint, and then covered immediately with a small glass. This creates a vacuum intended to draw out the "bad air" (Chan, 1992). For a period of several years, Patria visited the healer for periodic *ventosa* treatments. After emigrating to the United States, she located a Filipino healer not far from her new home and continued a similar pattern of treatment. At the insistence of her "Americanized" children, Patria also periodically visits a family practice physician who prescribes an anti-inflammatory drug that Patria takes faithfully.

While both Patria and Benigno view folk healing as natural and proper, their children are embarrassed by what they consider to be a "primitive" belief system. During a recent Sunday dinner, with her children and grandchildren present, Patria described the benefits of traditional Filipino folk medicine and encouraged her daughter, Cory, to consult a healer for chronic back pain. An argument developed, and two of Patria's sons, Richard and Robert, stormed out of the house because of what they considered to be their mother's superstitious and backward beliefs. Patria began to cry, and Benigno wondered how he and his wife produced such disrespectful and ignorant children.

Discussion Questions

1   Even though Patria and Benigno have lived in the United States since 1983, their beliefs regarding health and illness are much the same as they were when they lived in the Philippines. Why?

2   While Patria continues to apply folk remedies and visits the folk healer, she also visits a licensed physician and follows the prescribed professional medical treatment plan. How can Patria believe in *both* folk and "modern" medicine?

3 Why might Patria and Benigno's children be embarrassed by their parents' belief in folk healing?

4 Does anyone in your family engage in health practices or have health beliefs that could be considered superstitious or unscientific? If so, briefly describe one such practice or belief.

The next learning activity provides a framework through which you can learn about your own family's health beliefs and practices.

ACTIVE LEARNING EXPERIENCE: INTERVIEW WITH FAMILY ELDER ABOUT FAMILY HEALTH BELIEFS AND PRACTICES[1]

Purpose

The purpose of this activity is for you to gain insight into the beliefs of family elders regarding good health, diet, exercise, illness, folk medicine, and professional medicine. Upon completion of this activity, you will be able to:

1 Describe and understand health and illness beliefs of your family elders (or the beliefs of elders in another family).

2 Describe and understand health and illness practices of family elders.

3 Understand how current family health and illness beliefs and practices have been influenced by culture and family history.

Time Required

2.75 hours (1 hour for the interview, 1 hour to write out the results, and 45 minutes for discussion)

Procedure

1 Interview the oldest family member that you can. If it is not possible to interview a member of your family, locate an elder outside of your family but from within your ethnic/cultural group.

2 Ask your interviewee to answer the questions listed subsequently.

3 Prepare a one- to two-page summary of what you learned from the interview.

4 Discuss your findings with another person.

5 Your instructor may wish to lead a class discussion of findings contrasting the beliefs and practices of diverse families.

[1]The idea for this learning experience comes from R. E. Spector. (1996). *Cultural diversity in health & illness* (4th ed.). Stamford, CT: Appleton & Lange.

Interview With Family Elder About Family Health Beliefs and Practices

Ask the following questions of the family elder whom you are interviewing:

1   In what country (or countries) were your parents born?
2   When you were a child, what did your parents teach you about staying healthy?
3   What did your parents do when you or your brothers or sisters became ill? Did you go to a doctor? Did you go to another type of healer?
4   Did your parents use folk remedies when you were sick? For example, were you given herbs, roots, cod liver oil, or other types of home remedies? Which remedies were you given?
5   What special foods were you encouraged to eat in order to stay healthy?
6   What special foods were you given when you were ill?
7   What part did religion play when family members were sick?
8   When your parents experienced physical pain, did they tend to complain about it or tend to keep it to themselves?
9   What health practices have you continued to use as an adult that you learned from your parents or other family members?

After completing the interview, prepare a one- to two-page summary of your findings. Include a comparison of your health and illness attitudes and practices with those of the family elder you interviewed.

SOCIOECONOMIC CLASS, POVERTY, MEDICARE, AND MEDICAID

Socioeconomic class affects health and illness practices in profound ways, since social class is closely related to both income and access to health care services. Because of limited finances, poor elderly people are less likely to use health services, eat nutritious diets, and take prescription drugs.

According to Chen (1994), 12.2% of America's elderly population lived in poverty in 1990, with some groups being overrepresented among the roughly 3.7 million elderly poor. While only 10.1% of the 1990 elderly White population falls into the poverty category, 33.8% of older Blacks and 22.5% of older Hispanics are considered to be poor. In 1990, poverty levels in the United States were $6,268 for an individual more than 65 years of age and $7,905 for a two-person household in which one of the individuals was 65 or older (Chen, 1994). Poverty among older adults in the United States is closely related to gender. For example, while the median income for White male elders was $14,839 in 1990, it was only $8,463 for older White women. There are significant gender differences among the median incomes for Hispanic elders ($9,546 for men and $5,373 for women) and for Black elders ($7,450 for men and $5,617 for women) (Chen, 1994).

As shown in Table 3.1, a number of federal programs assist elders through various health and social services. Each program has its own rules governing eligibility and what services it will provide. Medicaid is a state-operated program designed primarily for persons with low incomes and few financial resources. While the federal government helps pay for Medicaid, each state has rules concerning who is eligible. Medicare is a federal health insurance program designed for those over the age of 65 as well as for certain persons with disabilities. Medicare has two parts: Part A (hospital insurance) and Part B (medical insurance). Part A includes deductibles and coinsurance. However, most people are not required to pay any premiums for Part A. On the other hand, Part B has premiums, deductibles, and coinsurance amounts that participants must pay themselves or through coverage by a private insurance plan. These premiums, deductibles, and coinsurance amounts are set each year on the basis of formulas established by law.

In the following learning experience, you are to interpret a form that Medicare sends to older adults informing them of the decision on their claim in regard to physician services.

ACTIVE LEARNING EXPERIENCE: EXPLANATION OF MEDICARE PART B BENEFITS NOTICE

Purpose

This activity creates an opportunity for you to interpret the Explanation of Medicare Part B Benefits form that Medicare sends to older adults to inform them of the decision on their claim regarding the services they have received from a physician. Upon completion of this activity, you will be able to:

1 Interpret the notice that Medicare sends to older adults after the physician submits a claim for services rendered.
2 Describe the computational procedures used in determining the amount to be paid by Medicare.
3 Explain the procedure used to determine the amount for which the care recipient will be responsible.

Time Required

40 minutes (25 minutes to complete the questions and 15 minutes to discuss the answers with another person).

Table 3.1 Major Federal Programs Supporting Long-Term Care Services for the Elderly and Persons with Disabilities

Program	Objectives	Administration	Long-term care services
Medicaid/Title XIX of the Social Security Act	Pays for medical assistance for certain low-income persons	Federal: HCFA/HHS State: state Medicaid agency	Nursing home care, home and community-based health and social services, facilities for persons with mental retardation, chronic care hospitals
Medicare/Title XVIII of the Social Security Act	Pays for acute medical care for the aged and selected disabled	Federal: HCFA/HHS State: none	Home health visits, limited skilled nursing facility care
Older Americans Act	Fosters development of a comprehensive and coordinated service system to serve the elderly	Federal: Administration on Aging/Office of Human Development, HHS State: state agency on aging	Nutrition services, home and community-based social services, protective services, and long-term care ombudsman
Rehabilitation Act	Promotes and supports vocational rehabilitation and independent living services for the disabled	Federal: Office of Special Education and Rehabilitative Services/Department of Education State: state vocational rehabilitation agencies	Rehabilitation services, attendant and personal care, centers for independent living
Social Services Block Grant/Title XX of the Social Security Act	Assists families and individuals in maintaining self-sufficiency and independence	Federal: Office of Human Development Services, HHS State: state social services or human resources agency; other state agencies may administer part of Title XX funds for certain groups; for example, State Agency on Aging	Services provided at the states' discretion, may include long-term care

Source: U.S. General Accounting Office, Health, Education, and Human Services Division. (1995). *Long-term care. Current issues and future directions* (GAO Publication No. 95-109). Washington, DC: Author.

Procedure

1 Either in a class setting or as a homework assignment, complete the questions included in this activity.

2 Discuss your responses with another individual.

3 Your instructor leads a discussion of responses to this activity.

Explanation of Medicare Part B Benefits

After a physician, provider, or supplier sends in a Part B claim, Medicare sends the older adult a notice called Explanation of Medicare Part B Benefits to inform the individual of the decision on the claim. Given the complexity of such notices, caregivers are often asked to interpret them. An illustration of the notice is shown in Figure 3.1.

Examine this notice carefully and then answer the following questions. After completing your responses, discuss them with another person.

1 What does the following statement mean: "Your provider did not accept assignment"?

2 Why is the Medicare-approved amount different from the total charges submitted by the physician?

3 What procedures were used to compute the amount that Medicare paid to the care recipient?

4 What out-of-pocket expenses will the care recipient pay for these services?

5 Who will pay $93 to the physician?

6 On a 5-point scale (1 = *very easy*, 5 = *very difficult*), how would you rate the level of difficulty involved in interpreting this notice?

7 Do you believe that the notice will be difficult for some elders to understand?

8 What specific changes would you suggest for making this notice easier to understand?

RURAL ISSUES IN HEALTH AND ILLNESS

Place of residence is a significant element of human diversity. While it is very difficult to know just "where rural stops and urban begins" (Coward, McLaughlin, Duncan, & Bull, 1994, p. 3), the following three measures of population have often been used in health services research: "(a) the total number of people living in a particular geographic area, (b) the distance of a place from a larger metropolitan service area, and (c) the population density of an area" (Coward et al., 1994, p. 3). When examining research regarding rural elders, it is important that one be aware of how the researcher defined the concept of "rural." Differing definitions of the term may, in part, give rise to seemingly inconsistent findings regarding the health status of the rural elders.

THIS IS NOT A BILL
Explanation of Your Medicare **Part B** Benefits

JOHN D DOE
APARTMENT 12 C
63 WOODLAWN DRIVE
BALTIMORE, MARYLAND 21207-1111

Summary of this notice dated February 1, 1994	
Total Charges:	$ 300.00
Total Medicare approved:	$ 180.00
We are paying you:	$ 144.00
Your total responsibility:	$ 207.00

Your Medicare number is: 123-45-6789A   Your provider <u>did not accept</u> assignment

---

Details about this notice

Control number 0000-0000-0000

BILL SUBMITTED BY: Elm Street Clinic
Mailing Address: 123 Elm Street, Baltimore, MD 21228

Dates	Services and Service Codes	Charges	Medicare Approved	See Notes Below
	Dr. Mary Smith			
Jan 10, 1994	3 office visits [00000]	$ 300.00	$ 180.00	a, b

Your provider did not accept assignment. We are paying you the amount that we owe you.

Notes:

a The approved amount is based on the fee schedule

b Your doctor did not accept assignment for this service. Under federal law, your doctor cannot charge more than $207.00.

Here's an explanation of this notice:

Of the total charges, Medicare approved	$180.00	
Your 20%	- 36.00	Your co-payment is 20%
The 80% Medicare pays	$144.00	
We are paying you	$144.00	
Of the total charges	$300.00	
Less amount exceeding charge limit	- 93.00	You are not responsible for this amount which is in excess of the Medicare limiting charge.
The total you are responsible for	$207.00	The provider may bill you for this amount.

IMPORTANT: If you have questions about this notice, call (carrier name) at (carrier telephone number) or see us at (carrier walk-in address). You will need this notice if you contact us.

To appeal our decision, you must WRITE to us before August 1, 1994.

Figure 3.1   Explanation of Medicare Part B benefits.

In summarizing studies of health indicators, Raymond Coward and associates (1994) concluded the following: (a) There are health differences between rural and urban elderly people, but such differences sometimes reflect positive indicators for rural elders; (b) the differences within the category of rural elders are large, particularly between those persons who farm and those who do not farm (elders who continue to farm are, as a group, very healthy, but rural elders who do not farm have among the poorest health of all elderly Americans); (c) nonfarm rural elders evidence the most medical conditions for all types of residence; and (d) rural elders, both farmers and nonfarmers, categorize their health in more negative terms than do urban dwellers.

Some of the research on rural and urban differences in regard to health issues seems difficult to explain. For example, Ries and Brown (1991), found, through their analysis of data collected under the auspices of the National Center for Health Statistics, that rural persons of various ages rated their health more negatively than their metropolitan counterparts but spent less time in the hospital and had fewer contacts with physicians (Thorson & Powell, 1993). In commenting on Ries and Brown's research, Thorson and Powell (1993) wrote: "Is it the case that rural people are healthier but less likely to admit it? . . . There may be some evidence to support this contention" (p. 139).

Thorson and Powell (1993) studied metropolitan and nonmetropolitan elders in Nebraska. Comparing 196 randomly selected elders from Douglas County (in the Omaha area) and 200 elders residing in the rural counties in the sand hills of western Nebraska, these researchers found that their rural interview respondents, while on average five years older than their urban subjects, reported less illness and briefer stays in the hospital. Two thirds of both samples viewed their health as excellent or good, and fewer than 1% indicated delays in securing health care services. Most of the rural counties included in this study had "no resident physician, hospital, or health department" (p. 141). There were some important demographic differences between the metropolitan and nonmetropolitan respondents, the former being younger (73.8 years vs. 76.6 years) and more likely to be married (55% vs. 47.5%). There was minority representation (7%), but there were no minority rural subjects.

While living in a rural community might not lead to self-perceptions of poorer health or health care, some rural elders do experience substantial difficulties with health and health delivery. This is especially the case with some minorities. As an example, almost half of all Native Americans reside in rural communities. As late as 1980, 21% of Indians more than 55 years of age residing on reservations or in rural settings either had incomplete plumbing or lacked plumbing all together, 14% did not have a refrigerator, and 14% were not receiving electrical service (John, 1994).

According to Robert John (1994), "Rural and reservation American Indian elders experience health care rationing through lack of funding, personnel, training, facilities, and services to address their needs" (p. 49). When health services are available, they may be situated at a great distance, which may limit elders' use of routine and preventative services (John, 1994). Many Native American elders lack awareness of available health services or may be unaware of how to make use of such services, even though their health is much poorer than that of rural White elders. Their isolation is related to the fact that a large percentage of rural American Indians do not have television sets or telephones, nor do they subscribe to newspapers (Bane, 1992).

PHYSICAL ILLNESS

Gender and Illness

Through the 1991 National Health Interview Survey (NCHS), more than 120,000 subjects provided information on incidence of chronic physical illness, on their disability status, and on the effect of these self-reported afflictions on their overall functioning (Jette, 1996; Ries & Brown, 1991; Verbrugge, 1990). According to the NCHS (Verbrugge, 1990), the most frequently reported conditions for the respondents who were 65 years of age and older were, in descending order, arthritis (48.4%); hypertension (37.2%); hearing impairments (32.0%); heart disease (29.5%); eye disease, meaning cataract or glaucoma (23.0%); orthopedic impairments (17.7%); chronic sinusitis (13.9%); diabetes (9.9%); and emphysema or chronic bronchitis (8.4%).

Of the chronic conditions just listed, only one (hearing impairments) is more likely to be reported by older men than by older women (Verbrugge, 1990). Elderly women report being ill more frequently and experience a greater prevalence of acute illnesses and nonfatal chronic illnesses (Verbrugge, 1983, 1990). As we discussed earlier, men's higher mortality rate results from a significantly greater incidence of serious maladies such as ischemic heart disease and arteriosclerosis.

Arthritis is the most common chronic disorder affecting both male and female American elders. Typical symptoms include stiffness, swelling, and pain in joints, which can affect activities like walking, bending, and reaching (Herzog, 1989). The most common types of this disease are osteoarthritis and rheumatoid arthritis. Affecting larger weight-bearing joints (e.g., knees), osteoarthritis is related to prior injury to the affected joint and to a lack of exercise. Rheumatoid arthritis, which usually begins in middle age, may affect joints throughout the body (Lorig & Fries, 1986). The exact causes of arthritic conditions are not known, nor are the reasons for their greater prevalence among older women. According to Herzog (1989), that "whether the higher prevalence among women is caused by their biology, the specific stresses that they experience, and interaction between those two sets of factors is not known" (p. 45).

Another disorder, osteoporosis (loss of bone mass), occurs in women significantly more often than in men. Data reported by Herzog (1989) indicate that, between the ages of 45 and 79, 29% of American women and 18% of men develop this disease. Treatments for women include estrogen replacement, exercise, and nutritional modification (Herzog, 1989). It is important to note that, for some women (e.g., those with breast cancer), hormone replacement may not be advised (Bellantoni & Blackman, 1996).

Why do older women report more morbidity—that is, more instances of acute and chronic illness—than do their male counterparts? Lois Verbrugge (1990) describes the following possible reasons for gender differences in morbidity: (a) biological risks due to genes or hormones; (b) acquired risks due to activities, habits, stress, or social environment; (c) psychosocial factors such as perceptions of symptoms and decisions to deal with personal health concerns; (d) health reporting behaviors; and (e) prior health care, involving how previous health-related actions affect current or future illnesses. Generally, research studies demonstrate that men are at a greater biological risk and receive less prior health care, while women perceive and report more symptoms. Some acquired risks lead to greater male morbidity (e.g., alcohol consumption), whereas others (e.g., role pressures) lead to greater female morbidity. On the basis of a thorough review of relevant empirical studies, Verbrugge (1990) concludes that "women's excess morbidity in contemporary life is driven by social factors, especially by risks stemming from lesser employment, higher felt stress and unhappiness, stronger feelings of illness vulnerability, fewer formal time constraints . . . and less physically strenuous leisure activities" (pp. 183–184).

Older men and women use health services at different rates. Thomas and Kelman (1990) found that elderly men are hospitalized more often, while elderly women visit physicians more frequently. Also, women report more disability days, as well as greater prescription and nonprescription drug use, than men do (Verbrugge, 1990; Verbrugge & Wingard, 1986).

Minorities and Physical Illness

We have described rural/urban residence and gender as elements of diversity affecting the health status of older Americans. A third important variable, minority group membership, can also profoundly influence the physical health of elders. There are numerous studies available on the physical health status of Blacks, but less research has been conducted on related issues for Hispanics and Asian Americans.

A number of studies have been undertaken to examine the double-jeopardy hypothesis as an explanation of health differences between minority and majority elders. As we discussed previously, the notion of double jeopardy argues that minority elders are apt to experience greater difficulties with aging (e.g., poorer health) as a result of their social, political, and economic inequality (Jackson, 1971). While this hypothesis may make some intuitive sense, it has not been supported by gerontological research (Burton, Dilworth-Anderson, & Bengtson, 1992; Ferraro, 1987; Markides & Black, 1996).

In contrast to the double-jeopardy hypothesis is the age-as-leveling theory, which suggests that, as they age, people experience similar issues and problems irrespective of their ethnic or minority group membership (Barresi, 1990; Kent, 1971). Few studies have attempted to test the veracity of this notion. Curiously, neither theoretical approach has proven to be a useful explanatory framework. Perhaps more longitudinal research viewing health, ethnicity, gender, cohort, and class as interacting variables will give rise to more adequate conceptual models (Barresi, 1990; Clark, Maddox, & Steinhauser, 1993).

During the past decade or so, a number of studies have examined the health status of elders from various groups. In the sections to follow, we review some of the major findings regarding the physical health of Black, Hispanic, Asian American, and Native American elders.

Black Elders

A number of studies have focused on physical health issues for older Blacks (e.g., Clark, Maddox, & Steinhauser, 1993; Edmonds, 1993; Gibson, 1991a; Gibson & Jackson, 1992). In a review of relevant research, Markides and Black (1996) concluded that: "Despite declines in differences with age, Blacks 65 and over were less healthy" (p. 158) in terms of such factors as self-ratings of health, limitation of activities, rates of bed disability, and incidence of hypertension. Daniel Clark and associates (1993) examined the hypothesis that Black elders are, on average, healthier than their White counterparts as a result of selective survival, meaning that those minority elders with more resilience are more likely to survive into old age. Declines in health differences between Black and White elders, particularly after the age of 85, may be symptomatic for Blacks of increases in early mortality and in disability at younger ages. Problems with access to health services, socioeconomic status, and health practices may all contribute to Black-White differences in health status (Markides & Black, 1996).

Blacks have higher rates of accidents, incapacitating arthritis, diabetes, glaucoma, hypertension and other cardiovascular diseases, and nephritis and nephrosis than their White counterparts (Johnson, Gibson, & Luckey, 1990; Manton & Johnson, 1987; Wykle & Kaskel, 1994). In comparison with any other group of Americans, Blacks have higher rates of all of the following types of cancers: esophagus, larynx, pancreas, prostate, and stomach (Gelfand, 1994). Blacks are more likely to die from breast, cervical, and uterine cancers than are Whites of the same age with similar diagnoses (Baquet, 1988; Wykle & Kaskel, 1994). Among Blacks, numerous chronic conditions are more prevalent at earlier ages and are more debilitating and limiting than is the case for White Americans (Johnson et al., 1990). For many disorders, Blacks have greater rates of morbidity but lower rates of mortality. This crossover effect occurs at different ages for some diseases and not at all for others (Gelfand, 1994). According to Gelfand (1994):

> Among men the crossover effect is seen in the prevalence of colon and rectal cancer. The age at which a crossover occurs is not the same for all these cancers. In the case of esophageal cancer, the crossover effect is visible at age 80. For lung cancer the crossover occurs at age 60. Among women, however, mortality rates from uterine cancer are greater at all ages among Blacks than Whites. (p. 70)

Black elders are pessimistic about their health (Baquet, 1988; Ferraro, 1993). In summarizing earlier research, Ferraro (1993) concludes that (a) following a diagnosis of a serious condition, such as cancer, older Blacks tend to be fatalistic (Baquet, 1988); (b) Blacks are less inclined to view early detection or treatment as useful; and (c) fatalism may contribute to Blacks' decreased likelihood of engaging in positive health behaviors (Colon, 1992) and their lower likelihood of seeking health care services (Gibbs, 1988). Certainly, such health fatalism and behaviors can be a consequence of a lack of available services, difficulties in accessing appropriate health care, financial constraints, and so forth. Ferraro (1993), through an analysis of data from the 1984 Supplement on Aging of the Health Interview Survey (Fiti & Kovar, 1987), concludes that, based on these self-report data, Black elders report more negative assessments of their health and more functional morbidity than do Whites and that Black female elders "report the highest levels of functional morbidity and the most negative assessments of health" (p. 201). In comparison with Black men, Black women may be at greater disadvantage on these health variables as a result of economic and family pressures (Ferraro, 1993).

Hispanics

Other than Blacks, Hispanics are the largest minority group in the United States (Markides & Black, 1996). Representing a broad diversity of cultures, most Hispanics include persons whose families originated in Central or South America or the Caribbean. Hispanics can be Black, White, or Asian, but they share the Spanish language.

While there are few comprehensive studies of the physical health of Hispanic elders, the findings, in general, demonstrate similarities in their health profile with that of non-Hispanic Whites. One possible reason for this apparent similarity seems to be that, because so many Hispanic elders are immigrants, and since immigrants tend to be in better health than native-born Americans, Hispanic immigrants may elevate the overall level of health among all Hispanic elders (Markides & Black, 1996; Sorlie, Backlund, Johnson, & Rogat, 1993).

On the other hand, there is research pointing to health decrements for Hispanics in comparison with non-Hispanic Whites (Gelfand, 1994; Markides, Coreil, & Rogers, 1989). Markides and his colleagues (1989) found that southwestern Hispanics demonstrated several indicators of disadvantage, including a higher incidence of diabetes, influenza and pneumonia (particularly for Hispanic women), and infectious and parasitic diseases. However, these same investigators found an advantage for Hispanic men relative to non-Hispanic men regarding incidence of cancer and cardiovascular disease.

Gelfand (1994) cautions that there are large differences between Hispanic groups in terms of the health of older adults. For example, among the statistics that he cites are the following: (a) The rate of mortality from cardiovascular disease is 20% higher for Puerto Rican men than for Cuban or Mexican American men; (b) among Hispanic groups, Mexican Americans have the highest rate of cerebrovascular disease; and (c) Cuban Americans show the highest rates of cancer. There is a need for additional research examining the health status of various

Hispanic groups so that health planners and providers will be better able to ascertain what health services are needed for these diverse groups of Americans.

Asian Americans

The third largest minority group in America is composed of those who trace their heritage to Asia and the Pacific Islands (Markides & Black, 1996). Perhaps no other American classification represents so many differing cultures. Included in this designation are such groups as Afghans, Arabic groups, Asian Indians, Cambodians, Chinese, Fijians, Filipinos, Guamians, Hawaiians, Japanese, Koreans, Laotians, Malayans, Micronesians, Pakistanis, Persians, Samoans, Thais, Tongans, Turks, and Vietnamese.

Despite great diversity among and within Asian groups, there have been few comprehensive studies regarding their health. What studies there are point to good health for a variety of Asian American elders relative to that of the White population (Gelfand, 1994; Markides & Black, 1996). However, there are several reasons why such findings may be incorrect and may misrepresent the relative health status of older adults from specific groups of Asian/Pacific Islanders (e.g., Laotians, Micronesians, and so forth) by failing to break down the data into subethnic groups (Tanjasiri, Wallace, & Shibata, 1995). While older Asian/Pacific Islanders constitute the fastest growing racial group age 65 and older, a number of health studies lack a meaningful sample from this population (Tanjasiri, Wallace, & Shibata, 1995; Yu & Liu, 1992, 1994). Also, as we stated in the earlier section on mortality, research studies using public health clinic records may contain incomplete or inaccurate health and demographic information (Takeuchi & Young, 1994).

The health research on elderly Asian/Pacific Islanders that is available tends to view them as healthier than other American elders. For example, Elena Yu (1986) analyzed patterns of morbidity and mortality using data from the National Center for Health Statistics and a cancer registry program managed by the National Cancer Institute, a part of the National Institutes of Health. Some significant findings from this study were as follows: (a) in general, Chinese American elders are healthier than White Americans; (b) both male and female Chinese Americans have much lower overall rates of cancer than their White peers; (c) Chinese Americans are at higher risk for nasopharyngeal cancer; (d) Chinese men, in comparison with White men, are more likely to develop cancer of the digestive system, but this is not the case for Chinese American women; and (e) Chinese American elders have a higher incidence of malignant neoplasms of the respiratory system.

Health studies that have broken down Asian/Pacific Islanders into specific subgroups have demonstrated a number of health concerns. Some research has identified high rates of tuberculosis, as well as hepatitis B virus, among a number of Asian groups. Also, one study revealed, among Filipinos who lived in California and were more than 50 years of age, a greater incidence of hypertension than among the overall California population (cited in Tanjasiri, Wallace, & Shibata, 1995). In reviewing community-based research on the health status of elderly Asian/Pacific Islanders, Tanjasiri and associates (1995) report studies concluding the following: (a) a majority of older Korean Americans view themselves to be in poor health; (b) Vietnamese American elders, as compared with older adults from other ethnic minorities, were least likely to consider themselves healthy; (c) a Boston study found one-third of Chinese American adults lacking health insurance coverage; and (d) a study of Koreans residing in Los Angeles indicated that 45% of this population was without health insurance.

Native Americans

Native Americans, representing American Indians, Eskimos, and Aleuts, include "approximately 278 federally recognized reservations, 500 tribes, bands, or Alaska Native villages, and an estimated 100 nonrecognized tribes in the U.S." (John, 1994, p. 46). There have been few systematic studies of the health of Native Americans. The Navajo, the largest Native American tribe, have received the most attention from researchers (Kunitz & Levy, 1989, 1991). Available data suggest that Native American elders, as compared with the general population, experience higher rates of a number of physical conditions, including diabetes, gallbladder disease, hearing impairments, kidney disease, liver disease, tuberculosis, and visual impairments. Among Native Americans, the most common chronic disorders are diabetes, arthritis, hypertension, cardiovascular disease, and gallbladder disease. In relation to the total population of American elders, Native American elders have a lower incidence of arthritis, cancer, emphysema, and hypertension (Gelfand, 1994). In addition, there have been significant improvements in the incidence of infectious disease among Native Americans as a result of the efforts of the Indian Health Service (John, 1994).

Through the following active learning experience, you will gain insight into the language barriers faced by non-English-speaking elders in their efforts to communicate effectively with many American health care professionals.

ACTIVE LEARNING EXPERIENCE: THE LANGUAGE BARRIER IN HEALTH CARE AND AGING[2]

Purpose

The purpose of this learning experience is to provide an opportunity for you to gain a sense of the frustration facing non-English-speaking elders in their efforts

---

[2]Ideas for this activity came from R. E. Spector. (1991). *Cultural diversity in health and illness* (3rd ed.). Stamford, CT: Appleton & Lange; K. H. Cavanaugh & P. H. Kennedy. (1992). *Promoting cultural diversity: Strategies for health care professionals.* Newbury Park, CA: Sage.

to obtain health care in the United States. Upon completion of this activity, you will be able to:

1   Better understand the difficulties involved in obtaining health care assistance when the client and the health care provider do not understand one another's language.
2   Appreciate the need for foreign language training, especially training in Spanish, of American health care personnel.

Time Required

30 minutes (15 minutes for role plays and 15 minutes to discuss the role play with another person or in a classroom setting).

Procedure

The following represent several different ways to engage in this learning activity.

Option A (Classroom Setting)

1   If you are completing this activity as a classroom exercise, your instructor can invite a guest to class, preferably an ethnic elder who speaks little or no English. The elder is to pretend to have a health problem and to communicate details about the health condition, symptoms, duration, and so forth.
2   Students are then permitted to ask the elder questions in English about the condition. Since the elder does not understand (or is to seem to not) English, this should prove to be quite frustrating.
3   Students then answer the questions on the answer sheet.
4   Your instructor leads a discussion about the experience.

Option B (Classroom Setting)

1   Your instructor divides the class into pairs.
2   One member of each pair role plays an ethnic elder who neither speaks nor understands English, and the other member plays the part of a public health nurse who does not understand the client's language.
3   The student playing the part of the health care provider attempts to answer the questions on the answer sheet.
4   Your instructor leads a discussion of the activity.

Option C (Independent Study)

1   If you are engaging in this activity for your own self-development, you are to ask a friend or acquaintance who is fluent in a language you do not understand.

2   Your acquaintance is to role play the part of the ethnic elder, and you will play the role of the public health nurse.

3   Attempt to provide written answers for the questions listed on the answer sheet.

4   Following this role play, discuss the frustrating nature of the role play with your acquaintance.

The Language Barrier in Health Care and Aging

The persons playing the part of the ethnic elder are to present a health care problem in a language foreign to students playing the part of the public health nurse. The latter is to ask the elder questions in English about his or her health problem. Afterward, the "nurses" are to try to respond in writing to the following questions:

1   What appear to be the physical complaints of the elder?

2   How long has the client shown symptoms of the problem?

3   Suppose that you figured out the cause of the client's problem and determined that she needs to take a certain medication and alter her diet. How would you communicate your suggestions for treatment to the client?

4   In real life, what can health care professionals and their organizations do to assist non-English-speaking elders in obtaining useful health care services?

Social Class and Morbidity

While culture relates to health and aging, health differences are also seen in terms of an older adult's socioeconomic level. Stoller and Gibson (1994) argue that gender, race, and social class create multiple hierarchies bestowing privilege on some older adults and disadvantage on others. These same authors assert that "research has demonstrated how a lifetime of poverty translates into poor health in later life" (p. xix).

In their studies of the impact of social stratification on health and ages, James House and associates (House, Kessler, Herzog, Mero, Kinney, & Breslow, 1992) conclude that, in general, higher status persons exhibit

> high levels of health until quite late in life, whereas people of lower SES [socioeconomic status] are much more likely to manifest significant declines in health by early middle age. . . . Furthermore, the relation of SES to health is very different at different points in the life course: SES differences in health are very small in early adulthood, increase steadily during middle age and early old age, and then diminish again in advanced old age. (pp. 1–2)

While there do appear to be relationships among health, social class, and aging, the effects seem to be complex. Complex variables such as gender and class may have confounding effects on research results (Longino, Warheit, &

Green, 1989). In other words, researchers may have difficulties in understanding whether some measure of health in old age is a consequence of aging, class, gender, ethnicity, or some combination of these variables.

ISSUES IN DIVERSITY, SEXUALITY, AND AGING

In this section of the chapter, we address the sexuality of older adults through narrative and active learning experiences. Topics include myths and misconceptions about the sexuality of elders, menopause, the physiology of the sexual response for older men and women, and issues affecting older gays and lesbians.

The following activity asks you to consider a series of common myths and misconceptions concerning the sexuality of older adults.

ACTIVE LEARNING EXPERIENCE: MYTHS AND MISCONCEPTIONS ABOUT THE SEXUALITY OF OLDER ADULTS

Purpose

The purpose of this activity is to offer an opportunity for you to explore your attitudes and beliefs concerning the sexuality of older adults. Upon completion of this activity, you will be able to:

1 Describe several myths and misconceptions about the sexuality of older adults.
2 Assess your beliefs about these misconceptions.
3 Understand the ageistic nature of these myths.

Time Required

50 minutes (20 minutes to complete the questions, 15 minutes to discuss your answer with another person or in a classroom group, and 15 minutes for your instructor to lead a class discussion).

Procedure

1 Answer the questions following the list of the nine myths and misconceptions.
2 Discuss your answers with another person or in a small group.
3 Your instructor leads a discussion of student responses.

Myths and Misconceptions About the Sexuality of Older Adults

The following represent some common myths about sex and elders.

- Most older people have no interest in having sex.
- Sex is more appropriate for young adults than for older ones.
- Most older adults are unable to have sexual intercourse.
- Those older persons who remain sexually active are weird.
- It is dangerous to their health for older people to have sexual intercourse.
- Most older persons are physically unattractive.
- The sexuality of older adults is both funny and cute.
- Older gay men are "dirty old men."
- Older gays and lesbians are promiscuous.

Please provide answers to the following questions:

1   Which of the misconceptions just listed most surprise you? In other words, which of the statements would you have thought to be basically true?

2   Explain.

3   Why do some young people believe that older people are not interested in having sex?

4   Why do many young adults have difficulty in understanding that their parents and grandparents have sexual interests and relationships?

5   Why do many younger adults view sex as dangerous for older adults?

6   Why do we often associate physical attractiveness with young adulthood?

7   In what ways is viewing elder sexuality as cute, funny, or weird an expression of ageism?

8   Why do many younger adults view older gay men and lesbians as promiscuous?

Gender Differences

A number of significant health differences between older men and older women emanate from reproductive functioning. Menopause, which typically occurs around age 50, brings numerous changes. It is defined as the cessation of menstruation and is said to have occurred if the individual has not experienced a menstrual period during the past 12 consecutive months (Block, Davidson, & Grambs, 1981; Rybash, Roodin, & Santrock, 1991). Menopause is characterized by a dramatic reduction in the primary female sex hormone, estrogen, the decline of which leads both to hot flashes and to the thinning of the vaginal walls. Usually affecting the upper body, hot flashes may include profound sweating. The atrophying of the vaginal walls is accompanied by vaginal shortening and decreased lubricants being secreted during sexual arousal (Fried, Van Booven,

& MacQuarrie, 1993; Rybash, Roodin, & Santrock, 1991). Interestingly, about one fifth of all women fail to report any severe symptoms accompanying their menopause.

Many women have hysterectomies, a form of artificial menopause and one of the most common of all surgeries performed in the United States. There are two kinds of hysterectomies: simple and total. In the former, the cervix and uterus are removed; in the latter, the ovaries and fallopian tubes are also removed. The most frequent reasons for this procedure are slippage of the uterus, fibroid tumors (these are not cancerous), and cancer.

Several physical and psychological problems have a relationship to menopause. Osteoporosis, a thinning of the bones due to lack of calcium, is a consequence of estrogen loss. There is an increase in cardiovascular disease following menopause. In addition, although menopause is not known to have a direct effect on psychological functioning, some women do demonstrate increased anxiety, insomnia, and/or depression (Rybash, Roodin, & Santrock, 1991). Depending on culture and individual personality, some women may mourn the loss of their capacity to bear children. When subcultures place a woman's worth in direct relationship to her reproductive potential, menopause may bring with it a decline in feelings of self-worth. Menopause may prove to be a liberating experience, freeing women from concerns of unwanted pregnancy.

With aging, women experience several minor changes in terms of the physiology of sex responses (Masters & Johnson, 1966). In younger women, breast size increases during sexual arousal; however, that is usually not the case for older women. With menopause, the vaginal walls become smoother, the clitoris and labia decrease in size, and vaginal secretions may decline, especially in women who do not continue to be sexually active.

The male climacteric is quite different from menopause. Beginning in middle age, the production of testosterone declines about 1% per year (Byer & Shainberg, 1991). However, men continue to be able to reproduce into old age. With age, men do experience physiological changes in the sexual process. In comparison with younger men, it takes longer for older men to develop an erection. There is a lessened need for older men to ejaculate, so they may be able to maintain their erections for a longer period of time than is the case with younger men. The necessary period of time between erections lengthens after the age of 50. It is common for older men to require between 12 and 24 hours before they are able to develop another erection. In addition, older men experience a flaccid penis sooner following ejaculation than do younger men. Older men may misunderstand their sexual response and misattribute these alterations to a loss of masculinity; as a result, they may develop fears of impotence. Changes may prove especially difficult for men who have been socialized in cultures that reinforce and exaggerate the importance of male sexual performance.

Societal messages about their sexuality or supposed lack of sexuality can have a negative impact on older men and women. Ageistic greeting cards and jokes demean and ridicule the sexuality of older adults by "making fun" of their appearance, physical loss, age concealment, or sexual interest or performance (Butler, Lewis, & Sunderland, 1991; Dillon & Jones, 1981; Palmore, 1981). Through a self-fulfilling prophecy, older adults may internalize such negative messages and believe that, because of their age, they are sexless, impotent, or weird for having erotic feelings. When younger family members or health care personnel deride or tease elders about sexual matters, such derision may reflect anxieties they may have about their own aging (Huyck & Duchon, 1986). Characterizing elders' expressions of sexuality as funny or "cute" is another way of "putting down" the worth of older adults. Health care staff (e.g., nursing home personnel) should attempt to allow the necessary privacy for competent elders to maintain their sexuality and sexual relationships (Lichtenberg & Strzepek, 1990; McCartney, Izeman, Roger, & Cohen, 1987).

Adults, as they age, may continue to demonstrate their sexuality through efforts to maintain physical attractiveness (e.g., through exercise, clothing, hair styles, and makeup), flirting, displays of affection (e.g., kissing, hand holding, hugging), dating, or long-term sexual relationships. Older women's sexual encounters may be affected by the availability of partners, since the number of older women so greatly exceeds the number of older men (AARP, 1994). Older women may have learned, through societal messages, the myth that they "are not supposed to be interested in sex," a myth that may have been learned more by some older cohorts and through some subcultures than through others. Sexual activities, specifically sexual intercourse, can be affected negatively by physical factors. For example, the ability to obtain an erection can be impeded by diabetes or by the use of various medications (e.g., antidepressants, antihistamines, sedatives, or alcohol) (Butler, Lewis, & Sunderland, 1991; Fried, Van Booven, & MacQuarrie, 1993). Also, psychological conditions, such as mood disorders, can contribute to erectile dysfunction (Rosen & Leiblum, 1991). Interestingly, the best predictor of continuing sexual interest in later life is a high level of sexual interest and activity during middle age (Belsky, 1990).

In the next learning activity, you will conduct interviews regarding attitudes and perceptions about menopause. You are to interview a female friend or family member 18–30 years of age, a female friend or family member 45–55 years of age, and a female friend or family member who is more than 65 years of age.

ACTIVE LEARNING EXPERIENCE: INTERVIEWS ON MENOPAUSE PERCEPTIONS

The purpose of this activity is to provide an opportunity for you to learn about the attitudes and perceptions that your family members or friends have about menopause. Upon completion of this activity, you will be able to:

1   Describe perceptions of menopause based on age and cohort.
2   Better understand cultural factors that influence such perceptions.

3 Understand the actual experience of menopause from the perspective of family members or friends.

Time Required

2 hours (90 minutes for three interviews and 30 minutes to discuss your answers with another person or in a classroom setting).

Procedure

1 Interview a friend or family member of either gender who is between 18 and 30 years old. Ask this individual the questions listed in Interview A.

2 Interview a female friend or family member between 45 and 55 years of age. Ask her the questions listed in Interview B.

3 Interview a female friend or family member who is more than 65 years of age. Ask her the questions listed in Interview C.

4 Your instructor will lead an in-class discussion of your findings from the interviews.

Note: We have found that many middle-aged and older women want to talk about their experience with menopause. However, if you find that your friend or family member does not want to share with you, please respect her wishes and find another person to interview.

Interview A: Perceptions About Menopause of an 18- to 30-Year-Old Woman

Ask your respondent the following questions and write down a summary of her responses.

1 What is menopause?

2 When you were growing up, did your mother, grandmother, or another female family member describe her experience of menopause to you?

3 Do you think that menopause is more a positive experience or more a negative one? Explain.

Interview B: Perceptions About Menopause of a 45- to 55-Year-Old Woman

Ask your respondent the following questions about menopause and write down summaries of her responses.

1 Have you experienced menopause personally? If yes, how would you describe it?

2 What were the symptoms (e.g., hot flashes)?

3   Do you view menopause as more of a positive or more of a negative experience? Why?

4   When you were growing up, did older family members (sisters, mothers, grandmothers, etc.) discuss menopause with you? If yes, do you recall what they said?

Interview C: Perceptions of Menopause of an Older Woman

Ask your respondent the following questions about menopause and write down summaries of her responses.

1   When you were growing up, did older family members (sisters, mothers, aunts, grandmothers) tell you about menopause? If yes, what kinds of things did they say?

2   Was your experience with your own menopause different from what you thought it would be? Explain.

3   What would help women prepare for the changes that may go along with menopause?

4   Should older female relatives tell younger female family members about menopause? If yes, what should they tell them?

Older Gay Males and Lesbians

Older adults may be heterosexual, bisexual, or homosexual in their orientation. As of the writing of this book, we do not know for certain why some people are homosexual or bisexual while most others are heterosexual. A number of scientists view sexual orientation as biologically determined. If this is the case, then people do not choose their sexual orientation, and neither can they change it (Seligman, 1994). Also, it is important to understand that sexual orientation occurs along a continuum with many individuals falling somewhere between exclusive heterosexuality and exclusive homosexuality (Byer & Shainberg, 1995). Sexual orientation is not an absolute, since some heterosexuals have had homosexual experiences, fantasies, or both, and some gay men and lesbians have had heterosexual experiences and/or fantasies (Engler & Goleman, 1992).

As a result of stereotyping, harassment, and other forms of discrimination, older gay men and lesbians may not communicate their sexual orientation to coworkers or even to some members of their biological families (Fullmer, 1995). While other minorities deal with bias and discrimination, lesbians and gays may likely be the only homosexual, or one of few, in their family of origin. Elise Fullmer (1995) suggests that "the special problems and concerns that . . . older lesbians and gay men face are primarily due to a social and institutional bias . . . rather than to deficiencies of older lesbians and gay men" (p. 103). American social institutions have policies that deny the reality of long-term, committed same-sex relationships (e.g., corporate benefits offered to heterosexual married mates but denied to gay or lesbian companions). Since gay men and lesbians in the oldest cohorts have experienced the most intolerance, many may present themselves as straight, which could cause great emotional pain.

For the most part, gays and lesbians deal with the same problems facing heterosexual elders. Elders, irrespective of their sexual orientation, cope with a wide array of change and loss (e.g., declining income and health, death of parents and companion) (Fullmer, 1995; Kimmel, 1992; Peplau, 1991).

It is important to note that lesbians and gay men tend to prefer long-term companionships, as is the case with their heterosexual counterparts (Fullmer, 1995; Kimmel, 1992). Also, according to L. Ann Peplau (1991): "Homosexual partnerships appear no more vulnerable to problems and dissatisfactions than their heterosexual counterparts" (p. 195).

There are some differences between gay male and lesbian couples. Male couples are more likely to reflect independence and competitiveness than skills in relationships. On the other hand, lesbians more frequently merge identities, are more likely to view sexuality as an expression of love, and tend to be more dependent on the combined income of both companions (Fullmer, 1995). This last difference is a result of the significant income differences between men and women.

Older gays and lesbians have variations of families within which they age. Kimmel (1992) has identified three such family configurations: (a) long-term, committed relationships; (b) networks of friends, significant others, and some biological family members; and (c) particular roles in the family of origin based on a special social position. Lesbians and gay men may be members of families that include children from a previous marriage, adoption, or natural or artificial insemination (Fullmer, 1995).

While a great many persons view and identify themselves as gay or lesbian during adolescence or even earlier, some persons may not come to terms with their sexual orientation until later in life. Those who "come out" in middle age or later may experience some of the same problems with sexuality and relationships facing adolescent and young adult heterosexuals (Fullmer, 1995).

SUMMARY

This chapter has centered on issues of diversity that affect the physical and mental health of American elders. Included were discussions of gender and mortality and of minority group membership and mortality. The latter included a discussion of the racial mortality crossover. Next, readers encountered material on health beliefs and behaviors, encompassing a description of the ways in which culture affects perceptions of health and illness. Particular emphasis was placed on the explanatory model framework, the *curanderismo* practiced by Mexican Americans in the Southwest, and Zborowski's classic study of ethnicity and the expression of pain. Then material was presented on social class and poverty, including information on Medicare and Medicaid. A section on rural issues in health and illness featured the finding that there are differences in the health of urban and rural elders but that studies have found some positive indicators for rural elders, particularly those who continue to farm. The units that followed were devoted to gender and physical illness and to minority group membership and physical illness. The former described the higher morbidity of older women; the latter included a discussion of the double-jeopardy concept, as well as research findings on Blacks, Hispanics, Asian/Pacific Islanders, and Native Americans. A brief section covering social class and morbidity followed. Another unit on sexuality included material on myths and misconceptions about elder sexuality, physical changes affecting sexual response, menopause, and a discussion of older gays and lesbians.

The following quiz serves as a review of this chapter.

ACTIVE LEARNING EXPERIENCE: ISSUES IN HEALTH AND SEXUALITY QUIZ

The goal of this activity is to assess your understanding of health issues in diversity and aging. Upon completion of this activity, you will be able to:

1   Assess your knowledge of health, sexuality, diversity, and aging.
2   Gain feedback regarding your knowledge of this topic.

Time Required

30 minutes (10 minutes to complete the quiz and 20 minutes to discuss your responses with another person or in a classroom setting).

Procedure

1   Complete the quiz.
2   Your instructor leads a review of the correct answers to the quiz in class.

Issues in Health and Sexuality Quiz

Indicate whether each of the following statements is true or false.

		True	False
1	After the age of 85, Blacks tend to outlive their White counterparts as a result of a racial mortality crossover.	_____	_____
2	In a number of Asian cultures, health is based on integration and balance among oneself, nature, and other people.	_____	_____

	True	False

3 *Curanderismo*, a form of Mexican American folk medicine, is based only on pagan rituals. _____ _____

4 Ethnic elders may view their illnesses from different meaning systems than those used by their adult children and physicians. _____ _____

5 On every significant measure, rural elders are ''sicker'' than their urban counterparts. _____ _____

6 The most common chronic physical disorder affecting older men and women is arthritis. _____ _____

7 Older immigrants experience more illness than do American-born elders of a similar age. _____ _____

8 Black elders are pessimistic about their health. _____ _____

9 All women experience menopause in much the same way. _____ _____

10 Older adults have little interest in sexual relationships. _____ _____

11 Research proves that older Blacks experience double jeopardy in regard to their health. _____ _____

12 Older women report more instances of acute and chronic illness than do older men. _____ _____

13 In general, Chinese American elders are healthier than White American elders. _____ _____

14 Menopause is characterized by a dramatic reduction in the primary female sex hormone, estrogen. _____ _____

15 Older gay men and lesbians, like their heterosexual peers, have problems associated with change and loss. _____ _____

GLOSSARY

Age-as-Leveling Theory A theory asserting that as people age they are faced with similar issues, regardless of ethnic group membership, and that, with age, there is a decline in differences between elders from minority groups and those from the dominant culture. This theory has received a great deal of criticism.

Arthritis The most common chronic disorder among American elders, its symptoms include stiffness, swelling, and pain in the joints. The most common types are osteoarthritis, which affects larger weight-bearing joints, and rheumatoid arthritis, which may affect joints throughout the body.

Curanderismo A form of folk medicine practiced by some Mexican Americans in the Southwest. It includes the belief that God heals the sick through *curanderos*, persons blessed with the don, a special gift. This system includes the idea that health and illness exist on material, mental, and spiritual levels.

Medicaid A state-operated health services program designed primarily for those with low incomes. Each state has rules governing eligibility, and the federal government helps pay for the program.

Menopause Occurs after 12 consecutive months without a menstrual period. There is a reduction of estrogen, resulting in symptoms such as hot flashes. While many women report very intense symptoms, 20% do not report any.

Morbidity The incidence and severity of illness.

Mortality Crossover Effect In old age, perhaps after the age of 85, there is a crossover effect in that Blacks tend to outlive their White peers.

SUGGESTED READINGS

Fried, S. B., Van Booven, D., & MacQuarrie, C. (1993). *Older adulthood: Learning activities for understandin g aging.* Baltimore: Health Professions Press.

This book includes 42 active learning experiences suitable for college courses, in-service settings, or self-development. Relevant activities include quizzes on physical aging, Alzheimer's disease, and elder sexuality, as well as structured experiences on ageism, loss and widowhood, fear of falling, and family guilt.

Fullmer, E. M. (1995). Challenging biases against families of older gays and les-bians. In G. C. Smith, S. S. Tobin, E. A. Roberterson-Tchabo, & P. W. Power (Eds.), *Strengthening aging families: Diversity in practice and policy* (pp. 99–119). Thousand Oaks, CA: Sage.

In this well-written and well-organized chapter, Fullmer describes how the stigma-tization of older gays and lesbians has led to inadequate social services and lack of information about role models for this segment of the older population. Specific sections of the chapter discuss defining the family within lesbian and gay communities, long-term committed relationships, biological families, relationships with children, legal and policy interventions, community interventions, and family counseling.

House, J. S., Kessler, R. C., Herzog, A. R., Regula, A., Mero, R., Kinney, A., & Breslow, M. (1992). Social stratification, age, and health. In K. W. Schaie, D. Blazer, & J. S. House (Eds.), *Aging, health behaviors, and health outcomes* (pp. 1–37). Hillsdale, NJ: Erlbaum.

This chapter, although difficult to read, presents an excellent overview of earlier studies on socioeconomic status, health, and aging, as well as an analysis of an ongoing longitudinal survey conducted by the Survey Research Center at the University of Mich-igan.

Markides, K. S. (Ed.). (1989). *Aging and health: Perspectives on gender, race, ethnicity, and class.* Newbury Park, CA: Sage.

This volume includes an overview chapter as well as chapters on gender, social class, the physical health of Black elders, the health of elderly Hispanics in the Southwest, and the health of Navajo elders. The authors include specialists in anthropology, medical sociology, and public health.

Spector, R. E. (1996). *Cultural diversity in health and illness* (4th ed.). Stamford, CT: Appleton & Lange.

This outstanding book, written by a nurse educator, is a solid and quite readable treatment of cultural differences in health and illness. The author presents such topics as familial folk remedies, healing traditions, health care delivery, and a wide variety of cultural views of health and illness. She includes an outline for her course in cultural diversity in health and illness in an appendix.

Tanjasiri, S. P., Wallace, S. P., & Shibata, K. (1995). Picture imperfect: Hidden problems among Asian Pacific Islander Americans. *The Gerontologist, 35*, 753–760.

This article examines issues surrounding the health and social needs of Asian/Pacific Islanders. The authors explain how aggregate data on this set of cultural groups distort their status relative to Whites. Specific sections of the article address such topics as population characteristics and socioeconomic status and health status.

KEY: ISSUES IN HEALTH AND SEXUALITY QUIZ

1 **True**. Blacks who live to the age of 85 have a greater life expectancy than Whites of a similar age. Elderly Blacks may outlive Whites as a result of their physical and psychological resilience (Markides & Black, 1996).

2 **True.** Among many Asian cultures, health is based largely on balance and integration of oneself with nature and with other people (Matsumoto, 1996).

3 **False**. This form of folk medicine, practiced by some Mexican Americans, includes a blending of Catholicism, medieval medicine, and the medicine of indigenous Indians (Gafner & Duckett, 1992).

4 **True**. Because of differing explanatory frameworks, elders, their children, and physicians may analyze a particular illness in quite different ways. Culture, class, cohort, and experience can all influence the formation of such models (Kleinman, 1980).

5 **False**. There are differences among health indicators for rural and urban elders, but sometimes these differences are positive for rural elders. For example, rural elders who continue to farm are, as a group, very healthy (Coward, McLaughlin, Duncan, & Bull, 1994).

6. **True**. Arthritis is the most chronic disorder affecting both male and female elders (Verbrugge, 1990).

7   **False**.   Immigrants are generally healthier than nonimmigrants at all ages (Markides & Black, 1996).

8   **True**.   Following the diagnosis of a serious condition, older Blacks tend to be fatalistic, and elderly Blacks are less inclined to view early treatment as useful. This fatalism may be a result of a lack of appropriate services, difficulties in accessing the health care system, and financial constraints (Baquet, 1988; Ferraro, 1993).

9   **False**.   While symptoms such as hot flashes are reported by a number of women during menopause, about one fifth of all women fail to report any severe symptoms (Rybash, Roodin, & Santrock, 1991).

10   **False**.   Older women and men continue to be interested in sexual relationships. Continued sexual intercourse is often related to patterns developed during earlier adulthood as well as the availability of sexual partners (Belsky, 1990; Fried, Van Booven, & MacQuarrie, 1993).

11   **False**.   This hypothesis has not been supported by gerontological research (Burton, Dilworth-Anderson, & Bengtson, 1992; Ferraro, 1987; Markides & Black, 1996).

12   **True**.   Older women do report being ill with greater frequency than do older men. Female elders experience a greater prevalence of many acute and nonfatal chronic illnesses (Verbrugge, 1983, 1990).

13.   **True**.   Generally, Chinese American elders are healthier than their White peers (Yu, 1986).

14   **True**.   With menopause, there is a reduction to 10% of the prior level of estrogen, the primary female sex hormone. Directly related to decreased estrogen are thinning of vaginal walls and hot flashes (Rybash, Roodin, & Santrock, 1991).

15.   **True**.   Irrespective of sexual orientation, older adults experience changes and loss associated with retirement, decreased income, death of loved ones, and declining health. Gay men and lesbians also experience problems resulting from social and institutional bias (Fullmer, 1995).

Chapter 4

Caregiving

OVERVIEW

Gender of Caregivers

- In what ways do the caregiving tasks performed by men differ from those performed by women?
- What are the competing values that often produce stress for female caregivers?
- Why do women from minority families face greater difficulties in their role as caregivers than women in the dominant culture?
- How do men and women differ in their reactions to stress resulting from caregiving?

Informal Caregiving Among Blacks

- What are the kin and nonkin networks that provide informal care for elderly Blacks?
- What are instrumental caregiving behaviors, and how do they differ from expressive caregiving behaviors?
- What factors influence the support networks for elderly Blacks?
- Why is intergenerational assistance so common in African American families?
- How do Black caregivers handle the stress that results from helping a person with Alzheimer's disease?

Informal Caregiving Among Hispanics

- What are some important characteristics of Hispanic elders, and what are the implications of these characteristics for informal care?
- What caregiving expectations do Hispanic women have of their adult children?
- Why does the use of formal services in Hispanic families often lead to depression among family caregivers?

- What support can be provided to Hispanic caregivers by (a) service providers and (b) churches?

Informal Caregiving Among Asian/Pacific Islanders

- What losses are experienced by older Asians after coming to the United States? How do these losses affect the need for informal care?
- What is filial piety? Why is this norm declining in the United States as well as in Asia?
- What are some of the factors responsible for the strain faced by many Asian families in the United States?

Informal Caregiving Among Native Americans

- What is the concept of extended family? Why does this norm continue to persist in Native American communities?
- How does the informal care used by urban Indian elders differ from that used by rural elders?

Formal Care

- What is formal care, and who provides it? What tasks are performed by various providers of formal care?
- What resources are available in the community for use by older adults?

Adult Day Care

- What is adult day care, and what services does it include?
- Why are many Chinese and Korean Americans unwilling to use the services of adult day-care centers?

Institutional Care

- Why are Asian/Pacific Islanders, Blacks, Hispanics, and American Indians significantly underrepresented in many nursing homes?

Barriers Hindering the Use of Formal Care

- Why do many ethnic elders lack knowledge and information about available services? What steps can be taken to promote greater awareness of the services they may need?
- How may location of services affect their use?
- How may the language barrier affect the use of services by ethnic elders, especially by those who are recent immigrants? What strategies would be effective in overcoming this barrier?
- What social psychological barriers prevent the use of services by ethnic and low-income elders? What approaches may be useful in overcoming these obstacles?

Ethnically Sensitive Care

- What model has been used by On Lok Health Care Services to address the health and social service needs of an ethnically diverse population?
- What principles underlie the On Lok model?

Summary

Diversity in Caregiving Quiz

Glossary

Suggested Readings

Key: Diversity in Caregiving Quiz

More people are now living to ages at which they are at risk of developing chronic disabilities. This creates an increased need for both informal and formal care. According to the report of the Senate Select Committee on Aging (1988), family or other informal caregivers provide 80% to 90% of the medical and personal care, household maintenance, transportation, and shopping needed by older adults. Furthermore, informal caregivers often work with formal caregiving sources such as physicians, hospitals, paid home care, adult day care, community long-term care services, and nursing homes. It is important to note that informal and formal care systems do not exist side by side as separate or independent processes. Instead, they are usually brought together through the efforts of the informal caregivers. How the two systems are integrated varies according to factors such as the gender of the caregiver, socioeconomic status of the caregiving unit, size of the community, and racial/ethnic group membership of the families.

In this chapter, we first discuss informal care and then examine the use of formal systems by older adults and their families.

INFORMAL CARE

To introduce our discussion of diversity and informal caregiving, we invite you to consider the following vignettes.

Vignette 1: Andy Johnson, a 35-year-old African American teacher in an elementary school, is the only surviving son in his family. His mother had given birth to four other sons, all of whom were stillborn or died shortly after birth. At this point, Andy is providing care for his 75-year-old father, who recently suffered a heart attack, and his sister, who has four children and whose husband died 2 years ago. When asked about his family caregiving, he indicated: ''I was asked by my family to provide care to all members of my family. My duties include (a) You will never get married; (b) You will continue to work full time; (c) You will take care of your parents in their old age; (d) You will take care of your sisters and their children; and (e) You will enjoy performing these tasks.'' Indeed, he has done nothing else with his life other than working and providing care for the members of his family. The decisions he has made about his life have always been influenced by his caregiving responsibilities. He says he feels good about what he has done to date and how he has faithfully met the expectations of his family.

Vignette 2: Irshad, now 68, came to the United States from Bangladesh when she was 40. Her son, Aziz, is now 42 and has started his own software business 200 miles away from home. Her 35-year-old daughter, Shaila, lived with her mother when she was a student at a local university. Upon graduation, she left her hometown to take up a position in the governor's office at the state capital 150 miles away from her mother. Two years after the move, she learned that her mother, Irshad, had developed cancer. She is now back living with her mother and devotes almost all of her time in providing the care her mother needs. While Aziz comes to see his mother at least once a month, Shaila serves as the primary caregiver. She cooks meals for the family, takes her mother to the clinic almost every week, manages all of the financial affairs, and keeps all of the relatives in Bangladesh, in Canada, and in England informed about her mother's changing health condition. The only people she sees are those who come to visit her mother. Irshad continues to do her prayers five times a day according to Islamic religious tradition, shares the teachings of Islam with her two children, and maintains contact with the religious leader, who lives in a neighboring community. In addition, she provides consultation to both Shaila and Aziz in matters related to employment, religious traditions, and social obligations. For their part, both adult children display a great deal of respect and affection for their ailing mother and do their best to provide the highest quality of care that is humanly possible.

Discussion Questions

1 In the first vignette, you learned about the caregiving responsibilities of Andy Johnson. How do these responsibilities affect other aspects of his life? What are the implications of Andy's responsibilities for his psychological well-being?

2 In the second vignette, what cultural influences did you notice in the daily lives of Shaila and Aziz?

3 What are the important similarities and differences in the two caregiving vignettes?

4 How would you handle the caregiving responsibilities if you were in a situation similar to those portrayed in the two vignettes? What values and preferences would affect the approach that you may take?

Gender of Caregivers

Providers of informal care are overwhelmingly women, mostly wives, daughters, and daughters-in-law. However, husbands, sons-in-law, brothers, and other men also take care of frail elderly family members. Although still a minority, men constitute up to a third of primary caregivers (Kaye & Applegate, 1990; Stone, Cafferata, & Sangl, 1987). As families continue to change and conceptions of gender roles broaden, the number of male caregivers is likely to grow.

Research comparing male and female caregivers appears to confirm some stereotypes regarding gender role. A traditional division of labor is particularly true of sons and daughters caring for their parents. Rathbone-McCuan and Coward (1985) found that daughters were eight times more involved in household chores and three times more likely to give personal care to their parents than sons. Sons, in turn, were nine times more likely than daughters to provide home repairs and maintenance. Similarly, Stone, Cafferata, and Sangl (1987) reported that daughters were more likely than sons to provide assistance with personal hygiene tasks. A similar pattern was observed among female caregivers other than wives and daughters as compared with their male counterparts. In more gender-neutral or traditionally male-oriented tasks such as financial management, financial assistance, and dealing with bureaucratic organizations, sons' involvement did not differ significantly from that of daughters, and sons had a more limited time and task commitment to caregiving than daughters. Along the caregiving continuum, as a parent's need for assistance progresses from a need for help with business matters and transportation to a need for more personal care, women are more likely to move into a primary role.

While caregiving can provide substantial personal satisfaction, it can also be a tremendous burden. Caregivers are left with less time for themselves and less privacy. This is especially true for women between the ages of 35 and 55, who experience pressure from two potentially competing values: (a) the traditional value that care of older adults is a family responsibility and (b) the newer value that women should be free to work outside the home if they wish. Elaine Brody (1981) has termed this group "women in the middle." As the phrase implies, such women are in middle age, in the middle from a generational standpoint, and in the middle in that the demands of their various roles compete for their time and energy. In short, the roles of paid workers and caregivers have been added to women's traditional roles of wives, homemakers, mothers, and grandmothers. Women face the challenge of how to balance the needs of their aging relatives, their own children, and their grandchildren while continuing to pursue their career interests.

Women in minority families face additional difficulties as caregivers. Since many minority elders experience chronic diseases and higher levels of disability at younger ages, they need care and assistance early in the family's life cycle when the women are still engaged in addressing the needs of younger members. On the other hand, there is a lower rate of nursing home use among minority groups than in the general population, indicating that a greater proportion of older persons in minority families are cared for at home. It follows that minority women are more likely to have competing responsibilities such as working outside the home, raising children, and providing care to older family members.

While caregiving can be stressful for both men and women, each may express the effects in different ways (Aneshensel, Rutter, & Lackenbruch, 1991). Female caregivers tend to take more antidepressants, report more symptoms of stress, and participate in fewer recreational and social activities than do male caregivers (George, 1984). They also report lower morale (Gilhooly, 1984) and higher levels of burden (Barusch & Spaid, 1989; Young & Kahana, 1989). In contrast, male caregivers are more likely to report physical health symptoms and loss of financial resources. Men's "getting-the-job-done" approach may help them keep greater emotional distance from their caregiving tasks and thus may shield them from some of the guilt, depression, and feelings of burden experienced by female caregivers. It is also possible that male caregivers may have learned to mask their feelings more effectively, living out the prevailing stereotype that they should "bear up" and suppress indications of personal vulnerability. Indeed, a number of studies suggest that, in contrast to women, men tend not to use caregiver support groups (Hlavaty, 1986; Snyder & Keefe, 1985). Those who do attend welcome information and appear more concerned with the specific issues of care provision than with discussing their feelings (Davies, Priddy, & Tinklenberg, 1986).

The following activity addresses differences in caregiving perceptions and responsibilities between men and women.

ACTIVE LEARNING EXPERIENCE: GENDER DIFFERENCES IN CAREGIVING

Purpose

The purpose of this activity is to provide you an opportunity to examine how gender influences the caregiving experience. Upon completion of this activity, you will be able to:

1 Describe gender differences in the experiences of caregiving spouses.
2 Explain how caregiving responsibilities may affect men and women differently.

Time Required

45 minutes (30 minutes to complete the questions and 15 minutes to discuss the answers with another person).

Procedure

1 Complete the questions included in this activity, either as a homework assignment or in a class setting.

2 Discuss your responses with another person.
3 Participate in a class discussion of student responses to the activity.

Gender Differences in Caregiving

Read the following case study, prepare written responses to the questions at the end of the study, and discuss these responses with another person.

Dr. Gordon is a physician in private practice. He has been providing in-home care to his wife, an Alzheimer's patient, for more than 8 years. As a result of the ongoing demands of caregiving, he has gradually reduced his professional practice but has continued to participate in professional and civic organizations. He has three sons and a daughter. All of them are married and live within a 2-hour drive of their parents' rural home. Dr. Gordon's daughter, Karen, who works full time and has her own three young children, plays an active role in the care of her mother. She knows what her father expects of her and does her best to meet these expectations. While the sons have more resources, they feel less distressed and are less involved in their mother's daily care. Occasionally they provide transportation for their mother, and they come to see her whenever they can. In contrast, their wives participate actively in providing care and support to Mrs. Gordon. They call her three or four times a day, take her out three times a week, call professionals regularly for consultation, and attend support group meetings.

Dr. Gordon approaches care for his wife as he has done for his patients. It appears that he views caregiving as problem solving that needs to be handled in a scientific manner. He manages his wife's money, medicines, and symptoms. The unfair division of responsibility among the various members of the family is of no importance to him. While he has adequate income, he has not hired in-home help because his daughter and three daughters-in-law are always available in that capacity.

Through the support group meetings, Karen recently learned about a day-care program available for elderly people with Alzheimer's disease. With the assistance of a county social worker, she has now been able to persuade her father to enroll Mrs. Gordon in this program. The day care provides much-needed respite to the family caregivers and provides a social environment for Mrs. Gordon. However, gradually she has become too impaired to attend day care. As in the past, Dr. Gordon expects that Karen and her three sisters-in-law will take on all caregiving responsibilities. However, these female caregivers feel physically and emotionally drained and are thinking of placing Mrs. Gordon in a nursing home. While they have done their best, they feel guilty and ineffective. On the other hand, Dr. Gordon and his sons feel no guilt or remorse. They believe that they have done their part as best they could.

Discussion Questions

1 Who are the caregivers in the Gordon family?
2 How does Dr. Gordon approach the tasks associated with providing care to his wife? What caregiving tasks does he perform?

3 What care-related tasks are performed by female caregivers?
4 How do the caregiving responsibilities affect these women?
5 What gender differences do you observe in this case study?
6 What are some possible consequences of the caregiving role for Dr. Gordon's daughter, Karen?
7 What sources of support are used by Dr. Gordon?
8 What sources of support are used by his daughter and daughters-in-law?

Informal Caregiving Among Blacks

Informal caregiving for older adults is the predominant type of caregiving among all racial/ethnic groups. However, older Blacks rely far more heavily on informal care than their White counterparts (Aschenbrenner, 1975; Devore, 1983; Gelfand, 1982; Hill, 1972; Jackson, 1980; Mindel, 1980; Woehrer, 1978). The major sources of caregiving for elderly Blacks are their kin and nonkin networks (informal support systems). Kin support includes immediate family (siblings and other relatives); nonkin networks, made up of friends, neighbors, and church members, also provide significant caregiving support (Chatters, Taylor, & Jackson, 1985; Gibson, 1982; Taylor & Chatters, 1986a, 1986b). In addition, the Black church also plays a special role in the support network of rural Blacks. It remains a significant provider of tangible services (e.g., assistance with shopping or housework and administering of medications) as well as emotional and social support in Black communities.

There are two categories of family caregiving behaviors: instrumental and expressive. Instrumental caregiving behaviors include (a) assistance with personal care functions (activities of daily living [ADLs]) such as dressing, feeding, or bathing and/or (b) assistance with instrumental activities of daily living such as managing finances, assisting with shopping or housework, or administering medications. Expressive caregiving behaviors include sharing in social activities, providing emotional support, and "being there" when the older adult needs someone. Instrumental and expressive care for Black elders is provided not only by family members, friends, and neighbors but also by ministers and church members (Sayles-Cross, 1990; Taylor & Chatters, 1986a; Wood & Parham, 1990).

Frequency and size of support networks for elderly Blacks are influenced by such factors as residential proximity of family members, family affection, presence of children in the household, being female, age, marital status, health status, and respect for youth and older persons (Chatters, Taylor, & Jackson, 1985; Taylor, 1985). In general, caregiving in Black families is influenced by levels of education and income, marital status, health, and number of children at home. In addition, social class continues to be an important factor that affects the caregiving behavior of Black adult children (Cantor, 1979; Mutram, 1985).

However, the prevalence of informal caregiving among African American families is not only a result of their economic status. In fact, there is a pervasive cultural tradition of providing care to parents, siblings, and other relatives (Angelou, 1969; Billingsley, 1968; Manns, 1981; Martin & Martin, 1978). Recent research indicates that African American daughters have a strong sense of filial responsibility, making them less receptive to the use of formal services (Price, 1994). Kelly (1994) reports that African American caregivers for elders with dementia cling to values of responsibilities to family, the extended family network, and in-home care for as long as possible. A particularly important aspect of informal caregiving in these situations is caregiver strain or family burden. Research reveals that there is no essential difference, based on race, in the burden experienced by family members providing care to frail elders (Morycz, Malloy, Bozich, & Martz, 1987). However, when the care recipient is a person with Alzheimer's disease who requires more step-by-step reminders to perform ADLs, White caregivers feel more burdened than Black caregivers. Wiley (1971) and Devore (1983) have suggested that Black families rely on extended kin more heavily than White families in times of strain. Black caregivers may use available extended family supports more often, because they are more used to doing so throughout the life cycle and because they have more experience in mastering stress.

Informal Caregiving Among Hispanics

In comparison with other older adults, Hispanic elders have poorer physical and mental health, have lower income levels, more often lose their family supports through movement of their children, and underuse formal support systems (Garcia, 1985; Lacayo, 1982; Maldonado, 1975; Torres-Gil & Negm, 1980). Within Hispanic cultures, adult children have traditionally acted as the main providers of assistance (Maldonado, 1975). In addition, caregiving between generations has been the basis for a natural helping network as well as for providing links with the formal system. Older Hispanics are viewed as wise, knowledgeable, and deserving of respect. They continue to expect, receive, and be satisfied with the help provided by their adult children and to feel that their support needs are being met adequately (Cox & Gelfand, 1987; Lopez & Pearson, 1985).

In a recent study of four generations of Hispanic women, Garcia, Kosberg, Mangum, Henderson, and Henderson (1992) found that (a) very high percentages of all four generations of Hispanic women believed that adult children—not formal services—should care for them, (b) children should share their homes with their elderly parents, and (c) no matter how inconvenient, contact should be maintained between children and their elderly parents. It is difficult to predict the extent to which such supports will persist in light of the increasing participation of adult children in the labor force and in light of their geographic mobility.

As noted earlier, providing care to dementia victims can impose substantial burdens and demands on caregivers' emotional and physical resources. As a result of these demands, Hispanic caregivers show a higher sense of burden and appear to be depressed (Cox & Monk, 1993). This is especially true for caregivers adhering to norms of filial support, according to which children should care for their parents and not use professional help. However, as the care recipients' physical condition deteriorates, caregivers tend to make more use of formal assistance. This decision to use formal services occurs only when the family is overwhelmed. Given the fact that use of formal services contradicts cultural norms of responsibility, it is not surprising that such use is associated with depression among caregivers, who view it as a failure to live up to their expected role.

Service providers should be aware that reaching out for assistance may be traumatic for persons who have been raised to view caregiving as a family responsibility. Counseling and reassurance to relieve caregivers' guilt should be incorporated into service programs, and counselors should be sensitive to the cultural experiences, norms, and values of the caregivers and have an understanding of the conflicts that may relate to the use of the formal system. In addition, churches should be encouraged to organize volunteer and support groups for providing caregivers with periodic relief or respite. Programs such as those offered through county social services, area agencies on aging, hospitals, and nursing homes could play very meaningful roles in terms of caregiver support.

Informal Caregiving Among Asian/Pacific Islanders

Asian Americans and Pacific Islanders represent more than 20 different ethnicities with origins in East Asia, Southeast Asia, the Indian subcontinent, Polynesia, Melanesia, and Micronesia. The vast cultural variation among these groups makes aggregating them for scientific purposes even more inappropriate than aggregating the various Hispanic groups, who at least share a common language.

It is important to note that more than 65% of Asian American elders were born outside the United States (American Association of Retired Persons [AARP], 1987; National Pacific/Asian Resource Center on Aging, 1989). Many have limited familiarity with the English language and American culture. This reduces their ability to advise younger family members about important decisions, a common practice in their native countries. As young family members take on the primary role as family mediators with American institutions (for example, the school or legal system and social services agencies), elders gradually lose some of their leadership roles in the eyes of their family and the larger American society. In short, older Asians experience more losses and fewer gains after coming to America than do their younger family members (Yee & Nguyen, 1987). Many of them become dependent on their adult children before they become physically disabled. Relative to the national average, Asian American groups show higher proportions of extended family living arrangements. In traditional Asian American cultures, filial piety continues to be an important norm in caring for aging parents; this norm includes issues of respect, responsibility, family harmony, and sacrifice (Sung, 1990). However, there are indications that these traditional norms are beginning to decline both in the United States and Asia. The factors producing this change are the same on both continents: the movement of children and family away from each other, large numbers of women in the work force, and the lack of availability of housing units that allow for intergenerational living. Furthermore, a strain faced by many Asian families in the United States is the duality of cultures within families and the inevitable clashes that result when different generations have different languages and values.

In brief, Asians who came to the United States in their youth or during early middle age have become acculturated to less traditional family relationships. However, in contrast to White families, the needs of their elders still take precedence for them. Given the variability among the various subgroups within this population, service providers should resist the temptation to treat Asian elders as if these subgroups were all alike.

Informal Caregiving Among Native Americans

Native Americans have traditionally placed a high value on the extended family (Lockery, 1991). This holds true even more for families living in rural America, where the elderly are more likely to live with close relatives. In addition to cultural traditions, poverty may be another determinant of extended families. A large number of older Indians in rural communities live with their children and grandchildren not only because of cultural norms, but also to share and exchange limited resources. These living arrangements also allow them to transmit cultural lore across generations, thus ensuring the cultural integrity of the group.

In addition, Native American families are more interdependent than those of Whites (Yee, 1990). This suggests a high value being placed in providing care for older family members. While this continues to be true to a great extent for those living on reservations, it may not be applicable for urban elders who have to augment their informal support through formal sources (National Indian Council on Aging, 1981; Shomaker, 1990). Research indicates that urban Native Americans use long-term care facilities at twice the rate of those who live in rural communities (Manson, 1993). However, this may, to some extent, be due to the availability of such facilities in urban areas. With the recent advent of nursing home construction in Native American communities, it will be important to monitor the use of these facilities and its impact on the tradition of informal caregiving.

In summary, the extended family continues to be the norm in Native American communities. All members of the household influence each other directly, the older members providing leadership. In addition, awareness of service needs, knowledge of service agencies, and use of agency services are higher for those living in extended family settings than for those living alone. Thus, family structure contributes not only to providing care and sharing resources but also to an increased awareness and accessibility of services available for older adults.

FORMAL CARE

Formal care includes nursing home care, but it also includes paid help for older adults who live in the community. In this section, we begin with a discussion of formal assistance for older people who live at home and then focus on institutional care. Estimates indicate that about 20% of older people living at home combine informal care with some paid assistance (Hing & Bloom, 1990). Formal assistance comes from sources such as public agencies, volunteer groups, private individuals, and businesses. Each source performs different tasks and addresses needs such as home health care, personal care, homemaking, nutrition, and home repairs (see Figure 4.1). How much paid home care is used by a particular person

Adult Day Care Centers provide health and social services to those who need daytime help with personal care.

Assistive Devices, such as phone amplification equipment, walkers, and emergency response systems for summoning help, can be obtained through special programs.

Friendly Visitors are volunteers who call upon older people regularly to provide companionship.

Home Adaptations, such as grab bars or wheelchair ramps, accommodate older people's changing needs.

Home Chore Services for yard work, household repairs, laundry, and cleaning are widely available.

Nutrition Programs, such as Meals-on-Wheels, bring nutritious meals to older people's homes. Other services provide inexpensive meals at senior centers and other group settings.

Home Health Care is available from nurses, physical therapists, and other health professionals.

Home Maintenance and Repair Programs offer emergency repairs and general upkeep of homes and property.

Homemaker Services help with grooming and dressing, light housekeeping, meal preparation, and food shopping.

Hospice Care in the home helps the terminally ill to cope with physical and emotional pain.

Respite Care offers short-term relief for family caregivers.

Senior Centers offer social, recreational, and educational programs for older people.

Telephone Reassurance is offered by volunteers who phone older people daily to confirm that they are well.

Figure 4.1   Resources for older adults in the community. Treas, J. (1995, May). Older Americans in the 1990s and beyond. *Population Bulletin, 50 (2)*. Washington, DC: Population Reference Bureau, Inc.

is determined by several factors, including the nature and severity of the disability or illness, access to informal care, and financial resources.

In the next active learning experience, you will investigate ways in which formal and informal care systems interact, as well as factors affecting the sharing of caregiving tasks between paid care providers and family members.

ACTIVE LEARNING EXPERIENCE: HOW THE FORMAL AND INFORMAL CARE SYSTEMS WORK TOGETHER

Purpose

The purpose of this activity is to provide you an opportunity to examine a variety of ways in which formal and informal systems work together to provide care to older adults. Upon completion of this activity, you will be able to:

    1 Describe various ways in which formal and informal systems may work together in providing care to older adults.

    2 Outline factors that affect how caregiving tasks are shared between a family member and a paid care provider.

Time Required

45 minutes (30 minutes to complete the questions and 15 minutes to discuss the answers with another person).

Procedure

    1 Complete the questions included in this activity either as a homework assignment or in a class setting.

    2 Discuss your responses with another person.

    3 Participate in a class discussion of student responses to the activity.

How the Informal and Formal Care Systems Work Together

Please read the following three vignettes, prepare written responses to the questions provided at the end of the vignettes, and discuss these responses with another person.

    Vignette 1: David Peterson, 82, lives in a one-room apartment in a large metropolitan area. He requires assistance to move from his bed to a wheelchair or from his chair to the toilet. He receives both personal care and homemaking services for a few hours every day. His 58-year-old daughter lives about a mile away from him and comes regularly to provide informal care. However, she is not able to lift her father or do extensive homemaking.

Vignette 2: Rosanne Sanchez is a 76-year-old widow who is both physically and mentally incapacitated from a recent stroke. She lives in a rural community of 5,000 people. Her son lives about 500 miles away. A paid caregiver, Andrea, was legally appointed as her guardian to manage her affairs. As a result of their ongoing association, Rosanne has developed a strong emotional attachment to and dependence on Andrea.

Vignette 3: Meg Rosenberg, an 85-year-old widow, lives alone in an apartment about 5 miles away from a comprehensive medical center. Her son lives about 1,500 miles away and maintains ongoing contact with her. He calls her on a regular basis and visits her three or four times a year. Meg Rosenberg subscribes to Lifeline, an emergency response system for summoning help in times of need. Recently, she made use of this system when she suffered a mild stroke. Her son came the same day she had been admitted to the local hospital.

   1 In the first vignette, how do the "formal" and "informal" systems of care work together to address David's needs?
   2 What conditions lead to cooperation between family caregivers and paid home care workers? What conditions may produce conflict among them?
   3 In the second vignette, how would you describe Rosanne's relationship with the paid caregiver? How does this relationship compare with that between David Peterson and his daughter in the first vignette?
   4 In the third vignette, how is the coordination between "formal" and "informal" systems of care different from what you observed in the first two cases?

Adult Day Care

Adult day care involves long-term care support to older adults who live in the community. As a structured, comprehensive program, it provides older adults with a variety of health, social, and related support services in a protective setting during any part of a day but less than 24-hour care (National Institute on Adult Daycare [NIAD], 1984). The program assists participants in remaining in the community, enabling informal caregivers to continue caring for impaired elders at home. Although a 1990 census identified more than 2,100 adult day-care centers nationwide, 40% of them were established after 1984 (Zawadski & Stuart, 1990).

   Despite the continuing increase in the number of day-care centers, fewer than half of Americans know what an adult day-care center is (Yu, Kim, Liu, & Wong, 1993). This is especially true for many Asian Americans and other recent immigrants. In a survey of Chinese and Korean elders from four congregate housing units in Chicago, interviewers had to explain what an adult day-care center was before the respondents could give their answers on using these services. Only 37% of the Chinese and 23% of the Koreans indicated their willingness to use the services of an adult day-care center. However, research with participants from day-care centers in Missouri shows that African American elders are more likely than older Whites to use these services and that they use them more frequently. As in the case of in-home services, a larger percentage of African Americans use Medicaid funding to pay for their day care (Wallace, Snyder, Walker, & Ingman, 1992).

Institutional Care

The institutional setting for the delivery of long-term care services is commonly referred to as a nursing home. The distinctive feature of nursing homes is the potential for meeting all of the residents' needs within the institution itself. Residents may be admitted to a facility during their process of recovery, returning to their community residence once the desired level of functioning is achieved.

Asian/Pacific Islanders, Blacks, Hispanics, and Native Americans are significantly underrepresented in nursing home populations in the United States. In spite of greater disability among most of these populations, their rates of nursing home residence are 40% to 80% the rates for Whites (AARP, 1987). This may be due to cost, discrimination, personal choice, or social and cultural differences (Moss & Halamandaris, 1977). Although all of these factors may have been operating to some extent among the four ethnic categories, their relative importance in explaining underrepresentation varies considerably across groups. Among the widely heterogeneous population of Asian/Pacific Islanders, language and cultural differences play an important role in their limited use of nursing home services. Blacks are more likely to identify cost and discrimination practices. American Indians list social and cultural factors as most important, with cost and personal choice close behind. Mexican Americans cite discrimination, cost, and the isolating factors of language and cultural differences as barriers.

Barriers Hindering the Use of Formal Care

In this section, we present four groups of obstacles that may hinder the use of available services by ethnic elders, women, and residents from rural communities. We also suggest strategies to help overcome these problems and promote the use of available services.

Lack of Knowledge and Information   People are not able to use services if they do not know about them. Research reveals that elders' degree of knowledge regarding medical and social services varies considerably from study to study and from service to service (Krout, 1983). For ethnic elders, this awareness also depends on factors such as the length of time they have lived in the United States, the type of community or neighborhood in which they now live, their mastery of English, and their use of media (Krout, 1983).

Ninety-eight percent of documents regarding essential services such as Medicare, Medicaid, Social Security, food stamps, public assistance, and Supplemental Security Income require a reading level of ninth grade or higher (Walmsley & Allington, 1982). This makes it difficult for many ethnic elders to read and understand the documents and gain access to the services. This is especially true for recent immigrants and refugees who may have a limited knowledge of English.

However, merely knowing about these services is not enough. They have to be perceived as culturally relevant and accessible. People become discouraged when they are "ping-ponged" from agency to agency and when they are asked to complete long, complicated forms in an unfamiliar language with technical jargon. Data from the National Conference on Social Welfare show that 60% of the people who seek social services are turned away from agencies (Hayes & Guttmann, 1986).

The following are some examples of approaches that have been effective in overcoming these obstacles.

- *Using church and neighborhood networks*. Geriatric professionals have been successful in reaching ethnic and minority elders, both in rural and urban areas, through informal networks such as families, friends, neighbors, and churches. Members of these networks can be helpful in communicating essential information about available services and providing links to service providers.
- *Using ethnic newspapers, radio, and television*. Wide use of media and non-English printed materials has been successful in targeting information about programs and services to various ethnic groups. In a study of Hispanic caregivers of dementia victims in New York City, researchers found that Spanish radio and television stations successfully reached and informed them about formal services (Cox & Monk, 1993).
- *Using outreach workers*. Elders in rural communities and ethnic neighborhoods feel isolated and lack knowledge about essential programs and services. Outreach workers with background concerning the special needs of ethnic elders can play an important role in making the needed services accessible to the target population.

Location of Service   The physical location of the service affects the extent to which it is used (Bell, Kasschau, & Zellman, 1976; Stanford, 1977). Traveling to an unfamiliar area outside an ethnic neighborhood means not only venturing into strange surroundings but negotiating new and often complex environments. Transportation difficulties are a consideration for recent immigrants, low-income elders, and residents of rural communities. If an adult day-care center is out of the immediate neighborhood and away from a mass transportation line, it may be available but not accessible.

The location of the nursing home plays an important role in making it possible for families to be closely involved in maintaining ongoing contact with residents. Research with nursing homes for Native Americans indicates that those built on reservations by tribal entities are defined as extensions of family care, demonstrating the continued value and esteem with which elders are treated

(Manson, 1989; Shomaker, 1981). Fandetti and Gelfand (1976) report similar findings with Italian and Polish respondents. Whereas most of these respondents preferred to care for their elderly family members in their own homes, there was a surprising willingness to consider placement in an institution connected with their respective ethnic communities. Merely locating health and social services in the racial or ethnic community may not necessarily solve the problem. Trust and faith in the efficacy of service providers also need to be developed.

Language Two particular obstacles to the use of formal programs by older adults are language barriers and programs that are insensitive to cultural traditions and beliefs (Harbert & Ginsberg, 1979). The greater the language barrier, the more isolated the group and the more unable its members are to participate in services provided in the wider society. This is especially true for elders who are recent immigrants. They differ markedly from the foreign-born individuals who have lived in the United States for many decades. These recent immigrants are less likely to speak English and more likely to trace their origin to Asia and Latin America than to Europe. While they may be able to get along in day-to-day life in the United States, they are more likely to experience difficulties in communicating personal problems involving the expression of feelings and emotions (Westermeyer, 1987). Furthermore, under severe stress or physical illness, they may lose the secondary language but still retain their native language (Marcos & Alpert, 1976).

Communication problems present obstacles not only for recent immigrants but also for native-born low-income minority and rural elders (Cormican, 1976, 1978; Hollis & Woods, 1981). Many service providers use unnecessary jargon, do not understand clients' dialect, or are not familiar with the expressions used by members of a particular ethnic group. It is also possible that clients may "choose not to understand" when understanding is anxiety provoking or demands activities that are viewed as difficult or unnecessary (Arroyo & Lopez, 1984; Sotomayer, 1971). Furthermore, many elders have difficulty in understanding the technical language used by service providers.

What steps can be taken to overcome the communication barrier?

- Health and social service agencies should continue their efforts to diversify their work force. Having bilingual-bicultural workers on their staff is helpful in providing services to non-English-speaking elders.
- Given the shortage of professionally trained ethnic workers, interpreters are necessary. It is essential to develop a pool of carefully selected and trained interpreters to ensure sensitivity, accuracy, confidentiality, and the ability to interpret cultural content (Baker, 1981).
- Communicating in a "user-friendly" language makes a difference. When documents use an abundance of technical jargon, clients appreciate an explanation in an easy-to-understand language. Service providers should consider their clients' educational level, socioeconomic status, and cultural background. They should remember that communication problems extend beyond

older persons who speak a foreign language and also include those who are illiterate. Providing services to these elders will continue to present a challenge.

Social Psychological Barriers   Even when formal services are available in the broader community, social psychological as well as bureaucratic and physical barriers may prevent their use by ethnic and low-income elders. Many older Blacks are reluctant to seek help from a formal service agency. They may view the use of such services as a reflection of defeat or powerlessness. Others may have a mistrust of helping professionals. One study notes that Blacks drop out of treatment earlier and more frequently than Whites as a result of negative experiences with helping professionals (Sue, McKinney, Allen, & Hall, 1974). In addition, historical cohort experiences may play a role in shaping an older person's view of help-taking. If in the past members of certain ethnic groups have experienced discrimination from service providers, they may continue to avoid using their services.

It is important to note that, within the same ethnic group, use levels may differ from one service to another. For example, Hispanic elders make frequent visits to their physician's office but do not typically use social services such as transportation, senior centers, meals-on-wheels, homemaker assistance, routine telephone checks, and church-based assistance. It is not clear whether the low rates of use actually represent unmet needs for this population or whether the group does not need more social services than what they use currently. Another possibility is that the design of these services does not take into account the cultural uniqueness of the older groups they are meant to serve. This problem can be addressed by involving ethnic elders in designing programs that are culturally sensitive. Research indicates that involving ethnic elders in designing programs makes services more culturally meaningful and promotes use (Chen & Soto, 1979). In addition, use is further increased by involving members of ethnic communities in the delivery of services for their elders.

In summary, use of many programs and services can be substantially increased if program design takes into account cultural values and practices of potential users. It is important that services be delivered in such a way that dignity, pride, and respect of recipients are preserved. Use is also increased by involving leaders and members of ethnic communities as full partners with professionals in all phases of the planning and delivery of services. This approach empowers communities and neighborhoods, connects the formal system with informal sources of support, increases elders' knowledge of available services, and promotes acceptance of services by ethnic elders and their families. Regardless of the model or approach used, it is essential to incorporate cultural practices in all programs and services aimed at meeting the needs of ethnic elders. Violating cultural norms shows disrespect to elders, their families, and their cultures.

An Example of Ethnically Sensitive Care

On Lok Senior Health Services represents a model that has been highly successful in meeting the health and social service needs of an ethnically diverse population in San Francisco (Van Steenberg, Ansak, & Chin-Hansen, 1993). On Lok's program serves 325 nursing-home-certified seniors. This population has few alternatives to permanent nursing home placement. Its ethnic mix is 87% Asian/Pacific Islander (mainly Chinese Americans), 9% Anglo (mainly Italian Americans), 1% Hispanic, 1% Native American or Alaskan Native, and 2% other. Participants include 71% women and 29% men. The program has been designed to:

• Provide care that meets the needs of and is satisfying to older persons and that costs no more than that provided in the "traditional" system.
• Encourage maximum self-help by the older person, work with family and friends to meet additional needs, and provide services for otherwise unmet needs.
• Help participants remain out of institutions as long as socially, medically, and economically feasible.

Figure 4.2 shows the service components of the On Lok program. Unlike traditional programs, On Lok consolidates the delivery of various services. Its extensive multidisciplinary team assesses participants' needs, develops care plans, delivers most services, manages the care given by contracted providers, monitors treatment results, and adjusts the care plans as needed.

Six principles underlie the On Lok model (Van Steenberg, Ansak, & Chin-Hansen, 1993):

1 It serves impaired and frail elders who need ongoing care for the rest of their lives. Participants have an average of more than seven medical diagnoses each. These diagnoses include dementia, hypertension, cerebral vascular disease, and arthritis.

2 Participants' continued residence in the community and the community's ongoing participation in the program are emphasized. Respect for the cultural preferences of the participants is a high priority.

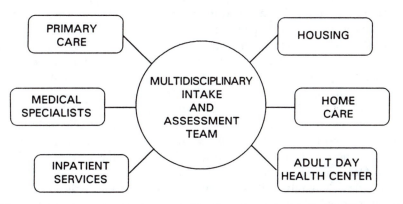

Figure 4.2 On Lok service components. (Van Steenberg, Ansak, & Chin-Hansen, 1993. Used with permission.)

3   Comprehensive medical, social, and supportive services are included. All services are available on a 24-hour basis. In-home care includes personal as well as skilled care.

4   Resources from Medicare, Medicaid, and private individuals are pooled to provide needed services, including preventative care.

5   The provider organization must be able to manage risk, that is, monitor clients, services, and costs and readily adapt to change. This assumption provides an incentive to increase the service system's efficiency and effectiveness.

On Lok also serves as a model for PACE—the Program for All-Inclusive Care for the Elderly—the national Medicare and Medicaid demonstration examining whether the On Lok model can work in other communities. With On Lok's close guidance, the model is being tested in a wide range of ethnic communities.

SUMMARY

Both informal caregivers and formal service providers work together to care for older adults. In what ways and how much each contributes varies with factors such as gender of the caregiver, socioeconomic status of the caregiving unit, size of the community, and racial/ethnic group membership of the families. Research reveals important gender differences in the provision of care. Women are much more likely than men to attend to the personal hygiene needs of the care recipients and engage in household tasks and meal preparation. In contrast, male caregivers typically provide transportation and help the older person with home repair and financial management. While caregiving can provide substantial personal satisfaction, it can also be a tremendous burden.

Informal caregiving for older adults is the predominant type of caregiving among all racial/ethnic groups. However, older Blacks rely far more heavily on informal care than their White counterparts. Within Hispanic cultures, adult children have traditionally served as the main providers of assistance. Although there is considerable variation among the major Asian American groups, values supporting the care of older adults appear to be strong, and rates of co-residences are higher than those found in the general population. The evidence on Native American groups also suggests high rates of co-residence and strong family support systems. However, ethnic families are changing with increased acculturation and assimilation into the larger society.

Formal care includes nursing home care, but it also includes paid help for older adults who live in the community. About 20% of older people living at home combine informal care with paid assistance available from a variety of sources. One example of such assistance is adult day care, which helps elders remain in the community while allowing caregivers to maintain their employment and other responsibilities. Nursing homes are an integral part of the continuum of long-term care services. Currently, ethnic elders from the four non-White categories are significantly underrepresented in nursing homes.

Having services available does not mean that they are easily accessible to all members of the older population. Barriers that hinder their use by ethnic elders, women, and residents of rural communities include lack of knowledge, location of services, communication problems, and insensitivity to cultural traditions and beliefs. We have presented some strategies that may be helpful in overcoming these barriers.

The following quiz can help you assess your knowledge of some of the concepts discussed in this chapter.

ACTIVE LEARNING EXPERIENCE: DIVERSITY IN CAREGIVING QUIZ

The aim of this activity is to gauge your present knowledge of issues related to caregiving and diversity. Upon completion of the activity, you will be able to:

1 Assess your knowledge of caregiving and diversity.
2 Gain feedback on your knowledge of important issues related to diversity and caregiving.

Time Required

30 minutes (10 minutes to complete the quiz and 20 minutes to discuss your answers with another person or in a classroom setting).

Procedure

1 Complete the quiz.
2 Your instructor leads an in-class review of the answers.

Diversity and Caregiving Quiz

Indicate whether each of the following statements is true or false.

		True	False
1	Husbands are more likely than wives to be sole caregivers.	____	____
2	Older Blacks rely far more heavily on informal care than do older Whites.	____	____
3	Native Americans have traditionally placed a high value on the extended family.	____	____

	True	False

4 Native American elders living in urban areas use long-term care facilities at twice the rate of those who live in rural communities.   _____   _____

5 In research with Alzheimer's caregivers, husbands were more likely to report mental health symptoms than were wives.   _____   _____

6 Older parents expect their sons to provide more personal care than their daughters.   _____   _____

7 The rate of nursing home use among minority groups is significantly higher than the rate in the general population.   _____   _____

8 Elderly women are more likely than elderly men to live alone.   _____   _____

9 In Asian/Pacific Islander families, adult children are expected to provide ongoing assistance to their parents.   _____   _____

10 Older Whites are more likely than older African Americans to use adult day-care services.   _____   _____

GLOSSARY

Community-Based Long-Term Care An individualized program delivering an array of social, nutritional, health, and other supportive services to the homes of impaired older adults living in the community.

Filial Piety Love and respect toward parents. Three important conditions for filial piety are respecting parents, bringing no dishonor to them, and taking care of them.

Formal Support System Includes public and voluntary service organizations that carry out the economic and social policies and programs mandated by agencies such as the Social Security Administration and the Administration on Aging. These agencies provide services requiring the application of technical knowledge uniformly and impartially to a large number of people.

Informal Caregivers Caregivers in the informal support system are distinguished from formal service providers in several ways: (a) They are chosen on the basis of intimacy and personal involvement; and (b) their assistance is generally nontechnical in nature (e.g., housekeeping, bathing, and feeding, as compared with specialized medical procedures).

Reciprocal Caregiving Patterns of care that are exchanged between parents and their adult children. For example, while adult children might assist elderly parents by providing them transportation to the physician's office, parents may provide financial support or advice.

SUGGESTED READINGS

Allen, J., & Pifer, A. (Eds.). (1993). *Women on the front lines: Meeting the challenge of an aging America.* Washington, DC: Urban Institute Press.

This book covers a wide range of issues, including high rates of poverty among older persons who live alone, middle-aged women's struggles to combine family care with paid work outside the home, women's prospects in the growing health care occupations, and older women's status in the labor force. The theme of caregiving and social values permeates the book and is the major focus of Chapter 3, "Caring Too Much? American Women and the Nation's Caregiving Crisis."

Barresi, C., & Stull, D. (Eds.). (1993). *Ethnic elderly and long-term care.* New York: Springer.

Barresi and Stull provide a rich survey of health care issues in a variety of ethnic communities. Chapters focus on factors related to caregiver burden, documentation of long-term care practices in different ethnic communities, and discussion of how ethnicity may influence the delivery of care and individual adaptation. Directly related to the focus of this chapter is Part 2 of the volume, which deals with caregiver issues in home-based long-term care, particularly informal care provided to rural elders and those suffering from dementia.

Harel, Z., McKinney, E., & Williams, M. (Eds.). (1990). *Black aged: Understanding diversity and service needs.* Newbury Park, CA: Sage.

This volume provides conceptual frameworks and extensive data for a better understanding of Black elders and the Black community, highlights the unique historical and collective experiences as well as cultural values and symbols of the current cohort of elderly Black Americans, and examines the service needs, service preferences, and service use of elderly Blacks. In Chapter 11, "Diversity in Black Caregiving," the authors review theoretical perspectives and applied data on informal support and caregiving.

Kaye, L. W., & Applegate, J. S. (1990). *Men as caregivers to the elderly: Understanding and aiding unrecognized family support.* Lexington, MA: Lexington Books.

This book reports the findings of a much-needed study addressing questions such as: (a) What do male caregivers do? (b) What are the attitudes, expectations, and needs of men acting as caregivers? (c) What are the distinctive characteristics and coping strategies of men performing this role? (d) What are the factors that instigate the allocation of caregiving to men in families? (e) What are the incentives and disincentives for successful male caregiving performance? and (f) To what extent have support groups responded to the unique needs of male caregivers?

Newhouse, J. K. (1995). *Rural and urban patterns: An exploration of how older adults use in-house care.* New York: Garland.

This book surveys a large, representative, statewide sample of Virginians who live in both rural and urban communities and explores how older adults use in-home services and what factors predict the use of such services. Although both rural and urban residents are included, the examination emphasizes the rural population.

Yee, B. (1992). Elders in Southeast Asian refugee families. *Generations, 17*(3), 24–27.

This article illustrates the intercultural and intergenerational conflicts that arise when younger family members adopt patterns of the dominant culture and discusses how elderly relatives' traditional roles as family advisers and decision makers are undermined by their lack of familiarity with the culture and language of their new country.

Zarit, S., Pearlin, L., & Schaie, K. (Eds.). (1993). *Caregiving systems: Informal and formal helpers.* Hillsdale, NJ: Erlbaum.

The authors present a number of research reports and discussion chapters on caregiving families and cross-cultural perspectives. Topics include (a) intergenerational transfer of resources, (b) ethnographic studies of multigeneration African American families, (c) the impact of caregiving in different family contexts, (d) barriers to the use of formal services among Alzheimer's caregivers, and (e) integrating informal and formal systems.

KEY: DIVERSITY IN CAREGIVING QUIZ

1 **False.**   Wives are more likely than husbands to be sole caregivers (Stone, Cafferata, & Sangl, 1987). Caregiving husbands, in contrast, are more likely than caregiving wives to receive supplemental assistance from informal helpers and to use formal services (Stone, Cafferata, & Sangl, 1987; Tennstedt, McKinlay, & Sullivan, 1989; Zarit, Todd, & Zarit, 1986).

2 **True.**   Numerous authors have indicated that older Blacks have more powerful kinship networks than do Whites and tend to rely far more heavily on informal care than do older Whites (Aschenbrenner, 1975; Devore, 1983; Gelfand, 1982; Hill, 1972; Jackson, 1980; Mindel, 1980; Woehrer, 1978).

3 **True.**   Native Americans have traditionally placed a high value on the extended family (Lockery, 1991). The exact form of the extended family is influenced by place of residence (urban or reservation), socioeconomic issues, and acculturation factors (John, 1991).

4 **True.**   Although older adults constitute a greater proportion of the rural (5.8%) than the urban population of Native Americans, the latter use long-term care facilities at twice the rate of the former. This may be due to the greater availability of facilities in urban areas than in rural communities.

5 **False.**   In studies of Alzheimer's caregivers, female caregivers were more likely to report mental health symptoms and less satisfaction with the quantity and quality of personal time (George & Gwyther, 1986). However, male caregivers were less likely to report subjective mental health symptoms and used fewer antidepressants (Clipp & George, 1990). In contrast, many men reported the use of alcohol as a coping response.

6 **False.** Older parents expect their daughters to provide more personal care than their sons (Horowitz, 1985; Zarit, Todd, & Zarit, 1986). Women are much more likely than men to take care of the personal hygiene needs of care recipients, including bathing, dressing, toileting, and cleaning and cooking (Senate Select Committee on Aging, 1988). In contrast, sons typically assist parents with transportation needs, home repairs, and financial management and devote fewer hours to caregiving commitments over shorter periods of time.

7 **True.** In spite of evidence regarding greater disability among minority elders (Asian/Pacific Islanders, Blacks, Hispanics, and Native Americans), their rates of nursing home residence are 40% to 80% the rates for Whites (AARP, 1987). This underrepresentation may be due to cost, discrimination, personal choice, and social and cultural differences.

8 **True.** Elderly women are more likely than elderly men to live alone, and as they age, the likelihood increases. In 1990, 9.2 million persons 65 years of age or older lived alone; 80% of these individuals were women (Saluter, 1991). Among noninstitutionalized persons 65 to 74 years old, one third of both Black and White women lived alone. These groups were more likely to live alone than were Hispanic women. Among noninstitutionalized persons 85 years old and older in 1990, White women were twice as likely to live alone as White men.

9 **True.** Many Asian cultures are influenced by Confucian ideology emphasizing filial piety and children's moral obligation for the care of family elders. In a study of older ethnic groups in San Diego (Weeks & Cuellar, 1981), high percentages of Filipino, Samoan, Guamanian, Japanese, Chinese, and Korean elders reported that they would turn to family members for help.

10 **False.** Wallace, Snyder, Walker, and Ingman (1992) examined a representative sample of 317 adult day-care (ADC) participants from most of the ADC centers in Missouri and found that African American elders used ADC at twice the rate of older Whites. No racial differences were found in the functional or cognitive need levels of participants, but African American participants were more likely than Whites to depend on their children as primary caregivers and to rely on Medicaid.

Chapter 5

Work and Retirement

OVERVIEW

Gender and Ethnic Differences in the Older Work Force

- Why is the older work force becoming increasingly female and ethnically diverse?
- How do employment patterns of women reflect a cohort effect?
- Why are older women overrepresented in some occupational categories and underrepresented in others?
- What are the employment patterns of older Black women, and how do these patterns differ from those for White women?
- Why are older Blacks overrepresented in occupations characterized by low wages, lack of health and retirement benefits, and the need for physical strength and endurance?
- Why do many older Blacks reduce work activities prior to retirement age?
- What are the characteristics of Blacks who have been labeled as unretired-retired?
- Why do older Mexican Americans have more difficulty adapting to the loss of work than socioeconomically advantaged older Anglos?
- What types of activities are generally undertaken by older American Indians?
- Why are Asian/Pacific Islanders often called the "model" minority? Why is this label misleading?
- What work-related difficulties are experienced by elderly refugees from Southeast Asia?

Barriers to Employment

- What is the concept of age discrimination? Give examples of age discrimination in the work force.
- What are the primary purposes of the Age Discrimination and Employment Act?

- What is the underlying intent of the Americans with Disabilities Act? What provisions does the act make to facilitate the employment of persons with disabilities?
- What are some misconceptions regarding older workers?
- What steps can be taken by employers interested in strengthening the role of older workers in the work force?
- Distinguish between individual obsolescence and job obsolescence.

Creating New Opportunities for Work

- Why is it important to provide employment to older adults? In what ways do they benefit from continued opportunities to work?
- What are some examples of programs that have been developed to create new work opportunities for older women and low-income minorities?
- What programs are supported by the Job Training Partnership Act? What populations are served by these programs?
- What are retiree job banks? Why are they offered?

Differences in Retirement Experiences Among Minority Groups

- Why do we need different conceptions and models to understand the retirement experiences of minority populations?
- Why is a preretirement phase not pertinent to many Mexican Americans and Blacks?
- In what ways do minority elders experience preretirement differently from elders from the dominant culture?
- Why does women's rate of participation in retirement preparation programs tend to be lower than that for men?
- What steps can be taken to promote the participation of women in retirement preparation programs?
- What factors should be taken into consideration in designing retirement planning programs for (a) low-income minorities and (b) women?
- What are some of the factors that affect retirement decisions of older Blacks, Hispanics, and members of other minorities?
- How do gender and marital status influence retirement decisions?
- What are important race- and gender-related differences in how retirement is experienced?

Leisure Pursuits

- What do people do with their time when they retire? What activities do they choose? What is the relationship between these activities and those they choose to do in their preretirement years?
- What gender differences have been identified with regard to leisure activities?
- What barriers are faced by women and low-income minorities in participating in leisure activities?

- Why are senior centers unsuccessful in attracting a large percentage of older adults?
- What supplementary programs and services may be offered by senior centers to address the needs of elderly refugees from Southeast Asia?
- Why is volunteering common among retired women and ethnic minorities?

Summary

Diversity in Work and Retirement Quiz

Glossary

Suggested Readings

Key: Diversity in Work and Retirement Quiz

In the first part of this chapter, we discuss the employment status of older adults in the context of their gender, socioeconomic status, and racial/ethnic group membership. We review the barriers to their employment and explore new models and approaches that may be fruitful in extending the periods of labor force participation. The second part of the chapter focuses on retirement and diversity, including topics such as retirement planning, the decision to retire, adjustment to retirement, and leisure activities.

As an introduction to our discussion of work and retirement, consider the following vignettes.

Vignette 1: Sarah Martin, a 58-year-old Black woman, works in a sales position at Anderson's Department Store. She enjoys working with the customers as well as with other employees. In recent years, the turnover at Anderson's has been quite high, especially in the women's division, where Sarah works. In less than 2 years, she has worked under the supervision of three division managers. Every time there is an opening, a salesperson from the women's division or from another division within the store is brought in to manage the division. All of them tend to be under the age of 40. Last month, Sarah requested that she be considered the next time there was an opening for the division manager's position. She knows that the position involves more responsibility than her current position. However, a higher salary, a commission on total sales within the division, and the availability of stock options make the position financially attractive for her. She feels that her 5 years of experience at Anderson's, together with her previous experience in similar companies, have prepared her well for the position.

During the past 8 months, she has been passed over for promotion on two occasions. At first she informally expressed her disappointment to Ronald Johnson, the store manager. On the second occasion, she demanded an explanation from him. Johnson finally agreed to meet with Sarah. He began by reviewing Sarah's work record. Although the company did not have a formal employee review policy,

Johnson referred to handwritten notes from Sarah's personnel file. He pointed out that her record was only average. While he acknowledged that she was a dependable worker with a good attendance record, he said that these qualities alone do not make her a first-rate candidate for the division manager's position.

Although Sarah is still working at Anderson's, she is disheartened by the lack of opportunities to handle new challenges and responsibilities. Some of her associates think that this may be a case of age discrimination and have encouraged her to discuss the situation with an attorney. She is hesitating to lodge an age discrimination complaint, because such an action may creative additional difficulties for her in the company and may lead to harassment by management.

Vignette 2: Claude Atwood, a 68-year-old Native American, retired from his position with the U.S. Forest Service about 3 years ago. At the same time his wife, Jean, also retired from her position with the Minnesota Department of Natural Resources. Upon retirement, the Atwoods decided to maintain their residence in Minneapolis, where they have lived for the past 10 years. They now spend about 5 hours a day in a Minneapolis high school that serves a large number of Native American students. In their role as teachers' aides, they work closely with the teachers, especially those responsible for classes in science and mathematics. Students appreciate the help they receive from Claude and Jean in understanding difficult concepts. It appears that the Atwoods have a knack for explaining complex ideas and principles in an easy-to-understand manner. Their examples from many years of work experience make abstract concepts concrete and meaningful for their students. In addition, their use of hands-on instruction seems to be highly effective with Native American students.

In addition to tutoring, the Atwoods have also been able to offer some invaluable career advice to a large number of students. Jean's ability to provide informal counseling to women and her sound knowledge of Indian traditions and culture have been much appreciated by the young Native American women who attend Minneapolis High. Both Claude and Jean have also brought to students' attention summer work opportunities available in state and federal agencies.

Students also enjoy the stories the Atwoods tell them about what life was like when they were teenagers 50 years ago: no indoor plumbing, central heat, TV, VCRs, or computers. The couple often share work-related experiences, stories from their travels, and the lessons they have learned in life. The principal and the teachers from Minneapolis High appreciate the perspectives the Atwoods bring to the school, the ongoing support they provide to students, and the interaction they promote between the school and the American Indian community. At a recent school board meeting, the principal reported that, since the Atwoods' arrival at her school, she has observed a significant increase in the participation of Native American parents in parent-teacher conferences and a variety of other school activities.

Discussion Questions

1   On what basis was Sarah Martin passed over for promotion?

2   Did Sarah receive periodic feedback regarding her performance? Does the company have a performance appraisal system that presents its employees with regular feedback on their strengths and weaknesses?

3 Based on the second vignette, outline the values held by Claude and Jean Atwood toward retirement.

4 How might their work at Minneapolis High School affect Claude and Jean Atwood?

5 What are the characteristics of retired seniors who undertake similar activities in schools, hospitals, and other nonprofit agencies?

GENDER AND ETHNIC DIFFERENCES IN THE OLDER WORK FORCE

Women

The older work force is becoming increasingly female and ethnically diverse. While middle-aged men have been withdrawing from the labor force, relatively fewer men working in their early 60s (Figure 5.1), middle-aged women have been marching into, not out of, the labor force. In particular, the participation rate of women 45 to 54 years of age, many of whom are displaced homemakers, is higher than for any other age group (Liebig, 1988). As a result, the older work force, like the work force as a whole, is increasingly female. It is important to note that women's participation rates also decline rapidly with age. This occurs for two reasons. First, as women get older, many leave their jobs and withdraw from the labor force. This is especially common at age 62, when eligibility begins for reduced Social Security benefits, and at age 65, when eligibility begins for full benefits. Second, the women in the 55-and-over group who were born earliest participated in the labor market to a lesser extent than those born 10 or 15 years later. Thus, some of the age differences observed at a given point in time are not totally a result of aging; they also represent a cohort effect. Cohort

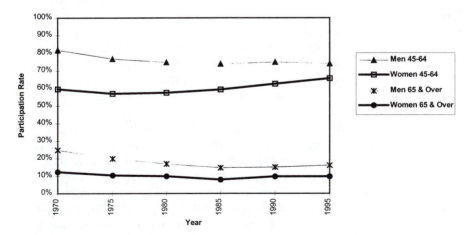

Figure 5.1 Labor force participation rates of midlife and older men and women (based on data provided by U.S. Bureau of the Census, 1996).

effects may include differences in work life patterns, attitudes, and education levels between groups of women born at different times.

Women who continue to work beyond normal retirement age often reduce their work activity in terms of hours, weeks, or both. Herz (1988) reports that the work schedules of women between the ages of 55 and 61 are similar to those of their middle-aged counterparts; more than half work full time and year round. That proportion edges down for those between 62 and 64 years of age, and only a quarter of women 65 or older have such schedules.

A majority of women, both older and younger, still work in traditional occupations. For example, nearly two thirds of working women 55 years of age and older and more than half of those between the ages of 25 and 34 are employed in three traditionally female job categories: sales, administrative support (including clerical), and services. Some reduction in occupational segregation has occurred in recent years, although new opportunities have been beneficial mainly to young women and new labor force entrants. The limited employment options available to women during their youth have largely determined the types of jobs held by women currently 55 or older. This explains why only 1 of 10 lawyers and judges between 55 and 64 years of age is a woman, as compared with 3 of 10 between the ages of 25 and 34 (Herz, 1988).

After age 55, the proportion of women employed in a particular occupation begins to reflect not only past opportunities but also other factors. Earnings, retirement income, and opportunities for part-time work all vary between occupations and greatly affect whether women work and what types of jobs they hold. In general, women in their 50s are about evenly represented across job groups, whereas those 65 years old and older are substantially overrepresented in some occupations and underrepresented in others (Herz, 1988). Research indicates that women 65 and over are overrepresented in both sales and service jobs. While the rigid hours required by many occupations force women to choose between full-time work and no work at all, those in sales and service jobs are often able to work part time for the same employer. Another reason for older women's overrepresentation in sales and service jobs may be low rates of pension coverage in the industries that employ these workers. Research reveals that women who do not receive a pension are about three times more likely to be working 18 to 30 months after first receipt of Social Security benefits than those who receive a pension.

Health also plays an important role in whether older women continue to work, and it is one reason the oldest groups of women are underrepresented in some physically demanding occupations, such as operators, fabricators, and laborers. A relatively small proportion of women who have been employed in such jobs are likely to be in poorer health than those who have performed less strenuous work. However, women's continued activity is affected less by their health than by the availability of a pension. Women who report physical limitations and do not receive pensions are two times more likely to be working than persons who have no health limitations and do receive pensions (Iams, 1986).

Racial Differences   Older Black women have a higher level of work activity than do older White women. However, Black female employment is concentrated in a narrow range of lower paying occupations. Analyses by Julianne Malveaux (1987) show that Black women continue to be crowded into not only typically *female* jobs but typically *Black female* jobs. Black women 55 years of age and older are about three times as likely as White women to be employed in service occupations. While there are significant differences between the youngest and oldest cohorts, a third of Black women in their late 60s are employed as household workers.

To some extent, the more extensive work activity of older Black women reflects differences in available retirement resources. Relative to Whites, Blacks (men and women together) are less likely to receive pension income, to own their own homes, or to own other valuable assets. In addition, since older Black women are much less likely than older Whites to be married, they have fewer resources for retirement and are likely to continue working to support themselves.

The labor force status of other minority women has rarely been studied. The U.S. Bureau of Labor Statistics has collected detailed labor force data on Blacks and Whites since 1960, and it began to collect data on Hispanic workers in 1976. Accurate data on Asian and Native American women are unavailable. However, Malveaux and Wallace (1987) report that Hispanic women are underrepresented in even "typically female" professional jobs (e.g., the health professions and noncollege teaching), and they further note that there are proportionally fewer Black women than Hispanic women in managerial positions. It should also be noted that there are differences within the population of Hispanic women in their representation in managerial positions, with Mexican Americans showing the lowest representation.

Blacks

In the preceding section, we discussed the employment status of women from different ethnic groups. We now proceed to review the work status of Black Americans 55 years of age and older. This group is of particular interest because they often leave the labor force despite inadequate incomes.

Many Blacks have more varied work histories than Whites. More often than not, these differences in work histories can be attributed to education, occupational status, and social discrimination. At all income levels, elderly Blacks are more disadvantaged educationally than their White counterparts. Furthermore, they are overrepresented in occupations characterized by low wages, lack of health and retirement benefits, and the need for sheer physical strength and endurance (Gibson, 1987). Unfortunately, Blacks 50–64 years of age are twice as likely as Whites to suffer a major physical disability that prevents them from working (Abbott, 1980). In addition, racial discrimination has led to major disparities in income between Black and White workers classified in the same occupational groups (Corcoran & Duncan, 1978; Gibson, 1987). Thus, older

Blacks have not received the benefits obtained by younger Black workers as a result of affirmative action and civil rights struggles (Abbott, 1980), and many of them may reach the end of a vicious employment cycle in financial destitution and ill health. They may work because of economic necessity or for survival rather than for fulfillment, recognition, or status (Jackson, 1988). However, many elderly Blacks reduce their work activities prior to retirement age as a result of health problems (Jackson & Gibson, 1985). It is not possible for them to continue working in blue-collar and service occupations that require physical strength and good health. The nature of their physical work in low-status occupations also contributes to the health problems they experience in later life.

It is important to note that there is substantial diversity among older Black Americans. In addition to workers and retirees, there is a third group referred to as unretired-retired (Gibson, 1986b). This group is composed of individuals who appear and behave as if they are retired but do not call themselves retired. These Black workers, many in early middle age, are making a gradual exodus out of the labor force, mainly for reasons of physical disability. Since they have never had a regular job, they have not accrued pension benefits, and there is no clear cessation of work for them. Without social interventions such as equalizing employment opportunities and creating jobs that would accommodate their declining physical abilities, this large group of Blacks may never work again in any systematic way; their work lives will effectively be over, and disability pay will become a mainstay for them.

Mexican Americans

Mexican Americans, like Blacks, are concentrated in urban areas, where many live in ghettos. Most older Mexican Americans today are unskilled or semiskilled workers who were employed for many years on farms, ranches, and factories and in service occupations throughout the Southwest. As in the case of older Blacks, their work experience has also been plagued by intermittent periods of unemployment. Many of them have worked, voluntarily or involuntarily, in part-time seasonal jobs for much of their working lives.

Mexican Americans are economically disadvantaged relative to Anglos (Briggs, Fogel, & Schmidt, 1977; Jaffe, Cullen, & Boswell, 1980). This disadvantage results from lower education, lower occupational status, and discrimination (Poston & Alvirez, 1973). While the income disadvantage of Mexican Americans is large for all age groups, it becomes even greater in late life (Dowd & Bengtson, 1978). In this regard, there may be some variability in findings from different studies; on the whole, however, older Mexican Americans tend to have substantially lower incomes than older Anglos. Research with older Mexican Americans in San Antonio—a largely lower-class group—showed poor adaptation to loss of work in comparison with that of socioeconomically advantaged older Anglos. Furthermore, more Mexican Americans than Anglos reported that they would go back to work if they could find a job (Markides, 1978).

It appears that many of them are among a group labeled as "discouraged workers" (Flaim, 1973), people who have dropped out of the labor force after being unsuccessful in their job-seeking efforts. Given the continuing increase in the population of older Mexican Americans and the difficulties they face in adjusting to life without work, the challenge is how to design innovative programs that would make effective use of this valuable resource.

The following learning activity concerns barriers to employment facing older ethnic minorities.

ACTIVE LEARNING EXPERIENCE: BARRIERS TO EMPLOYMENT FOR MINORITY ELDERS—THE CASE OF JOSÉ CERVENTES

Purpose

This activity will engage you in thinking about the difficulties faced by older adults representing ethnic minority immigrants. Upon completion of this activity, you will be able to:

1 Understand the obstacles many older immigrants face in finding employment that is consistent with their educational preparation and experience.

2 Identify some possible strategies that can be used by this population to overcome barriers to finding adequate employment.

3 Outline the losses experienced by older immigrants upon arrival in the United States.

4 Describe why some older adults prefer to continue working.

Time Required

1 hour (30 minutes to read the case and answer the questions and 30 minutes to discuss responses in class).

Procedure

1 Prepare written responses to the questions following the case as a homework assignment.

2 Your instructor will ask you to discuss your responses with a classmate during the class session in which this assignment is due.

3 Your instructor will lead a discussion of the losses experienced by older immigrants, the barriers they face in finding adequate employment, and the approaches that may be helpful to them in overcoming the barriers.

The Case of José Cerventes

José Cerventes is a 55-year-old Hispanic man who lives with his son in Evanston, a Chicago suburb. He is originally from Colombia and first came to the United States at the age of 53. His wife died of cancer before he immigrated to the United States. He has since moved from New York to Florida, back to Colombia, to California, and then to Illinois. Most of his moves have been precipitated by job searches. When he first came to the United States, he had a Colombian license as a civil engineer but quickly learned that his educational credentials were not recognized in America. While this had a serious effect on his potential for employment, he accepted the reality and decided to take any job he could find. This led to a varied work history for José. For example, he has made blueprints and cables for microwaves, worked in gas stations, distributed telephone books, supervised construction for swimming pools, served as an interpreter for a travel agency, and worked in warehouses and factories. While living in Florida, he worked for a consulting firm that moved him back to Colombia, but the firm had financial difficulties and he had to come back to the United States. He has now resumed his search for employment. He says that work is important for him to maintain his mental health. It makes him feel good, provides him with opportunities for social interaction with a variety of interesting people, and allows him to maintain financial independence. While his son is always willing to support him, he prefers not to ask him for money. In fact, José would rather give him the money, as he would have done if they had continued to live in Colombia. He feels strongly that older adults should be able to find employment, regardless of their chronological age, and that the most important criteria for employment should be applicants' health and their ability to do quality work.

Discussion Questions

1   Why did José Cerventes face difficulties in finding employment consistent with his educational preparation and experience?
2   What losses did he experience upon arrival in the United States?
3   Why does he consider it important to continue working?
4   What strategies can he use to make himself more marketable in the world of work?

Native Americans

Native Americans, like Blacks and Mexican Americans, have long suffered from economic discrimination that has kept them on the periphery of the American economy. The concepts of work and retirement, in their conventional sense, are even less applicable to the Native American experience than to the experience of Blacks and Mexican Americans. In the aboriginal state, there was no retirement for older persons. They continued to serve in constructive roles that provided them with prestige and respect. As observed by Levy (1967), "the older Indian was actively engaged in leading, educating, and advising, the very roles generally associated with middle age and prime of life in contemporary American society'' (p. 228). However, this advantaged position was enjoyed only as long as the older person was able to be productive.

While the educational backgrounds of the Native American population as a whole are rather limited, this is especially the case with the older population. Limited education has led to low incomes over their life course. A 1986 study conducted by the National Indian Council on Aging reported that 87% of a sample of 620 older Native Americans had incomes below $400 per month, a figure that placed them below the federal poverty level. However, it should also be noted that, among the American Indian population, there are low levels of participation in the Social Security and Supplemental Security Income (SSI) programs (John, 1994). While the lack of sustained labor force attachment over the life course is a partial explanation for nonparticipation in the Social Security program, this rationale does not explain the lack of participation in SSI. Perhaps the program eligibility guidelines, which do not take into account cultural values and the unique legal relationship between the United States and American Indians, make it difficult for this group of elders to qualify for benefits.

Despite considerable changes in recent years, elderly Native Americans, especially those who live on reservations, continue to perform meaningful functions in the family and the community (Roger & Galleon, 1978; Williams, 1980). However, as suggested by Gibson and Stoller (1994), using paid work as the only measure of Native Americans' contribution does not provide a complete picture of their productivity. Their contributions to society are underestimated when unpaid work is not considered.

Asian/Pacific Islanders

Older Asian/Pacific Islanders (APIs) constitute a small but rapidly growing group of ethnic minority elders in the United States. The diversity of API elderly subgroups is vast. The limited aggregate data currently available tend to paint a deceptively positive picture of a ''model'' minority. However, when these data are separated into specific subcategories, such as income and education, we find a large variation in the health and socioeconomic indices for APIs of all ages. Recent immigration, especially by API refugees, has contributed to the bipolar nature of the socioeconomic and health status of the group (Asian American Health Forum, 1990; Lin-Fu, 1988), and it becomes important to distinguish between foreign-born Asian elders and American-born Asian elders.

Table 5.1 presents one way of viewing 1990 census data in which APIs show higher levels of educational attainment than Whites and Blacks. Concentration on only the higher end of the income spectrum also suggests the relative success of API elders. Specifically, in comparison with Whites and Blacks, a higher proportion of API elderly households with married couples appear to enjoy incomes of $50,000 or more, and higher proportions of API elders living alone have incomes of $35,000 and more.

Table 5.1   Positive Socioeconomic Indicators for API Elderly Relative to Whites and Blacks, United States, 1990

	Asian/ Pacific Islanders (%)	Whites (%)	Blacks (%)
Education			
Completed high school or more	46.9	56.2	27.4
Completed some college or more	24.5	23.1	12.2
Income			
Married-couple families with incomes of $50,000+, householder 65+ years old	27.6	18.1	10.4
Persons living alone with incomes of $35,000+, 65+ years old	7.3	7.3	1.4

Source: U.S. Bureau of the Census, 1993.

Table 5.2   Negative Socioeconomic Indicators for API Elderly by Education and Poverty Relative to Whites and Blacks, United States, 1990

	Asian/ Pacific Islanders (%)	Whites (%)	Blacks (%)
Education			
No formal education	12.7	1.4	5.7
Below poverty line			
Families with persons 65+ years old	10.1	5.4	22.4
Persons 65+ years old	12.0	10.8	31.9

Source: U.S. Bureau of the Census, 1992, 1993.

While positive images of API elders continue to persist, researchers also point to negative realities for many members of this population (Tanjasiri, Wallace, & Shibata, 1995). Within the API population, there are specific subethnic groups that tend to have lower income levels. These groups include Vietnamese, Samoans, Asian Indians, Chinese, and Koreans (Morioka-Douglas & Yeo, 1990). Finally, families with foreign-born household heads are poorer than those with American-born household heads (Liu, 1986; Morioka-Douglas & Yeo, 1990).

Data from the 1990 census document the existence of two different subgroups in terms of income and education among API older adults. As can be seen in Table 5.2, about 13% of API elderly have received no education (U.S. Bureau of the Census, 1992, 1993). In addition, gender differences in educational attainment are also wide; about 16% of API elderly women have no education, as compared with 8% of API men. Thus, the relative standing in socioeconomic status of API older adults in comparison with Whites shifts depending on whether one is focusing on the high or low end of the bimodal distribution.

It should be noted that the low end of the distribution includes a sizable population of refugees from Southeast Asia. As Yee (1992) has indicated, there is a constriction of work and family roles for middle-aged and elderly men in this group. Elderly male refugees experience significant downward mobility. Migration has created the loss of high-status work, family, and community roles. Many of these individuals may not be able to recover their formal status because their job skills are not transferable to the United States or employers may be unwilling to hire older workers. Their lack of facility with English may be another barrier, making it difficult to pass professional licensing examinations such as those required in medicine, dentistry, and architecture.

BARRIERS TO EMPLOYMENT

As we noted in the earlier sections of this chapter, older women and ethnic minorities continue to face a variety of obstacles in their search for employment. In this section, we outline major barriers and present some possible strategies for overcoming these obstacles.

Age Discrimination

Many employers engage in a variety of personnel practices that differentiate among employees or applicants based on their age (Levine, 1980). Mandatory retirement, refusal to hire middle-aged persons, and a preference for promoting younger workers are examples of these common practices. In order to prohibit these age/work practices, Congress enacted the Age Discrimination in Employment Act (ADEA) in 1967. This act was amended in 1978 to prohibit the use of pension plans as justification for not hiring older workers and to raise the mandatory retirement age to 70. In 1986, the mandatory retirement age was eliminated for businesses with more than 20 employees. The ADEA is a hybrid statute whose provisions were drawn from both Title VII of the Federal Civil Rights Act of 1964 and the Federal Fair Labor Standards Act (FLSA). The ADEA has three purposes: (a) to promote the employment of older persons based on their ability rather than their age, (b) to prohibit arbitrary age discrimination in employment, and (c) to help employers and workers meet problems arising from the impact of age on employment. It protects individuals 40 years of age and older (Eglit, 1992) and is enforced by the Equal Employment Opportunity Commission, a federal agency. Despite such legislation, age discrimination alleged as the basis for loss of employment is the fastest-growing form of unfair dismissal litigation.

Discrimination Against Individuals With Disabilities

In addition to discrimination based on age and race, older women and members of minority groups also face discrimination in employment stemming from their disabilities, including impairments in sensory, manual, or speaking skills. In October 1990, Congress enacted the Americans with Disabilities Act (ADA). This law, which prohibits discrimination in employment against individuals with disabilities, may be used by older workers to challenge discrimination in seeking or retaining employment.

The law requires that employers make ''reasonable accommodations'' to the known physical or mental limitations of an otherwise qualified individual with a disability unless doing so would impose an ''undue hardship'' on the operations of their business. Reasonable accommodations include job restructuring, part-time or modified work schedules, reassignment to vacant positions, the use of qualified readers or sign interpreters, and attendants for travel. The law prohibits the use of employment tests, qualification standards, or other selection criteria that disproportionately screen out individuals with disabilities unless they can be proven to be job related and meet the business necessity standard set in the ADA. While ADA encourages older people with disabilities to stay at work or to return to work by promoting the ''carrot'' of increased accommodation, it also includes the ''stick'' of strict criteria for Social Security disability eligibility. To what extent the law will significantly increase accommodation, especially to older workers with handicaps, remains to be seen.

Through the next learning activity, you will become more familiar with obstacles in the workplace affecting elders with disabilities.

ACTIVE LEARNING EXPERIENCE: OLDER WORKERS WITH DISABILITIES AND THE WORKPLACE

Purpose

The purpose of this activity is to acquaint you with some of the obstacles confronting older employees with disabilities. Upon completion of this activity, you will be able to:

  1 List several types of problems in the workplace facing elders with disabilities.
  2 Analyze case material relevant to the Americans with Disabilities Act of 1990.

Time Required

40 minutes (20 minutes to read the cases and answer the questions and 20 minutes for class discussion).

Procedure

1 Read the cases and answer the questions following them.
2 Discuss your responses with another person.
3 Your instructor will lead a discussion of student responses.

Older Workers With Disabilities and the Workplace

Read each of the following cases. After reading each case, prepare written responses to the accompanying questions and discuss them with another person.

Case 1: For 22 years, Ruby Kelso has worked as a cashier at the cafeteria operated for the students and staff of Wordsworth College. She has been a good employee, witnessed by the fact that, several times, she has been named College Employee of the Year. Although 67 years old, Ruby wants to continue to work; she needs to work. Ruby's husband died of cancer last year. She misses him and finds that most of her social interaction involves her job. She also needs the money. Her salary is small, but it's better than for her to try to scrape by on Social Security. As a result of arthritis and back pain, Ruby performs her job at a slower pace than she used to. She could really use a more comfortable chair that would give her back more support. She has mentioned this to her supervisor, Sara Kennon. Ms. Kennon told Ruby that the college couldn't afford to buy the chair, and she has made veiled threats that if Ruby doesn't get faster at her job, she could be let go.

Discussion Questions

1 What options does Ruby Kelso have?
2 Under the Americans with Disabilities Act of 1990 (ADA), what is her employer, Wordsworth College, required to do in terms of accommodating her disabilities?
3 What rights does Ruby Kelso have under the ADA?
4 How could Sara Kennon have better handled the situation?

Case 2: Sam Nkrumah works in the office of the regional telephone company. A 58-year-old manager, Sam is in charge of a staff of 30. As a result of a motorcycle accident at the age of 19, Sam is confined to a wheelchair. After receiving a master's degree in business administration at the age of 24, Mr. Nkrumah went to work for the phone company, and he has been there ever since. He has received numerous promotions and is eligible to be named as general manager. However, he has been told by his boss, Russ Merdly, a company vice-president, that he would not present the kind of image the company wants. His boss makes overtures suggesting that Sam consider planning to retire. Sam is furious and feels betrayed by the company to which he has given so much.

Discussion Questions

1 What are Sam Nkrumah's options?
2 Under the ADA and other civil rights legislation, what obligations does Sam's employer have regarding Sam's employment?
3 If you were Sam Nkrumah, what would you do?

Negative Stereotypes

In addition to the unfounded stereotypes that depict older workers as lower in intelligence, performance capacity, and potential for development, other stereotypes persist about the work behaviors of ethnic minorities. These include misconceptions such as that Black and Hispanic workers are lazy, Asian Americans are model minorities, and Native Americans are interested only in hunting and fishing. Furthermore, older women and minorities also experience additional bias. It is therefore essential to design effective educational programs that provide employers with objective information related to unfounded beliefs and assumptions that are present in the use of fair employment practices. In addition, performance appraisals should receive critical and effective priority in personnel management (Mehrotra, 1984). Involving employees in the design of the appraisal system, evaluating their performance on a regular schedule, and making decisions based on performance rather than age would be helpful in strengthening the role of older adults in the work force. Shuster and Miller (1981) have documented that records of employees' performance appraisal play the most critical role in a defense against a charge of age discrimination.

Individual and Job Obsolescence

When employees fall behind in understanding how to use new tools and techniques or fail to recognize how the application of new knowledge can improve their performance, they become vulnerable to obsolescence. In addition, jobs themselves may become obsolete or disappear when demands for certain products or services decline or new manufacturing techniques replace older, less efficient processes. Older workers are particularly vulnerable to both job obsolescence and individual obsolescence. The greater vulnerability of older women and minorities to job obsolescence is reflected in the longer period of unemployment that they typically experience. Other factors responsible for these difficulties include limited educational preparation, reluctance to admit that certain essential skills have become rusty, and fear of learning the use of new technology. These problems may be exacerbated by reluctance on the part of employers to invest in upgrading the skills of older workers.

In summary, there are a great many barriers that prohibit employment of older women and minority workers. What steps can an employer take to remove these barriers? Employers should consider the following guidelines:

- Examine policies or procedures to determine whether they discriminate against or have a negative effect on older women and minority employees. Use the findings to modify negative policies or procedures with the goal of ensuring age-neutral policies.
- Analyze recruitment messages and other external communications regarding employment.
- Design effective performance appraisal systems and use them on a regular schedule.
- Make part-time work more attractive by prorating employee benefits in proportion to full-time work.
- Consider redesigning jobs as an approach to reducing undue stress, whether physical or mental. Such stress often impairs the performance of older workers.

CREATING NEW OPPORTUNITIES FOR WORK

There is substantial evidence that employment has a positive effect on the mental health, life satisfaction, marital satisfaction, and perceived health of older adults. For example, Bossé, Aldwin, Levinson, and Ekerdt (1987) examined psychological symptoms in a sample of older men and found that retirees reported more psychological symptoms than did workers, even after controlling for physical health status. Another study found that the prestige associated with a spouse's employment had a positive effect on marital satisfaction among older adults (Cassidy, 1985). Furthermore, a study of a nationally representative sample of elderly women indicated that employed women reported significantly higher levels of life satisfaction than did members of the same cohort who were homemakers or retirees (Riddick, 1985). In addition to mental health and life satisfaction, significant differences in perceived health have also been found between older workers and retirees (see, for example, Soumerai & Avon, 1983). Improved health is generally reported more frequently by older workers, and declining health is more prevalent among retirees. Given this relationship between work and well-being, a variety of employment and training programs have been designed for low-income older adults, especially women and minorities. Examples of successful programs are presented subsequently.

Senior Community Service Employment Program (SCSEP)

This program, funded under Title V of the Older Americans Act (OAA), targets disadvantaged older persons. It provides training to older people, serves as a source of income, and places them in community service organizations (Rothstein, 1988). The program is administered through state sponsors and 10 national agencies. Participants receive the minimum wage for work averaging 20 to 25 hours per week and work up to 1,300 hours in a year.

Displaced Homemakers Network

Displaced homemakers, because of age and lack of work experience and updated skills, face multiple barriers upon reentry to the labor force. They need training, advice on how to find jobs, other supportive services, and income. One of the prime sources of support and information for this special population is the Displaced Homemakers Network (DHN). Local programs, aided by a national umbrella organization, work to improve employment and training opportunities. Despite low levels of funding, local DHN programs have been instrumental in enhancing the employment opportunities for many members of this population.

Job Training Partnership Act Programs

The Job Training Partnership Act (JTPA), funded by the U.S. Department of Labor, earmarks 3% of all training funds for economically disadvantaged individuals who are 55 years of age or older. Displaced homemakers are also eligible to participate in these programs if they are economically disadvantaged. In addition, the JTPA singles out displaced homemakers as a group facing special employment barriers. Furthermore, up to 10% of JTPA's funds may be used to assist such individuals, even if they are not economically disadvantaged. However, at the present time, JTPA funds do not allow use of supportive services such as skills assessment, counseling, and intensive training that displaced homemakers often need. Finally, participants in JTPA programs are typically trained for clerical or health field jobs, employment that is not especially lucrative.

Other Programs

In addition to those just outlined, there are a number of other employment-related programs that could be used to expand employment opportunities for older adults. For example, Green Thumb, administered by the Farmers Union and funded by the U.S. Department of Labor, seeks to involve people 70 years old and older in working with children in rural schools, and the Conservation Employment Program, administered by the U.S. Forest Service, seeks to engage older adults in improving national parklands. Retiree job banks, such as those offered by the Travelers Company, Banker's Life and Casualty, and Wells Fargo, provide a variety of opportunities for employees interested in working after retirement, and the Project with Industry Program of Aging in America offers job-seeking skills and training sessions targeting older disabled adults (Cronin, 1988).

DIFFERENCES IN RETIREMENT EXPERIENCES AMONG MINORITY GROUPS

Theories and research on retirement focusing primarily on White men may not generalize to minorities. The traditional retirement criteria (e.g., age 65, a clear line between work and nonwork, income from primarily retirement sources, and viewing oneself as retired) do not apply to Blacks, Mexican Americans, Asian Americans, and other minorities. Gibson's (1987) research with Blacks, Zsembik and Singer's (1990) work with Mexican Americans, and Palmore, Burchett, Fillenbaum, George, and Wallman's (1985) analysis of racial differences confirm that different conceptions and models are needed to interpret and understand minority retirement experiences. It is clear that these populations view retirement in ways different from the dominant culture, experience retirement differently, have access to fewer sources of retirement benefits, and face a variety of adjustment problems during retirement.

On the other hand, retirement experiences within each ethnic group also vary widely depending on the retiree's economic, occupational, and professional resources. Careful investigation of these variations is especially warranted in view of the dearth of adequate data representing a full range of retirement experiences for each group. Markides and Mindel (1987) remind us that much of what we know about the retirement experiences of these populations has more to do with social class than with ethnicity. Studies in which researchers carefully control status and class variations are more likely to reveal similarities than differences in the preretirement and retirement experiences of Blacks and Whites (Richardson & Kilty, 1989).

Variations in the Preretirement Phase

The preretirement phase is a preparatory stage in which older workers first start thinking about and preparing for retirement. Before entering this phase, they must first conceptualize retirement as a distinct and meaningful phase of life. However, it is questionable whether a large proportion of minority populations experience a preretirement phase. For example, Gibson (1987) reports that many older Blacks who are not working prefer to call themselves disabled rather than retired, such a status providing them with economic, social, and psychological benefits. Similarly, Zsembik and Singer (1990) report that Mexican Americans perceive retirement differently than nonminority groups. Given their lifetime work patterns that yield no clear line between work and nonwork, lack of access to private pensions, low levels of public pension, and long periods of unemployment, a preretirement phase is not pertinent to many Mexican Americans.

In addition to Blacks and Mexican Americans, Asian Americans also differ from the dominant culture in their perceptions of retirement. Some Asian Americans, especially Japanese Americans, avoid thinking about retirement and continue to work in their later years (O'Hare & Felt, 1991). The preretirement experiences of the more established Asian Americans—Chinese, Japanese, and Asian Indians—differ substantially from those of Mexican Americans because many of the former have worked in professional and managerial positions. It may be fruitless to discuss with Native Americans the planning of their retirement years because they already know what to do with their time (Curley, 1978).

The most significant way in which minority elders experience preretirement differently from the dominant culture concerns financial preparation. The factors that make a difference in the economics of retirement among minority elders include the sector—public or private—in which a person works, the occupational category of the job held, and the longest time worked at a particular job (Rhodes, 1982). Minorities are at a disadvantage, since fewer work in the public sector (with its better pension coverage) than Whites. Also, they are in lower occupational categories (and therefore have lower incomes) and have a more erratic and unstable work tenure. They are thus less likely to accumulate vesting rights and wage provisions necessary for receiving the maximum postretirement incomes from pension and Social Security (Social Security Administration, 1982). In addition, many older immigrants (e.g., newly arrived Pacific Islanders and Vietnamese) have not worked long enough to be eligible for Social Security benefits (Kitano & Daniels, 1995; O'Hare & Felt, 1991).

Given the difficult circumstances in which today's older minorities find themselves, it is important to begin involving younger cohorts in retirement preparation programs specifically designed to address their needs. (See Figure 5.2 for a discussion of factors relevant to retirement planning for minorities.) As Richardson and Kilty (1989) have suggested, retirement specialists should begin by reaching out to groups that are able to accumulate pensions and benefits and are ready to plan for retirement. They should then focus on low-income groups that have limited financial resources to invest and save. (See Figure 5.3 for tips on saving and investing for retirement.) While financial planning is an important component of all retirement preparation programs, it is important that these programs also include health promotion, health enhancement, and prevention of illnesses.

Gender Differences   So far, our discussion on variability during the preretirement phase has focused mainly on members of minority groups. But what about women? Are there gender differences in the area of retirement preparation? Available research on this topic suggests that women and men engage in different types and amounts of retirement preparation. In a study comparing retirement among professionals, Newman, Sherman, and Higgins (1982) found that men had more positive attitudes toward retirement and had made more retirement plans than did women. In a sample from New York City, Kroeger (1982) examined both formal (i.e., structured retirement preparation programs) and informal (i.e., talking to others and seeking information through the media) retirement preparation experiences of preretirees. The findings indicated that, in comparison with men, women are less likely to engage in retirement preparation. Among those preretirees who participated in retirement planning, women were more likely than men to enroll in formal programs. In contrast, men were more likely than women to engage in informal retirement preparation.

Individuals who retire suddenly have far less time to formulate a strategy than those who have anticipated their retirement. This is true for many women

In developing programs and educational packages for use with the minority population, it will be helpful to consider the following factors:

- Language. Many older minorities do not speak English or prefer another language. This is especially true for low income elderly and recent immigrants.

- Social factors. It is important to take into account the distinct characteristics of the target group. Be aware of the needs of different cohorts within each ethnic group. For example, middle-aged and younger cohorts of African Americans have benefited from the availability of educational opportunities, reduction of discrimination, and the affluence of recent years. This is, however, not true for older cohorts.

- Attitudes. It will require a reversal of attitudes toward retirement on the part of middle-aged minorities to become active participants in retirement planning. These attitudes are shaped not only by their social and economic conditions, but by their heritage and cultural values as well. It will be helpful to emphasize the changes that may occur over a life time in family and social relationships and how these changes will affect traditional patterns of support during retirement years.

- Informal support networks. Given the extensive reliance by minorities on informal support from family, church, and neighborhood groups, retirement preparation programs should include a discussion regarding the role of these networks. In addition, their input should be obtained in the design and conduct of such programs.

- Financial planning. While some members of minority groups have been able to accumulate savings, assets, and pensions, there are others with extremely low incomes. The needs of these two groups are quite different. The first group will benefit from a discussion of financial planning concepts such as spendable income in retirement, reducing expenses to increase one's net worth, and investing. The second group should be made aware of the various public benefit programs and services that are available.

- Health promotion. Like other components of retirement preparation, health promotion activities should begin at the participants' educational level and use materials and presentation styles that take into account their needs and life experiences.

Figure 5.2 Factors relevant to retirement planning for minorities. Adapted from Torres-Gil, F. (1984). Preretirement issues that affect minorities. In H. Dennis (Ed.), *Retirement preparation* (pp. 109–128). Lexington, MA: Lexington Books.

who are forced into retirement before they are ready because their husband or an aging parent unexpectedly falls ill. In addition, other women need to retire simply because their husbands have retired. These women, who retire because of family obligations, are unlikely to engage in retirement preparation programs because they had not yet expected to retire.

For many women, the greatest deterrent to retirement preparation is inadequate access to preretirement programs. Such programs are not generally offered in small businesses and service industries, where most women are employed. When women are able to participate in a retirement education program, they often find that its content is targeted toward male retirees, with little or no emphasis on the specific concerns of female retirees. (See Figure 5.4 for a discussion of factors relevant to retirement planning for women.)

It should be noted that most of the research on gender differences in retirement preparation does not take into account participants' race. While we do not

Given the financial difficulties faced by many women and minorities during retirement, we offer the following tips on saving and investing for retirement:

- Pay yourself first! Each month before you pay your bills, place money in a savings account, money market fund, or mutual fund.
- Reduce personal debt! As you can, pay off credit card debt and try to only charge what you can pay off when your next payment is due. Any amount carried over to future payment periods incurs very large interest debt.
- Start your retirement saving and investing as early as possible. It makes a huge difference. Suppose that at age 22 Juanita begins investing $2,000 a year in her Individual Retirement Account (IRA) every year until she reaches the age of 30, but her friend, Xavier, begins investing $2,000 at the age of 33 and continues to do so until the age of 65. Assuming a growth rate of 8% per year, Juanita will have $398,807 by the time she is 65, but Xavier will only have $315,253 even though he invested $66,000 compared to Juanita's $18,000. This is all due to the effects of the compounding of earnings on earnings (Planning Today, Enjoying Tomorrow, 1994).
- If possible, fully fund your Individual Retirement Account each year. As of the writing of this book, an individual can place up to $4,000 each year in an IRA and $2,000 for a married couple.
- If your employer has a pension program, maximize the amount that you invest in it. Many large employers have 401(k) plans or 403(b) plans, in which employee contributions are deducted from paychecks before taxes. These plans have a number of advantages, including the fact that many employers match a part of what an employee contributes.
- Diversify your investments. Many people find that mutual funds, which typically own a number of stocks (shares of ownership of a public corporation), bonds (interest-bearing corporate or government securities), or a combination of stocks, bonds, and other investment instruments, provide them with an appropriate amount of diversification.

Figure 5.3 Investing for retirement. Adapted from *Planning today, enjoying tomorrow* (1994). Kansas City, MO: Twentieth Century Mutual Funds.

have adequate data on gender differences within various ethnic groups, Gibson's (1987) research with a Black elderly cohort shows that men and women are remarkably alike in aspects of work that affect their self-definitions of retirement. As Gibson suggests, applying White gender differences in retirement-related experiences to Blacks will hide important similarities of older Black men and women. Future research will need to identify more precisely the relationships among race, gender, and retirement experiences.

Variations in the Retirement Decision Phase

The decision to retire is influenced by several factors. Certainly, the availability of Social Security and/or a private pension affects decisions about the feasibility of retirement. Blacks, Hispanics, and other minorities, as a result of discrimination, inequitable access to education, and other factors, are less likely to have economic security at any point in their lives, particularly at the age of traditional retirement (Rhodes, 1982). Issues other than economics also affect the retirement decision. Self-reported health measures have been found quite useful in predicting and analyzing various types of retirement patterns. These measures are commonly used in research, because clinical evaluations of health are difficult to obtain. In fact, poor self-reported health has been found to be a significant predictor of retirement status in many studies (Anderson & Burkhauser, 1985;

Key factors to be considered in retirement planning for women include:

- Financial planning. Economic insecurity is the single greatest difficulty faced by female retirees. Retirement preparation programs should encourage participants to calculate probable benefit amounts and likely expenses after retirement. They should also understand the effect of their marital status on Social Security benefits, including whether they should collect benefits based on their own work history, as a dependent spouse, or as a widow. Alert them to the inheritance laws in their state of legal residence to prepare them to plan for the best ways to dispose of their estate, regardless of which spouse dies first.
- Health. Participants should be reminded that (a) usually health insurance coverage provided by employers does not continue after retirement; (b) Medicare covers, on average, less than 50% of healthcare expenses and does not cover many conditions that are highly prevalent among older women; (c) it is beneficial to identify alternate services and resources to reduce healthcare costs; and (d) health promotion and prevention strategies provide long-term benefits.
- Interpersonal relationships. Since a large number of women survive their husbands, retirement planning should include a discussion of issues related to widowhood. Factors contributing to the satisfaction and well-being of retired widows include adequate income and health, ability and support to absorb household functions formerly undertaken by a husband, and ongoing social support. Given the demands on female retirees from their children and parents, it would also be helpful to include a discussion of effective caregiving strategies as a part of retirement planning. Women with narrow support networks should also be encouraged to expand them before retirement in order to reduce the likelihood of isolation.
- Use of time. For many women self-worth is related to work. They are willing to retire if they can find an alternate way to make a meaningful contribution to society. Retirement preparation for this group should include a discussion of opportunities for second careers, educational pursuits, volunteer services, and leisure activities. This would allow them to remain mentally active and would provide a range of opportunities to interact with peers who have similar interests.

Figure 5.4 Factors relevant to retirement planning for women. Adapted from Block, M. (1984). Retirement preparation needs of women. In H. Dennis (Ed.), *Retirement preparation* (pp. 129–140). Lexington, MA: Lexington Books.

George, Fillenbaum, & Palmore, 1984; Hayward, 1986). Research with retired Mexican Americans indicates that poor health has a significant effect on their early retirement decisions (Stanford, Happersett, Morton, Molgaard, & Peddecord, 1991).

Workers in blue-collar occupations retire earlier than those in white-collar positions, with service workers falling in between. Industry patterns indicate that employees in service and trades tend to delay retirement and that those in manufacturing, transportation, and construction retire earlier (Burtless, 1987). These differences have been attributed to factors such as job satisfaction, injury, illness on the job, and job productivity. Research also indicates that blue-collar workers (i.e., those in more physically demanding jobs) are more likely to report health-related work limitations and retire early because of physical limitations (Mitchell, Levine, & Pozzebon, 1988). As long as Mexican Americans and Blacks are concentrated in occupations that require manual, backbreaking, physical work (for example, agriculture, warehouse, assembly line), they will continue to experience low job satisfaction, increased physical impairment, and early retirement.

In contrast to this population, Asian Americans tend to retire later than their White counterparts. For example, in 1990, 62% of Asian Americans between the ages of 55 and 64 were in the labor force, as compared with 57% of Whites (O'Hare & Felt, 1991). However, it should be remembered that the timing of retirement within this population varies a great deal depending on the worker's ethnic background.

The effects of gender on retirement decisions are not clear cut. This is, to some extent, due to limited research on women and retirement (Haug, Belgrave, & Jones, 1992). Given their late entry into the labor force, many women continue working for economic reasons (Hatch, 1992). In addition, economic factors are especially salient for women who are divorced or widowed or who have a discontinuous employment history. Current income and receipt of a private pension other than Social Security play an important role in women's decision to continue working beyond "normal" retirement age (Belgrave, 1989; U.S. Department of Labor, 1989). Unmarried women tend to remain in the labor force longer than do married ones (Logue, 1991), especially if they have experienced delayed entry into the labor force and have few financial resources. For these women, the work setting often functions as an environment that is both confidence affirming and the center of generative behavior. In other words, supporting and nurturing the younger generation is especially meaningful for them. "Career women" of retirement age are often involved in jobs that demand interpersonal caring and nurturance: teaching, nursing, office supervision, and the like. Many of these women are quite articulate about the generative function of their work. While they may desire to relinquish specific duties through retirement, they may find it difficult to adjust to the loss of psychological aspects of work-related relationships. However, this conclusion is not consistently supported by research.

Women who retire early tend to be of upper status, married, and in good health (Atchley, 1982). Timing of retirement at a younger age for women may be related to the tendency for women to marry older men (Hooyman & Kiyak, 1996) who reach retirement age at an earlier time. In addition, spouses tend to retire at about the same time. It is less likely that wives will continue working if their husbands are retired. Similarly, husbands are less likely to continue working if their wives are retired. Retiring at about the same time allows them to spend more leisure time together.

Black women retire later than Whites (Belgrave, 1988). This may be a reflection of their discontinuous work history and a lifetime of inferior earnings. They do not have the financial resources they need to have a comfortable retirement. The same is true for a large proportion of Black men as well.

Variations in Retirement Adjustment Experiences

Retirement, like other critical transitions, often affects one or more of the basic elements of an individual's life, including self-identity, self-worth, relationships with others, financial status, and daily activities. Since American society values youth and productivity, men and women who retire may lose status, income, and personal and social worth (Atchley, 1976; Belsky, 1990). Some people await retirement eagerly, whereas others dread the end of their working years (Hornstein & Wapner, 1984, 1985). In addition to individual differences, there are important race/ethnicity and gender-related differences in how retirement is experienced.

Racial/Ethnic Differences   Retirement is a relatively new experience for Blacks as well as for other minority elders since, until very recently, few lived to be old enough to retire and receive a pension. Even today, few such individuals retire with more than just Social Security, and some Blacks have to live on much less. It has, however, been suggested that Blacks in less economically secure situations may have an advantage over Whites regarding their ability to cope with scarce resources in their later years. The reason is that those who experience less abrupt changes in income would have to make less radical changes in their lifestyles and hence would be more content in their retirement years (Rhodes, 1982). Furthermore, income supports and subsidies have been important in maintaining the economic well-being of the current cohort of elderly Blacks.

In their research with Mexican Americans, Markides and Mindel (1987) reported that their subjects, in comparison with socially advantaged Anglo elders, adjusted more poorly to retirement. Given that many Mexican Americans have dropped out of the labor force after being unsuccessful in their job-seeking efforts, these findings corroborate previous studies documenting greater adjustment problems among involuntary retirees. In addition to these patterns, it is also believed that some retirees do not apply for Social Security benefits because they are unsure of their legal status in the United States, are afraid of dealing with government agencies as a result of past negative experiences, or simply do not know how to apply for benefits (Garcia, 1993). For some, ineligibility for benefits may result from intermittent work patterns, late-in-life migration to the United States, work in noncovered employment, and unscrupulous employers who do not report employee contributions to Social Security.

Gender Effects   Research on the meaningfulness of work shows that paid employment is as central to the lives of women as it is to men. In a study of retired teachers and telephone company retirees, respondents were asked to check from a list of goals the areas in which failure would be most troublesome (Atchley, 1975, 1976). Work was found to be valued by most of the respondents regardless of their gender, a finding that runs counter to the common assumption that work is a less important activity for women than for men. In addition, the retired men in this study were more likely than the retired women to become accustomed to retirement in 3 months or less, a finding that contradicts the thinking that retirement adjustment is easier for women, because they can go back to the homemaker role. Perhaps they have become so used to the routine, rewards, and sociability of paid employment that adjustment to a full-time home-maker role becomes difficult (Szinovacz, 1989).

Other reasons for the gender differences in adjustment to retirement may be that women (a) are more likely than men to have interrupted work histories and (b) tend to be segregated in a limited range of occupations and industries. Many of these occupations are characterized by relatively low wages and a decreased likelihood of pension coverage. Thus, women who have worked in such jobs may face a difficult economic transition at retirement.

In the next learning activity, you will examine some issues faced by gay and lesbian retirees as they cope financially with the death of a companion.

ACTIVE LEARNING EXPERIENCE: CASE OF FINANCES AND THE DEATH OF A COMPANION

Purpose

This activity will engage you in thinking about the transition difficulties and adjustment problems experienced by some gays and lesbians during retirement. Upon completion of the activity, you will be able to:

1   Understand the concerns about income sufficiency faced by some gays and lesbians upon retirement.
2   Identify the limitations of current regulations related to Social Security benefits for same-sex partners.
3   Outline some specific strategies useful for this population in preparing for retirement.

Time Required

40 minutes (20 minutes to complete the activity and 20 minutes to discuss responses in class).

Procedure

1   Prepare written responses to the questions as a homework assignment.
2   Your instructor will ask you to discuss your responses with a classmate during the class session in which the assignment is due.
3   Your instructor will lead a discussion of retirement-related concerns experienced by gays and lesbians.

Margaret and Jenny had lived together for 35 years. Fortunately, their families had been somewhat accepting of their lifestyle. Interestingly, Margaret and Jenny's relationship outlasted the marriages of both of their siblings. Last month, Jenny died as the result of a massive heart attack. Margaret is making every effort to deal with the grief associated with the tremendous loss. After all, Jenny and Margaret had been so very close for so long.

In addition to dealing with all of the emotional issues associated with Jenny's death, Margaret is experiencing financial uncertainty for the first time in her life. Margaret has been retired for 7 years from a sales position at a local department store. She does not receive a pension from the store, which is operated by a local company. Jenny worked in management for a utility company and had been receiving a generous monthly check from her former employer during the 4 years since she retired. Under current policy, Margaret is not eligible to receive benefits from Jenny's pension because she and Jenny were not considered legal spouses. The house in which Margaret resides is in both of their names. Of course, Jenny named Margaret as the primary beneficiary in her will.

Margaret assumed that she would be the first to go, since Jenny was younger and had appeared to be healthier throughout adulthood. How is Margaret going to manage? She is not even eligible for spousal benefits from Social Security.

Discussion Questions

1   As of the writing of this book, same-sex couples are not eligible for spousal benefits from Social Security. Please comment.

2   Many company pension plans allocate benefits to surviving spouses but do not recognize same-sex partners as eligible. Comment.

3   Both Jenny and Margaret were aware of the fact that, under Jenny's company pension and under the Social Security system, they were not considered to be spouses. Specifically, how could they have planned more effectively for their eventual deaths?

4   Margaret doesn't owe anything on her two-story house except for the yearly taxes. She has a relatively new midsized automobile for which she makes monthly payments. Margaret is generally in pretty good health, but she does have arthritis and a lifelong case of asthma. What can she do to manage on a substantially lower income?

LEISURE PURSUITS

Leisure has been defined as personally expressive discretionary activity that varies in intensity of involvement from relaxation and diversion through personal development and creativity up to sensual transcendence (Gordon, Gaitz, & Scott, 1976). There are important differences in how men and women, as well as people in different ethnic/racial groups, view leisure (Henderson, 1990). For example, one study of Black women reported that they view leisure as both freedom from the constraint of needing to work and as a form of self-expression (Allen & Chin-Sang, 1990). What do people do with their time when they retire? Studies reveal that they engage in many more activities with an increase in free time (Pepper, 1976). The most common leisure activities chosen by retirees are reading or writing, television, arts and crafts, games, walking, visiting family and friends, physical activity, gardening, travel or camping, organization and club activities, and outings. In comparison with 20 years ago, older people are choosing activities far more like those of people 20 years younger than themselves (Horn & Meer, 1987). Despite a pattern of age-related constriction in activity, the image of "active old" continues to be more accurate than that of voids of time and commitment. Furthermore, the activity patterns of retirees are characterized by considerable continuity with the activities and relationships that were meaningful to them in their preretirement years.

Cutler and Hendricks (1990) have identified gender differences with regard to leisure activities. Women tend to engage in sociocultural and home-centered activities, whereas men seem to prefer outdoor activities (fishing, hunting), sports (both playing and observing), and travel. Type of residence also makes a difference. People who live in retirement housing participate more frequently in leisure activities than people living in typical neighborhoods (Moss & Lawton, 1982). This may be due to the fact that retirement communities often provide structured activities for their residents, while many age-integrated neighborhoods and communities do not.

Older adults' leisure activities also vary by socioeconomic status. Not surprisingly, those with high incomes tend to be more active in leisure pursuits than low-income elders (Riddick & Stewart, 1994). These differences may be due to the costs of pursuing leisure activities rather than to inherent differences in people with low and high income levels. Older men tend to do more household maintenance and paid work outside the home; older women perform more housework, child care, and volunteer work and participate in more voluntary associations (Danigelis & McIntosh, 1993).

Older adults, especially women and low-income minorities, may face barriers to leisure participation such as health problems and lack of transportation. These barriers are especially important for understanding the participation patterns of these populations. Indeed, health problems are the primary reason given when older adults explain their lack of participation in leisure activities (McGuire, Dottavio, & O'Leary, 1986). A challenge for service providers is to create leisure opportunities that are both meaningful and accessible to this segment of the population. Participation in such activities is especially important for single elders who lack daily companionship (Larson, Zuzanek, & Mannel, 1985).

Senior Centers   Senior centers are one mechanism providing such opportunities to older adults. While these centers offer a large variety of services, they attract only about 15% of older persons (Krout, Cutler, & Coward, 1990). This may be due to reasons such as the following: (a) Individuals may be busy elsewhere; (b) they may be uninterested in the activities offered by the center; (c) they may be in poor health; or (d) they may not have the necessary transportation. As Hooyman and Kiyak (1996) remind us, people are more likely to participate in senior centers that are physically close to their homes. Also, some older people do not participate because they "don't want to be with only older people," and the low proportion of men in many centers discourages other men from taking part. Overall, older adults who are generally less advantaged, but not those who are least advantaged, are more likely to participate in senior center activities (Krout, Cutler, & Coward, 1990). Those who participate tend to do so because they need social interaction and have been invited by friends (Bazargan, Barbre, & Torres-Gil, 1992).

Many communities with ethnic minority neighborhoods have established senior centers and have been successful in attracting diverse elders who would not have participated otherwise. As suggested by Gelfand (1994), there are a number of supplementary programs and services that the centers may find worthwhile to offer. They may offer classes in English, which may be useful for recent immigrants negotiating the American service-delivery system. Facility in English would also make it possible for Latino or Asian elders to shop, use public transportation, or develop friendships with individuals outside their own ethnic group. The centers may also consider offering classes that would provide participants with knowledge of other cultures, including history, rituals, and native crafts.

Volunteering   One of the most popular forms of leisure involvement among retirees is volunteering. The reasons for volunteering vary. Some retirees engage in voluntary activities to meet people, and some do so to keep active or to fulfill a sense of duty; however, most volunteer because it provides them with a sense of satisfaction (AARP, 1988).

Which groups of older people are most likely to volunteer? A study by Caro and Bass (1995) revealed that volunteering is more common among women, those with education beyond high school, those with professional or technical skills, those in good health, and those active in religion. Differences in volunteering have also been observed among minorities. Volunteering as a way to help others through informal social networks is common in minority communities. Black community churches are extensively involved in providing support to their members. This may represent a history of self-reliance and indicate the tradition of incorporating hard work into leisure experiences and service to others (Allen & Chin-Sang, 1990). Providing mutual assistance (such as food and lodging to older adults) is a common practice in American Indian communities. Volunteer activities among Asian/Pacific Islanders tend to be ethnically specific and reinforce the continuation of their value systems. Hispanic communities tend to emphasize self-help, mutual aid, neighborhood assistance, and advocacy for older members (Height, Toya, Kamekawa, & Maldonaldo, 1981).

The next learning activity will engage you in investigating opportunities for older adults to volunteer in your community.

ACTIVE LEARNING EXPERIENCE: OPPORTUNITIES FOR VOLUNTEERING

Purpose

Through this activity, you will learn about possibilities for older adults to volunteer in your community. Upon completion of this activity, you will be able to:

1   List several specific opportunities in your community for elders to volunteer their time and talents.

2   Discuss some of the benefits that arise from the efforts of older volunteers.

Time Required

60 minutes (30 minutes to conduct telephone interviews and 30 minutes to discuss results in a classroom setting or with another individual).

Procedure

1   Call at least two service agencies at which you believe elders may volunteer. Ask to speak with whomever is in charge of volunteers. Introduce yourself and explain the reason why you are calling. Ask each of the people whom you interview the questions listed below.

2   Answer the questions twice, once for each of the two people you interview.

3   Discuss your telephone interviews with your classmates.

Opportunities for Volunteering

Telephone at least two social service organizations (hospitals, nursing homes, homeless kitchens, churches, etc.) and ask whether the organizations use volunteers. Ask to speak to whomever is in charge of volunteers at the organization, introduce yourself, and ask whether he or she would mind answering a few questions to aid you in your studies of older adults. If the person agrees, ask the questions listed subsequently. Complete one answer sheet for each of your two interviews.

1   What kinds of volunteer services do older adults provide to your organization?

2   In what ways does the work of older volunteers benefit your organization and the people it serves?

3   What kind of training does your organization provide to volunteers?

4   In what ways do you think older persons benefit by being volunteers in your organization?

5   What do you believe are some of the qualities of an excellent older volunteer?

6   Could your organization benefit from additional older volunteers?

SUMMARY

The older work force has become increasingly female and ethnically diverse. While middle-aged men have been withdrawing from the labor force, with relatively fewer men working in their early 60s, middle-aged women have been entering the labor force in large numbers. In fact, women 45 to 54 years of age tend to participate in the work force at a higher rate than any other age group. Although older Black women have higher levels of work activity than their White counterparts, their employment is concentrated in a narrow range of lower paying occupations.

Given the income disparities for Black and White workers in the same occupational groups, many elderly Blacks continue their employment as a result of economic necessity. However, many of them are employed in blue-collar and service occupations that require physical strength and good health. Thus, they are more likely to retire early as a result of declining health and physical limitations. In addition to workers and the retirees, there is a third group of Black Americans, those who are labeled as unretired-retired. This group is composed of Blacks, many in early middle age, who exit the labor force mainly for reasons of physical disability.

Older Mexican Americans also have substantially lower incomes than older Anglos. Many of them have dropped out of the labor force after being unsuccessful in their job-seeking efforts. Despite the low income levels in the American Indian population, their rate of participation in the Social Security and Supplemental Security Income programs tends to be rather low. Although Asian/ Pacific Islanders are often referred to as the "model" minority, they also include specific subethnic groups with lower income levels. Older women and ethnic minorities continue to face a variety of obstacles in their search for employment. These barriers include age discrimination, negative stereotypes, job harassment, individual and job obsolescence, and discrimination against individuals with disabilities. We have suggested some steps that may be helpful in removing these barriers.

Women and minorities view retirement in ways different from the dominant culture, experience retirement differently, have access to fewer sources of retirement benefits, and face a variety of adjustment problems during retirement. In addition, retirement experiences within ethnic groups vary widely depending on the retiree's economic, occupational, and professional resources. In fact, what we know about the retirement experiences of these populations has more to do with social class than with ethnicity.

Planning for the transition ahead of time can make a difference in adjustment to retirement. However, the existing retirement preparation programs do not adequately address the needs of a heterogeneous population differing in regard to sex, language, race, and economic status. This chapter has included a discussion of factors to be considered in designing retirement preparation programs for these populations. Many retirees like to explore new opportunities for second careers, educational pursuits, volunteer services, and leisure activities. However, there are important differences in how men and women, as well as people in different ethnic groups, view leisure and what they do with their time when they retire.

Complete the following quiz as a means of assessing your knowledge of the concepts presented in this chapter.

ACTIVE LEARNING EXPERIENCE: DIVERSITY IN WORK AND RETIREMENT QUIZ

The aim of this activity is to gauge your present knowledge of issues related to diversity in work, retirement, and leisure. Upon completion of this activity, you will be able to:

1 Assess your knowledge of diversity in work and retirement.
2 Gain feedback on your knowledge of important issues related to diversity in work and retirement.

Time Required

30 minutes (10 minutes to complete the quiz and 20 minutes to discuss your answers with another person or in a classroom setting).

Procedure

1 Complete the quiz.
2 Your instructor leads an in-class review of the answers to the quiz.

Diversity in Work and Retirement Quiz

Indicate whether each of the following statements is true or false.

	True	False
1 If layoffs were determined solely on the basis of performance, older employees would be hurt.	____	____
2 Workers in blue-collar occupations retire earlier than those in white-collar positions.	____	____
3 The older labor force has become increasingly female.	____	____
4 Retirement for health reasons is much more common among Blacks than among Whites.	____	____
5 Part-time employment is especially common among the oldest female labor force participants.	____	____

		True	False
6	Black men report a higher incidence of disability than their White peers.	___	___
7	Members of minority groups prepare for retirement as efficiently as the White majority.	___	___
8	Single women tend to retire earlier than do married women.	___	___
9	In comparison with Whites, minorities are more dependent on Social Security and other forms of government support in retirement.	___	___
10	Early retirement is more prevalent among Whites than among Mexican Americans.	___	___
11	Relative to men, women are less likely to experience financial difficulties in retirement.	___	___
12	Black men and women have more similar work histories and retirement experiences than do their White counterparts.	___	___
13	Those who choose early retirement have lower income levels than their still-working counterparts.	___	___
14	Spouses tend to retire at about the same time.	___	___
15	Retired Mexican Americans have less positive attitudes toward retirement than do Whites.	___	___

GLOSSARY

401(k) Plan   A type of pension program in which employee contributions are deducted from paychecks prior to taxes. Employers may match a part or all of the amount of an employee's contributions. There are many advantages to this type of plan, including current tax savings and the fact that these investments are tax deferred until money is removed.

403(b) Plan   Similar to a 401(k) plan, this pension plan is offered by colleges and universities, research institutes, hospitals, and an assortment of not-for-profit organizations.

Age Discrimination in Employment Act (ADEA)   Legislation enacted to promote the employment of older persons (age 40 and above) on the basis of their ability rather than age. It prohibits discrimination in "compensation, terms, conditions, or principles of employment because of an individual's age."

Americans with Disabilities Act (ADA)   Prohibits discrimination in employment against individuals with disabilities.

Cohort Effect   Sociocultural influences specific to a group of persons sharing a common set of experiences.

Displaced Homemakers   Primarily middle-aged and older women who have lost, generally through divorce or widowhood, the financial support they had while caring for a family.

Double Jeopardy   The idea that older adults from minority groups experience a dual disadvantage resulting from age as well as minority group membership.

Individual Obsolescence   Refers to a gradual reduction in workers' effectiveness. When they fall behind in understanding how to use new tools, techniques, and technology or fail to recognize how the application of new knowledge can enhance their performance, they become vulnerable to obsolescence.

Job Obsolescence   Jobs become obsolete and gradually disappear when demands for certain products or services decline or new techniques replace older processes that are comparatively less efficient.

Primary Labor Market Jobs   These are generally thought of as regular, full-time occupations.

Secondary Labor Market Jobs   These are generally thought of as part-time jobs, "moonlighting" jobs, second employment, or occasional employment with temporary agencies.

Senior Center   A community facility in which older people come together to fulfill many of their social, physical, and intellectual needs. The Older Americans Act identifies senior centers as preferred focal points for comprehensive, coordinated delivery of services.

SUGGESTED READINGS

Biracree, T., & Biracree, N. (1991). *Over fifty: The resource book for the better half of your life*. New York: Harper Perennial.

This self-help book provides directory information on a host of practical topics, including financial planning. It contains material on investing, banking credit cards, and determining one's net worth. This work is recommended for adults in planning their own retirement and for those who counsel older adults on financially related issues.

Hayes, C. L., & Deren, J. M. (1990). *Pre-retirement planning for women: Program design and research*. New York: Springer.

This book provides a well-documented look at a broad array of issues related to retirement planning, including the financial issues of retirement for women, social and emotional issues facing midlife women, health care, retirement planning for wives of military personnel, predictions of adjustment in retirement, and future research needs. Of special interest to program designers is a discussion of the need for and resistance to information and materials on the social and psychological needs of midlife women in retirement planning programs.

Kitano, H. M. L., & Daniels, R. (1995). *Asian Americans: Emerging minorities* (2nd ed.). Englewood Cliffs, NJ: Prentice Hall.

This book provides an interdisciplinary account of Asian American experiences, including census material, historical data, and social psychological perspectives. Separate chapters on various Asian American groups examine their patterns of adaptation.

Scott, D. (1988). *Wall Street words*. Boston: Houghton Mifflin.

Scott's book is a compendium of relatively simple explanations of more than 3,600 investment terms as well as numerous investing tips from a panel of experts. The definitions of common financial words are written so that readers unfamiliar with finance can grasp their meaning quickly.

Weaver, D. A. (1994). The work and retirement decisions of older women: A literature review. *Social Security Bulletin, 57*(1), 3–24.

This article presents detailed reviews of 13 studies on work and retirement decisions of older women. The author reviews each study individually. The article includes some recent labor force data on older women as well as a discussion of how these data relate to work and retirement decisions. Prospects for future research and some policy issues are also described.

KEY: DIVERSITY IN WORK AND RETIREMENT QUIZ

1 **False**.   Older workers are extremely productive. For example, when Grumman Corporation laid off workers on the basis of detailed performance evaluations, the average age of the work force rose from 37 years to 45 years (Shea, 1991).

2 **True**.   Various studies have shown that workers in blue-collar occupations retire earlier than those in white-collar positions (Burtless, 1987). These differences have been attributed to several factors, including job satisfaction, injury/illness on the job, and job productivity (Mitchell, Levine, & Pozzebon, 1988).

3 **True**.   Early retirement by men and increased labor force participation by women in their mid-50s have rapidly enlarged the female share of the older paid work force. While the labor force participation of men 55 years of age and older has declined dramatically, that of older women as a group has remained stable (Herz, 1988).

4 **True**.   In retirement decisions, although health is important for both Blacks and Whites, it seems to play a more central role for Blacks. Bound, Schuenbann, and Waidmann (1996) found consistent evidence suggesting that Blacks in poor health are more likely to leave the work force than Whites in poor health.

5 **True**.   While part-time work is prevalent among employed women of all ages, this trend increases dramatically with age (Quinn & Kozy, 1996).

6 **True**.   Research by Chirikos and Nestel (1983) and Gibson (1987, 1991b) indicates that economic need has a powerful influence on Blacks' tendency to report work disability. Individuals who expect their wages to be lower in the future are more likely than others

to say they are work disabled. The influence of expected low wages on self-reported disability has been found to be much stronger for Blacks than Whites.

7 **False**. People who are better educated spend more time on retirement planning than those who have less education, and members of minority groups spend less time planning than those in the White majority (Ferraro, 1990). Torres-Gil (1984) has identified a number of factors contributing to this underrepresentation, from culture and language to job level and income, and has suggested strategies for reaching these populations.

8 **False**. Single women tend to retire later than married women because they have fewer family considerations and must depend on their own pension incomes for retirement. Since their pensions are often inadequate owing to low-paying jobs, they are more likely than their married counterparts to continue working past the age of 65 (Atchley, 1991).

9 **True**. In comparison with those of Whites, the total retirement income packages of minorities contain larger proportions of Social Security and Supplemental Security Income. Among minorities, Blacks and Hispanics are less likely to be employed in positions with pension benefits. In addition, they have less stable occupational histories, many of them working more sporadically than Whites (Markides & Mindel, 1987; Rhodes, 1982).

10 **False**. Stanford, Happersett, Morton, Molgaard, and Peddecord (1991) found that Mexican Americans were more than twice as likely as Whites to have reported retirement status, as well as to have retired at an earlier age. These investigators also found that early retired Whites tend to be in white-collar positions, as compared with Blacks and Mexican Americans, the majority of whom are blue-collar and service workers.

11 **True**. Despite their growing labor force participation rates and employment choices and opportunities, women's earnings over the life course are significantly lower than those for men. These factors lead to retirement benefits that are substantially inferior to those for men (Rix, 1990).

12 **True**. Research by Gibson (1987) reveals that older Black men and women have more similar work histories and retirement experiences than do their White counterparts.

13 **True**. Several studies have noted that people who choose early retirement have lower income levels than those of their still-working counterparts (Belgrave, Haug, & Gomez-Bellenge, 1987; Holtzman, Berman, & Ham, 1980).

14 **True**. Spouses tend to retire at about the same time (Gustman & Steinmeier, 1994). This allows the couple to make specific plans to spend more leisure time together.

15 **True**. Dieppa (1978) found that retired Mexican Americans have less positive attitudes toward retirement than do Whites. Since many of them are not in a position to choose retirement, continued work being essential for their survival, their attitudes may reflect a negative association with retirement.

Chapter 6

Religion and Spirituality

OVERVIEW

Defining Spirituality and Religion
- What is the concept of spirituality, and how does it differ from religion?
- What procedures are used to assess religiosity?
- What dimensions of religiosity are included in the assessment process?
- What approaches can be used to measure spirituality?
- In what ways can we use the findings from such assessments?
- Why is it important to include religion and spirituality in the study of diversity and aging?

Religious Participation Among African American Elders
- Why is there such a high prevalence of religious activity among older Blacks?
- What programs and services do Black churches make available to Blacks?
- What activities are generally included in examining nonorganizational religious involvement among older adults?
- What are the key findings regarding the participation of older Blacks in nonorganizational religious activities?
- What are the implications of a high prevalence of religiosity for the well-being of African American elders?

The Role of Religion Among Hispanic Elders
- What religious traditions have influenced the current practices of the Hispanic population?
- What religious activities are popular among Hispanic elders?
- What role is played by religion in their lives?
- What is the concept of *fe*, and what purposes does it serve for older Hispanics?

Religious Practices Among American Indians

- What religious practices are followed by American Indians?
- What are some important religious beliefs of this population?
- How do American Indians view older adults?
- What role is played by elders in American Indian communities?
- How is this role different from that in the dominant culture?

Religious Traditions Among Asian/Pacific Islanders

- What are the distinctive characteristics of Hinduism?
- How does Hinduism view the process of aging?
- How do Hindu immigrants view other religions?
- What are the implications of this perspective for their everyday life in the United States?
- What are the distinctive characteristics of Buddhism?
- Which of these characteristics have special relevance for the study of aging? Why?
- What are the characteristic features of the Islamic vision of human life?
- What are the common themes and differences in Hinduism, Buddhism, and Islam?
- How do each of these religions view the aging process?

Summary

Diversity in Religion, Spirituality, and Aging Quiz

Glossary

Suggested Readings

Key: Diversity in Religion, Spirituality, and Aging Quiz

In this chapter, we examine religion and spirituality among Black Americans, Hispanics, and American Indians. In addition, we provide an introduction to Hinduism, Buddhism, and Islam, the three major religions represented among the older population of Asian Americans. In each case, we outline the distinctive characteristics of the religion, its views on aging and family life, and implications for its followers in the United States.

Consider the following vignettes as an introduction to our discussion of spirituality and aging.

Vignette 1: Lester C. Dale, a 67-year-old African American accountant, has been active in his Baptist church for more than 40 years. He has been a deacon, taught Sunday school, served as treasurer, and provided a variety of services to fellow members. The church has always been an important part of his life; after his recent retirement, however, he has begun to spend even more time there. He helps members who need assistance in filing their income tax, in preparing paperwork for Social Security benefits, and in selecting adequate health insurance for their older relatives. For the last 2 months, he has also been providing transportation to Chuck Johnson, a senior member of his church who needs to see his physician at a local clinic almost every week. As a result of this experience, Lester is now developing a pool of volunteers to make transportation available for other elders who are unable to drive.

When asked why he continues to do so many things at the church, he says that he is performing God's work. He feels that God has truly blessed him. His energy to do all that he does comes from his faith in God, and the work that he does helps him in developing new relationships. Mr. Dale often says that the role of the church is not only to offer Sunday services but to provide social support to Black individuals and their families.

Vignette 2: Rama Sharma, 63, is a physician at University Hospital in Minneapolis. Born and raised in India, he came to the United States after obtaining his medical degree in New Delhi. He completed his residency in pediatrics at University Hospital and decided to stay in America to engage in research and open a medical practice. For the past 10 years, he and his wife have taken leadership roles in the Hindu temple that they helped to establish in an old church building. The temple does not have a priest. Instead, Dr. Sharma and other senior members of the community take turns in leading a discussion on teachings of Bhagvad Gita and Ramayana. Every Sunday, one or two families bring vegetarian food that is served after the worship service. During the summer months, Dr. Sharma and his colleagues organize a summer camp for Hindu children from Minneapolis and neighboring communities with the goal of enhancing their awareness of culture and religion. This allows the children to interact with their counterparts from other communities, to learn about their cultural heritage, and to develop relationships with older adults who bring wisdom and insights from their experiences. In addition, the children learn to respect all religions when they attend festivities associated with birthdays of leaders representing a full range of religions. This makes them aware that all religions aim toward the same goals and differ only in rituals and other day-to-day practices.

Discussion Questions

1 Why does Lester Dale perform so many different tasks at his church?

2 What services are provided by the Black church for individuals and families in the community?

3 Discuss the goals of the summer camp organized by the Hindu temple described in the second vignette.

4 How do the operations of the Hindu temple differ from what you have experienced in your church, synagogue, or other place of worship?

DEFINING SPIRITUALITY AND RELIGION

It is important to distinguish spirituality from religion. Although these two terms are related, they are not synonymous. Religion is generally defined as a formal system of belief in God or another supernatural being and refers to efforts aimed at relating the human to the divine. Other approaches to defining religion emphasize its usefulness in providing meaning in the face of the unknown and its stabilizing effects on social groups. Thus, while the first definition depicts religiosity as an end in itself, the second approach portrays religion as a means to some end.

The term *spirituality* pertains to (a) one's inner resources, especially one's ultimate concern; (b) the basic values around which all other values are focused; (c) the central philosophy of life—religious, nonreligious, or antireligious—that guides day-to-day living; and (d) the supernatural and nonmaterial dimensions of human nature. This generic nonreligious spirit, then, is the energy that enables one to reach out and embrace one's basic life-enhancing value, ethic, and ultimate concern, however those concepts are defined. The term *spirituality* flows from this definition and refers to a particular spiritual "style," the way the person seeks, finds, creates, uses, and expands personal meaning in the context of the entire universe (Thibault, Ellor, & Netting, 1991). In other words, spirituality is the human drive for meaning and purpose. This implies that spiritual activities and perspectives are interwoven with all other aspects of life and, hence, are found in a wide range of contexts, not simply those related to institutional religion (Moberg, 1971).

While spirituality cannot be equated with religion, religion provides many people with narratives, symbols, rituals, and beliefs that not only guide the quest for meaning, but illuminate a destination of ultimate meaning (Pargament, 1992). At the present time, we do not have a strong knowledge base regarding the differential outcomes that result from taking one spiritual pathway over another. However, developing a better understanding of various options and their effectiveness has important implications for various segments of the older population.

Assessment

Since religion includes participation in services at one's church, temple, or synagogue and also includes involvement in nonorganizational activities (such as reading religious literature, watching or listening to religious programs, and praying), research on religion and aging should use measures that include both types of activities. One example of such assessment procedures is the Springfield Religiosity Schedule (SRS). Developed by Koenig, Smiley, and Gonzales (1988), the SRS acknowledges the complexity of religion by including measures of the four dimensions of religiosity: belief, ritual (both organizational and nonorganizational activities), experience, and religious knowledge.

Because researchers have only recently begun to consider dimensions of spirituality apart from religious beliefs and behaviors, few assessment tools are currently available. Ellor and Bracki (1995) designed a structured interview process to assess the spiritual needs of older persons. This approach is particularly useful for clergy, psychologists, social workers, nurses, and others working with older adults and their caregivers. A number of other investigators have developed measures of spiritual well-being (see, for example, Moberg, 1984) that can be used in conducting research, providing psychological and pastoral counseling, and planning and evaluating new programs and services.

While the idea of measuring the abstract concept of spirituality may seem difficult, creative assessment approaches such as in-depth interviews with older persons provide valuable insights into the ways in which a sense of spirituality promotes creativity, concern for others, and hopefulness amid life in a nursing home or any other setting. In fact, some health promotion screening measures include questions on individuals' spiritual or philosophic values, life goal setting, and approaches to answering questions such as "What is the meaning of my life?" and "How can I increase the quality of my life?" This approach implies that health care providers have received adequate training to include such questions on spiritual well-being in order to respond to their clients' needs (McSherry, 1983).

Although religion is an enduring characteristic of human behavior, issues of religion and spirituality have not been widely addressed in gerontology. A review of research in major journals indicates that religious variables are seldom included in quantitative studies with older adults. This situation is perplexing, because national surveys document that older adults attach a high value to their religious beliefs and behaviors. This is particularly true of ethnic and minority elders, who consistently show a high degree of religious involvement (Jackson, Antonucci, & Gibson, 1990; Levin, Taylor, & Chatters, 1994). Although religious faith and religious institutions have played crucial roles in their lives, it does not mean that the various subgroups of minority elders have identical beliefs and values and engage in the same religious activities. A discussion of these topics is the focus of our attention in the rest of the chapter.

Through the following learning experience, you will analyze your religious and philosophical beliefs regarding aging and the meaning of life.

ACTIVE LEARNING EXPERIENCE: PERSONAL BELIEFS ABOUT AGING AND THE MEANING OF LIFE

Purpose

This activity will engage you in an analysis of your beliefs concerning aging and the meaning of life. Upon completion of this activity, you will be able to:

1 Describe personal beliefs about aging and the meaning of life.
2 Appreciate the diversity of personal belief systems.

Time Required

40 minutes (20 minutes to answer the questions and 20 minutes to discuss responses in class or with another individual).

Procedure

1 Complete the answer sheet as a homework assignment.
2 Discuss responses in class or with another person.

Personal Beliefs About Aging and the Meaning of Life

Prepare written responses to the following questions.
1 When you were a child, what religion(s) did your parent(s) or guardian(s) consider themselves to be?
2 Were you raised in a particular religion? If yes, what was the religion?
3 With what religion or philosophy of life (e.g., humanism) do you identify?
4 In what ways does your religion or philosophy of life help you in coping with disappointments, sadness, and loss?
5 What does your religion or philosophy of life have to say about the meaning of life?
6 How does your religion or philosophy view aging and the value of elders?

RELIGIOUS PARTICIPATION AMONG AFRICAN AMERICANS

Religion and churches occupy an important position in the lives of Black Americans in general and older Blacks in particular. Black churches are a unique social entity. They were developed by an oppressed group that was refused access to the institutional life of the broader American society (Morris, 1984). Black churches have assumed many social functions and have been involved in a variety of health and social welfare, educational, political, and community activities, as well as in addressing spiritual needs (Cone, 1985).

Given the prominent standing of the church in the Black community, it is not surprising to find that religious commitment is particularly strong among older Blacks. More specifically, the literature consistently shows that elderly Blacks are more likely than their White counterparts to attend religious services, read the Bible, and pray on a regular basis (e.g., Gallup Report, 1984). Moreover, research by Chatters and Taylor (1989) suggests that, even within the Black community, older Blacks tend to go to church services more frequently and have a higher degree of subjective religious involvement than do Blacks in younger age groups. Within the Black community, religion is especially important to women. Black women are more active in church groups and attend services more frequently than Black men and White men and women (Taylor, 1993). However, the gender differences diminish in the Black population over the age of 70, indicating that religion becomes more important for Black men as well.

Church Members as a Source of Informal Support

Historical and present-day evidence suggests that Black churches are extensively involved in providing support to their members, and frequency of church attendance is a critical indicator of both the frequency of receiving assistance and the amount of aid provided (Taylor & Chatters, 1986a, 1986b). In addition, for elderly persons with adult children, advanced age is associated with more frequent assistance from church members. But among childless elders, advanced age is associated with dramatic decreases in the frequency of support from church members. These results suggest that adult children may facilitate linkages to church support networks on behalf of their elderly parents. What type of support is provided by church members? Taylor and Chatters (1986a, 1986b) report that Black elders receive advice and encouragement, help during sickness, and prayer from church members. While families provide total support to their older relatives, for certain groups of elderly Blacks, friends and church members may be of even greater importance than has been previously thought (Taylor, 1993).

Church-Based Programs

In addition to promoting contact and social integration among members, churches provide concrete help in the form of day centers for older adults (Negstad & Arnholt, 1986) and medical screening for various diseases (Eng, Hatch, & Callan, 1985; Tobin, Ellor, & Anderson-Ray, 1986). Furthermore, they offer outreach programs such as (a) home-care services that assist the elderly with household cleaning and related tasks, (b) fellowship activities that help maintain the seniors' involvement in the community, (c) meals-on-wheels that provide home delivery of meals, (d) senior citizen housing, and (e) multiservice programs that refer older adults to a variety of formal service agencies (Caldwell, Chatters, Billingsley, & Taylor, 1995).

Church-based programs, such as home care and meals-on-wheels, reduce the likelihood of premature placement of older adults in nursing homes or other long-term care facilities by helping them live independently. These programs also provide needed assistance to family caregivers by addressing the burden and stress of their caregiving responsibilities. It is important to note that many churches collaborate with social agencies in operating a variety of programs and services for older adults. Because of their proximity to both the family and the formal system of service delivery, these churches are in an excellent position to provide direct services and to refer those in need to appropriate professionals.

Nonorganizational Forms of Religious Involvement

Up to this point, our discussion has focused mainly on formal religious participation such as church attendance and church membership. But what are the private, nonorganizational forms of religious involvement among this population? This is the focus of our discussion in the present section.

What indicators would be of use in examining nonorganizational religious involvement among older people? Taylor and Chatters (1991) used the following indicators in a study with elderly Black adults: (a) reading religious materials, (b) watching or listening to religious programs, (c) engaging in prayers, and (d) requesting prayer. Close to half of the respondents reported reading religious books and materials nearly every day, and another 24% read religious books at least weekly. Women reported reading religious materials more frequently than men. One third of the respondents indicated that they watched or listened to broadcasts of religious programs nearly every day, and about half reported doing so at least once a week. The respondents reported that they engage in prayer on a frequent basis, 9 of every 10 indicating that they prayed nearly every day. Finally, 18% of the respondents reported that they ask someone to pray for them nearly every day and about one fourth at least once a week. In short, a majority of elderly Black respondents engaged in daily prayer, read religious materials and watched or listened to religious programs on a weekly basis, and requested prayer on their behalf several times a month. Gender is the strongest and most consistent predictor of participation in nonorganizational religious activities. Elderly Black women read religious materials, pray, and ask others to pray for them on a more frequent basis than do their male counterparts. These findings are similar to those we presented earlier with regard to participation in formal religious activities.

In addition to gender differences, pervasive age differences are observed in terms of private prayer among older Black adults (Taylor & Chatters, 1991). It appears that this behavior is distinct from formal participation and other nonorganizational practices. Similar findings reported by other investigators in regard to strength of religious beliefs, private devotional practices, and self-perceptions of being religious suggest that age bears a special relationship to these most personal and intrinsic dimensions of religiosity.

Stress, Religiosity, and Psychological Well-Being

Religion performs an important function for members of this population. Some indications of this function are seen in the literature on stress and coping. Research with older adults from different ethnic/racial groups suggests that they turn to religion in an effort to cope with the stressful experiences confronting them. In addition, there is some evidence that older people who turn to religion during stressful times are less likely to experience psychological distress than those who are not involved in religious activities (see, for example, Idler, 1987; Koenig, Smiley, & Gonzales, 1988).

The central role of the church in the Black community, coupled with high levels of religious commitment among older Blacks, indicates that religiosity provides an important coping resource for members of this minority group. While church members provide assistance to each other, religious commitment affects psychological well-being independently of the effects of social support (Krause, 1992). It is important to note that older Blacks do not increase their levels of religious involvement when stressors arise (i.e., religion is not stress responsive). Instead, the effects of ongoing and stable religious commitments appear to offset the negative impact of bereavement on depressive symptoms. In other words, the negative effects of stress are offset by the positive effects of religiosity or feelings of self-worth.

Prayer serves as a coping mechanism for both older Blacks and older Whites (Husaini, Moore, & Cain, 1991; Koenig, George, & Siegler, 1988). The use of prayer as a help-seeking behavior is stronger among older Black and White women than it is among men. Prayer may also partly account for the lower rate of suicide for Black as compared with White elders (Gibson, 1986a). In addition, church attendance has been found to be related to a reduced risk of mortality among older African Americans (Bryant & Rakowski, 1992). This effect may be indicative of the role of the church as a source for both informal and formal support to its members.

Involvement of older adults in religious activities also contributes to their life satisfaction. Research indicates that older Blacks report a higher degree of life satisfaction than their White counterparts. This difference is explained by their more extensive contact with church friends, even though older Whites have a large number of friends. The church may also serve as a "pseudo-family," particularly for Black elders in the South whose children haved moved to the North (Ortega, Crutchfield, & Rushing, 1983).

In summary, an emerging profile of religiosity among older Black adults emphasizes a high degree of organized religious participation such as church attendance and church membership (Taylor, 1986), along with extensive involvement in private religious activities. This ongoing participation in both organized and nonorganizational religious activities provides an important coping resource, contributes to life satisfaction, and promotes feelings of self-worth.

The following activity addresses the significant role that church plays in the lives of three elderly women.

ACTIVE LEARNING EXPERIENCE: THE CASE OF THE MARSHALL SISTERS AND THEIR CHURCH

Purpose

This activity presents case material on the role of church in the lives of three elderly sisters. Upon completion of this activity, you will be able to:

1 Understand the important role religious institutions play in the lives of some African American elders.
2 Describe spiritual, social, and psychological needs met by an elder's affiliation with an organized religion.

Time Required

30 minutes (15 minutes to read the case and answer the questions and 15 minutes to discuss the case in class or with another person).

Procedure

1 If the activity is part of a class, the instructor divides students into groups of four or five.
2 In groups, students discuss the case and answer the questions that follow it.
3 The instructor leads a discussion of group responses.
4 If the students are completing the activity for self-development, they prepare written responses to the questions and discuss their responses with another person.

The Case of the Marshall Sisters and Their Church

Read the following case and prepare answers to the accompanying questions.

The Marshall sisters view the Baptist church as the center of their lives. Ella, 74; Wanda, 70; and Dorothy, 67, attend services almost every Sunday morning, as well as Sunday and Wednesday evenings. In addition, Dorothy teaches a scripture class for adult Sunday School, and the Marshall home is the site of another weekly Bible study class. The church has been of great importance to them since their childhood as the daughters of sharecroppers in Alabama. Ella is a widow, Wanda never married, and Dorothy is divorced. Ella has three children, one of whom lives just across town. Dorothy has two children, who both live in their birthplace some hundred miles away. Between them, Ella and Dorothy have nine grandchildren and seven great-grandchildren. Some of the children and their families are very active in their churches, while the others attend church only a few times a year, including Easter.

The Marshall sisters consider the members of their congregation to be family as well. When church members are sick, the sisters visit them in the hospital or take them food if they are at home, and when members die, the sisters grieve with the family members of the deceased. Even though they live on Dorothy's meager pension and Social Security, the Marshall sisters have been known to quietly donate money to other church members they believe to be in need. All of their close friends either belong to the church or are members of their family.

Discussion Questions

1 By the sisters being so active in their church, what personal psychological needs are met?
2 The church occupies a central place in the sisters' social life. Explain.
3 The sisters not only believe in the religious doctrine of Christianity, but they try to live their religion as well. Explain.

4 What do religious institutions, such as a Baptist church, have to offer to older adults?

RELIGION AND HISPANIC ELDERS

Religion, as practiced by older persons of Mexican heritage, can be seen as a blending of different rituals and doctrines including both Aztec and European influences. For the Aztecs, religion was historically an all-encompassing, daily activity. The gods were to be prayed to, and sometimes to die for; to be sacrificed for a god was the greatest honor one could receive. Even more important than sacrifice were the land, sun, moon, and water. All things in nature were respected. A typical day began with prayer to the sun, and the prayers continued throughout the day (Hall, 1988; Jennings, 1980). Since many older persons of Mexican heritage came to the United States from an agrarian lifestyle, they have continued to view the land as something to respect and value.

With the coming of the Europeans, indigenous people of Mexico were forced to accept Catholicism. However, they managed to save some of their traditional religions through covert practices, and they accepted some aspects of this new religion more readily than others. Those aspects that were accepted had some parallels in the indigenous religion. It is this version of Catholicism that is practiced today by the majority of older persons of Mexican heritage.

Although Catholicism is still important to the older members of this population, there is a trend toward conversion to other religions (Korte & Villa, 1988). An underlying reason for this trend may be that Catholicism is centered around in-church activities and formal participation outside the home. For older adults, a home visit may be the motivating factor for adopting other religions. What needs to be emphasized is not the importance of belonging to any particular religious group but the fact that religion, in and of itself, remains an important aspect of these individuals' lives (Villa & Jaime, 1993).

As noted earlier, in the everyday life of older Mexicans, both Aztec and European influences are still in place today, and out of this mixture of Indian and European ideologies has evolved the unique concept of *fe*, which can be completely communicated only through the Spanish language. The notion of *fe* incorporates varying degrees of faith, spirituality, hope, cultural values, and beliefs. *Fe* does not necessarily imply that people identify with a specific religious group. Rather, they identify with a cultural value or ideology. We return later to the concept of *fe* as a coping strategy.

Religion, Faith, and Spirituality

Before proceeding further, it is important to distinguish religion from *fe*. Religion makes one feel a part of a cosmic plan in which everyone has a role to play as a child of God. Religious beliefs help make life more bearable by explaining the unexplainable. Everyday difficulties that older adults must endure are, to some extent, buffered by religion (Gallego, 1988). In this section, we discuss the participation of older Hispanics in both organizational and nonorganizational religious activities.

Organized Activities

As noted earlier for older Black adults, attending religious services appears to be a weekly activity among a high percentage of older Hispanics. Three fourths of the older persons surveyed by Maldonaldo (1995) in San Antonio reported attending a religious activity once a week. The participation rate for women was higher than that for men. In addition, older Hispanics perceive themselves as more active in religious activities and would like to be even more active. One important benefit of participation in organized activities is that it allows elders to remain integrated in a value system, family, neighborhood, religious community, and the larger society. While older women would like to be more active in organized activities, many of them are not able to continue such participation. This may be due to poor health, lack of transportation, and disabilities (Markides, Levin, & Ray, 1987).

Nonorganized Religious Practices

As is true for older Blacks, private prayer devotion is the most commonly used religious practice among older Hispanics. The second most commonly used practice among this population is that of meditation. A majority of both the men and the women in the San Antonio survey (Maldonado, 1995) reported that they meditate daily, although it is not clear how they define meditation. It is noteworthy that a majority of older Hispanics view themselves as religious, with women reporting higher levels of self-perceived religiosity (Maldonado, 1995; Markides & Martin, 1983).

Faith

Faith represents a way of being, living, and imagining and is considered a prerequisite for spiritual growth. While some people believe that faith is a gift from a supreme being, others think that it can be developed in response to life events (Carson, 1989). The concept of *fe* incorporates varying degrees of faith, spirituality, hope, cultural values, and beliefs. *Fe* can be conceptualized as a continuum of behaviors and beliefs that begin with conception and include the baptismal ceremony, the birthday, and the last rites, and continue in the remembrance of the departed loved one throughout the year and especially on the death anniversary (Villa & Jaime, 1993). *Fe* includes the sharing of food and drink to celebrate a birth as well as a death. It is used in involving divine will in curing the sick.

The concept of *fe* embodies a way of life as well as the culture in which it is lived; out of this life experience has developed a unique world view that is both Indian and Spanish (Villa & Jaime, 1993). The symbolic embellishment of these two influences is found in *la fe de la gente*: the faith of the people. It should be noted that *fe* is defined by each person in a way that makes the most sense to that individual. In order to understand how a person copes with the negative effects of social forces, one must understand his or her unique *fe*. In other words, *fe* serves as a coping mechanism and helps people maintain a positive attitude when dealing with the harsh realities of life. It is a method of coping with poor health, poverty, and death. As Villa and Jaime (1993) remind us, it is essential that service providers working with this population be sensitive to the cultural values placed on religiosity and *fe*. They need to view *fe* as a valid coping mechanism important not only to the client but to themselves as well. In other words, they should view *fe* as their clients see and experience it.

RELIGIOUS PRACTICES AMONG AMERICAN INDIANS

There are a great variety of religious practices among the American Indians. According to the 1990 census, only about 25% of the members of this group identify themselves as Christians. This means that a large majority have maintained their native religions. Also, many have merged Christian and Native American religious beliefs. They consider it essential that Indian Christianity be rooted in their culture and practices (see Weaver, 1993, for a discussion of forging a relevant spiritual identity among Indian Christians).

The American Indian population has traditionally been highly religious and spiritual. For example, the Lakota peoples, one of the hundreds of distinct groups in North America, have a short prayer that captures the general cultural and spiritual sentiment of all American Indians. "Mitakuye ouyasin," they pray for all relatives. In this prayer, relatives are understood to include not just tribal members but all living, moving things. All of these are part of an incomprehensible totality that always was and always will be. Onandoza Chief Oren Lyons expresses this eloquently and simply by stating that all things are equal because all things are part of the whole (Arden & Wall, 1990). It is for this reason, then, that not even an animal or a tree is harmed without appropriate spiritual reciprocity. To act without such responsibility is to introduce imbalance and disharmony into the world. In other words, maintaining harmony among humans, nature, and the supernatural represents an important religious belief for this population.

The elderly have had a special place in the cultures and religions of the American Indian population. They are honored and respected and serve as elders of the tribe and the clan. In Indian communities, older adults are the "wisdomkeepers," the repositories of the sacred ways and natural world philosophies that extend indefinitely back in time (Arden & Wall, 1990). Older Indians serve the larger world not from mystic sentimentalism but from a felt experience, and they provide spiritual direction to the members of their community. The wisdom of thousands of years flows through their lips. Many Indians view the world as one family connected through bonds of love. Their deepened sense of time, along with their sense of responsibility, heightens the intimate care they extend to all creation. Thus, they serve as sacred ecologists who protect all of their "relatives," including human, animal, and plant life. Through the next active learning experience, you will develop a deeper understanding of a religion different from your own as well as how that religious system operates in the life of a particular older adult.

ACTIVE LEARNING EXPERIENCE: INTERVIEW WITH AN ELDER FROM A DIFFERENT RELIGIOUS TRADITION

Purpose

The goal of this activity is to provide an opportunity for you to develop an appreciation and a better understanding of a religion different from your own and of how the system functions in the life of a diverse elder. Upon completion of this activity, you will be able to:

1   Describe several aspects of a religion that differs from yours.
2   Understand the role of a particular religion in the life of a diverse elder.
3   Discuss differences between your own religion and another one.

Time Required

90 minutes (40 minutes to conduct the interview, 20 minutes to write up the results, and 30 minutes to discuss the results in class or with another individual).

Procedure

1   Interview an older adult from a religious or other spiritual tradition that differs from yours.
2   The structure of the interview is to follow the questions listed on the next page.
3   After completing the interview, prepare written responses to the questions.
4.   Discuss your responses in class or with another individual.

Note: Instructors should be sensitive to students' feelings and experiences with religious traditions. Some students may have difficulties with this activity. Instructors should provide a classroom climate in which students are comfortable in sharing experiences or free not to share.

Interview With an Elder From a
Different Religious Tradition

Use the following questions to guide your interview. Following the interview, prepare written responses to each of the interview questions.

1 What is your religion?
2 In what ways does your religion influence the way in which you live?
3 What does your religion have to say about the role of the family and respect for elders?
4 Does your religion or philosophy of life include a belief in an afterlife (life after death), heaven, or hell?
5 Do you attend religious services? If yes, how often do you attend?
6 Do you consider yourself to be more or less religious than you were when you were growing up? Explain.

Following the interview, write down responses to the questions just listed as well as those listed subsequently.

1 In what ways are the elder's spiritual/religious beliefs and practices similar to your own?
2 In what ways do the elder's religious beliefs and practices differ from yours?
3 How does the elder's religion affect his or her adjustment in the dominant society?
4 Why is it essential for service providers to have some knowledge regarding the religious beliefs and practices of the elders they serve?

RELIGIOUS TRADITIONS OF
ASIAN/PACIFIC ISLANDERS

As noted in earlier chapters, Asian/Pacific Islanders (APIs) represent an example of combining diverse groups under one label. Since this group is composed of 26 census-defined subethnic groups, there is a tremendous diversity in their religious beliefs and practices. Space limitations do not allow us to cover all of them. Our focus is limited to examining Hindu, Buddhist, and Islamic conceptions of aging.

Hinduism

As of 1990, there were more than 800,000 persons in the United States of Asian Indian birth or ancestry (Kitano & Daniels, 1995). Since the overwhelming majority of people in India are Hindus, it is reasonable to estimate that more than 85% of Asian Indians in the United States are Hindus. Research also indicates that the Asian Indian community is putting down its roots in the United

States. In Cincinnati, Ohio, for example, some 400 Indian families recently raised $700,000 to build a Hindu temple that would serve as a community center as well as a place for religious observances (Kitano & Daniels, 1995). While many observers have argued that Asian Indians in the United States have been reluctant to make the crucial break with their past and become completely assimilated, evidence regarding their acculturation is also accumulating. The reader may see some similarity in this regard with what we presented in our discussion of the religious beliefs and practices of Mexican Americans and American Indians. In spite of their ongoing assimilation into schools, the workplace, and social groupings, members of these populations continue to maintain their ethnic identity. Religion and religious observances are helpful in retaining their ethnic ways. It is in this context that we now proceed to examine distinctive features of Hinduism and their relevance to the study of aging.

Distinctive Characteristics   As a religion, Hinduism is neither hierarchical nor dogmatic. It has not been made but has been grown. It deals in images and metaphors. Perhaps the idea that has had the widest and most penetrating influence on Indian thought is the conception of the universe, which is known as *Samsâra*, the world of change and transmigration. As a child grows into youth and adulthood, so the soul passes from life to life in continuity if not identity. This idea presents a sense of transitoriness, but continuity of everything. Nothing is eternal or permanent, not even the gods, for they must die, and not even death, for it must turn into new life.

The character of the successive appearance of the soul is determined by the law of Karma (simply meaning deeds), which forms the basis of views about the universe. According to this law, all deeds bring upon the doer an accurately proportionate consequence either in this existence or, more often, in a future birth. At the end of a person's life, his or her character or personality is practically the sum of his or her acts. When extraneous circumstances disappear, the soul is left with nothing but the acts and the character formed, and it is these acts and this character that determine the next stage.

Other characteristics of Hinduism include (a) a belief in the efficacy of self-mortification as a means of obtaining superhuman powers or final salvation, (b) an even more deeply rooted conviction that salvation can be obtained by knowledge, and (c) the doctrine that faith or devotion to a particular deity is the best way to salvation. Hinduism emphasizes that various religions are alternate paths to the same goal. To claim salvation as the monopoly of any one religion is like claiming that God can be found in this room but not in the next, in this attire but not in another. In other words, according to Hinduism, various religions are simply different languages through which God speaks to the human heart. Truth is one; sages call it by different names. It is this belief in the unity of great religions that has important implications for how Asian Indian Hindus in the United States interact with followers of other religions.

Images of Aging   Hinduism presents a variety of images to depict the march of life through time and space. On one hand, these images assert that aging is pain and suffering and that true liberation can be achieved only when the process of aging is stopped. On the other hand, Hinduism insists that self-liberation is possible only in the embodied state, which is under the sway of the aging process. Thus, aging is a necessary vehicle or energy that unfolds the path of liberation before the embodied self. The suffering and losses related to aging are the key to the liberation experience. The pain of aging, from this perspective, is a useful shock mechanism to wake people from the mirage of their worldly existence (Tilak, 1989). But in order for this to happen, one must develop a proper awareness of the body, its life span, and meaning. As indicated in the preceding section, knowledge is the key ingredient for alleviating the pain and suffering of aging. From this standpoint, the wise and liberated individual is one who has lived in harmony with life's true meaning and purpose.

While the concepts of disengagement and retreat are included in Hinduism, disengagement from active household duties is undertaken to re-engage in the tasks of self-realization. According to this perspective, old age is the time for developing a philosophy and then adapting that philosophy into a way of life, a time for transcending the senses to find, and dwell with, the reality that underlies the natural world. This approach is useful in coping with the stressors of old age, in maintaining high morale and life satisfaction, and in avoiding boredom (Tilak, 1989).

Implications   Given the acceptance of other religions and receptivity to other beliefs and practices, it becomes easier for the members of the Hindu population to accept the cultural traditions of their host country while maintaining some core beliefs of their own heritage. Although in recent years, some Hindu temples have been constructed (or established in old church buildings) in a number of metropolitan areas, such opportunities for religious and cultural gatherings are generally not available to a large number of Asian Americans who live in smaller communities. However, this does not deter them from following key religious traditions. What they generally do tends to be individualized, private, philosophical, and contemplative. Many of them study their religious books, practice meditation, do prayers at their in-home shrine, and follow their religious philosophy in day-to-day life.

Buddhism

The term *Buddha* literally means "enlightened" or "mentally awakened." According to Buddhism, one becomes a great or a liberated person when one's mind (by the power that is within it) becomes enlightened enough to look at life realistically. Buddhism began with a man who shook off the daze, the doze, the dreamlike vagaries of ordinary awareness. It began with a man who woke up.

This man was Siddhartha Gautama. Gautama's understanding of the reality of life is traditionally presented as four visions:

- A man weakened with age.
- A sick man with infected skin and bones.
- A dead man being taken from the cemetery.
- A recluse with a calm and serene face.

The first three visions show facets of the reality of ailing humanity. The last shows one possible relief from it. If correctly understood, the four visions can give us an insight into the doctrine that later taught by Gautama: a way of escaping the suffering caused by old age, sickness, and death. The way is the life of renunciation. Of course, even a monk who renounces the world does not escape sickness, old age, and death. But he does escape the agony caused by them inasmuch as his mind is not unduly attached to transient aspects of life, and he does not consider them to be ultimate values.

In this regard, it is important to note the differences among Islam, Hinduism, and Buddhism. Islam promotes family life. Hinduism reveres the renouncer but seeks to protect family values by establishing a balance between worldly responsibilities and spiritual pursuits that require their renunciation. In short, the Hindu ethos favors the family. While Islam and Hinduism tip the scale of values toward the home and the world, the early and determining orientation of Buddhism was toward the celibate, homeless, wandering world renouncer (Thursby, 1992).

Both Buddhism and Hinduism share a view in which the fate of all beings, as determined by their own Karma or modes of action over successive lifetimes, is to suffer a ceaseless round of rebirths into various bodies until they are able to discover and dedicate themselves to an effective method for attaining release. In other words, human beings are emancipated by their self-effort, without supernatural aid.

Distinctive Characteristics   In this section, we outline distinctive characteristics of Buddhism that are especially relevant to the study of aging.

- *Renunciation of worldly values:* Status distinctions determined by birth are spiritually irrelevant, and freedom from worldly values is required for release from *Samsara*. It is important to cultivate an attitude of detachment that eventually turns toward a renunciation of worldly values.
- *Four basic qualities:* The qualities that characterize a liberated person are friendliness or loving kindness, compassion, gentleness, and equanimity.
- *The four noble truths:* Suffering abounds; it is occasioned by the drive for private fulfillment; that drive can be tempered; and the way to temper is by traveling the eightfold path.
- *The eightfold path:* Traveling this path implies a right view, right thought, right speech, right action, right livelihood, right effort, right mindfulness, and right meditation. It is this approach that brings insight, provides knowl-

edge, and leads to tranquillity, to highest awareness, to full enlightenment, to *Nirvana*.

• *Meditation:* As indicated earlier, meditation is one of the elements of the eightfold path. Buddhist meditation is designed to perform two functions: (a) calming of the mind (through tranquillity meditation) and (b) widening of the mind's vision of the reality of life (through insight meditation).

• *Detachment:* Buddhism values giving up attachment to the seemingly enduring personal identity that is created by interaction with family, friends, and institutions. This perspective leads to viewing aging as a problem.

Buddhists in America   Since Buddhism is followed in almost all parts of Asia (e.g., Thailand, Cambodia, Laos, Vietnam, China, Japan, Korea, Tibet, and Nepal) and a large number of recent immigrants have come from these countries, there is a substantial Buddhist population in the United States. As indicated earlier for other Asian groups, Buddhists are also spread out, often with too few people in any one area observing a similar form of Buddhism to form a religious community. Only in metropolitan areas, especially on the West Coast, are Buddhist temples available. In addition, there is a shortage of monks in the United States. Many of the monks are older and do not speak English. This creates a barrier for younger members of this population raised in the United States.

In the next learning activity, you will become familiar with how some Japanese Americans use customs from other religious traditions.

ACTIVE LEARNING EXPERIENCE: MULTIRELIGIOUS CUSTOMS AMONG JAPANESE AMERICANS[1]

Purpose

This activity provides an opportunity for you to examine multireligious customs of Japanese Americans and to analyze how some Buddhists remain open to customs, traditions, and values from a variety of other religions. Upon completion of this activity, you will be able to:

1   Outline benefits of accepting and respecting others' religions in a spirit of mutual give and take.
2   Share examples of how some other groups in the United States take an active part in learning from other religions.
3   Discuss how such interactions among members of different religious groups affect the quality of life for older adults.

[1]Megumi Kondo designed this activity.

Time Required

30 minutes (15 minutes to read the case and prepare group answers to the questions and 15 minutes for a general class discussion).

Procedure

1 The instructor divides the class into groups of five to seven students.
2 Each group selects a member who is responsible for writing down the group's answers and for reporting them to the class.
3 Groups answer the questions that follow the case.
4 Group recorders report their group's answers to the class.
5 The instructor leads a discussion reflecting group responses.

Multireligious Customs Among Japanese Americans

Read the following case and answer the accompanying questions.

Buddhism and Shintoism are two major religions of Japanese Americans. A family uses both Buddhist and Shinto customs in daily life. Some Christian customs are also used in annual life events. This is a case of a family that uses Buddhism, Shintoism, and Christianity in their life events.

Fumi Ito is a 70-year-old widow who lives with her first daughter's family. Since Fumi and her husband did not have a son, their first daughter, Akiko, has taken a role to keep their last name. Her son-in-law, Nobuo, has accepted the change of his last name Yamaguchi to Ito when they married. Fumi's husband, Akio, died 2 years ago. His funeral was observed with the traditional Buddhist custom. The third anniversary of his death was observed last month. Fumi visits his grave once a week. She pours water over the gravestone, makes floral offerings, lights the incense, and prays for him. Fumi's family also visits the grave at least once a month (usually on the date of his death). When they visit the grave, they offer rice cakes or Akio's favorite things and pray.

Akiko and Nobuo have a son, Koichi, and a daughter, Mika, so Mika does not need to keep their last name. When Koichi married, Koichi and his wife, Sachiko, had a wedding ceremony at a Shinto shrine. For marriage, Shinto is the most common religion. Many wedding ceremonial halls in Japan have a room for Shinto wedding ceremonies. Only the closest family can attend the ceremony. During the ceremony, a Shinto priest prays for a new couple, and a bride and groom exchange nuptial cups for their marriage pledge and then exchange their rings. The ceremony is about 30 minutes long, and the reception follows the ceremony in another hall.

Mika married last month. She and her husband, Takayuki, had their wedding ceremony at church. Mika's favorite singer had a wedding ceremony at this church, and she longed to have a wedding ceremony at the same church. Neither Mika nor Takayuki are Christian. However, the pastor allowed them to have a wedding ceremony at the church. Both of them had to go to church at least four times to learn about Christianity and marriage before their wedding ceremony. Some Christian churches allow any couple to have a wedding ceremony with some conditions.

All of the Ito family members attended these events. They used Buddhism, Shintoism, and Christianity each time. Many Japanese people use Shintoism, Buddhism, and Christianity in their lives. Christmas is an annual event for many Japanese people, even if they are not Christians. Many Japanese Buddhists use a variety of religious events in their daily lives. Social interaction among members of different religious groups provides them with ongoing opportunities to see important similarities in different faiths, promotes acceptance and respect for each other, and allows them to live together in a spirit of mutual give and take.

Discussion Questions

1   What aspects of Japanese multireligious customs did you find unique? Why?

2   Why has intercommunication between religions become important in Japan?

3   Given the large number of Buddhist immigrants in the United States, what are the benefits of their accepting and respecting other religions?

4   Give examples of creative approaches that may be useful in promoting interaction among older adults representing different religious traditions in the United States.

5   What other religious traditions that you have studied in this chapter view all religions as having the same goal?

Islam

The word *Islam* is closely related to *salam*, which means peace or salvation. Thus, its full connotation is "the peace that comes when one's life is surrendered to God" (Smith, 1991). In other words, Islam seeks to cultivate the attribute that life is total surrender to God. Those who adhere to Islam are known as Muslims. They believe that Islam reached its definitive form through the prophet Mohammed. While there had been authentic prophets of God before Mohammed, he was their culmination; hence, he is called "The Seal of Prophets." No valid Islamic prophets will follow him.

The language of scripture and divine revelation in Islam is Arabic, and nearly all of the key terms and concepts of religious life are derived from that language. Allah is the Arabic name of God. This revered name refers to the sole divine creator (Williams, 1963), of incomparable majesty, who is to be supremely praised and respected. Allah is believed to have revealed perfectly in the Quran, the holy scripture that was transmitted through Mohammed, how he intends people to live. Because translations cannot possibly convey the emotions, the fervor, and the mystery that the Quran holds in the original, Muslims have preferred to teach others the language in which they believe Allah spoke with incomparable force and directness.

Language, however, is not the only barrier the Quran presents to outsiders. In its content, it is like no other religious text. It does not ground its theology in dramatic narratives, as do the Indian epics of Ramayana and Mahabharata, or in historical ones, as do the Hebrew scriptures; nor is God revealed in human form as in the Gospels and Bhagvad-Gita. Whereas the Old and New Testaments are directly historical and indirectly doctrinal, the Quran is directly doctrinal and indirectly historical. In the Quran, God speaks in the first person. Allah describes himself and makes known his laws. The Muslims consider each sentence as a separate revelation and experience the words themselves as a means of grace. As pointed out by Cragg (1988), the Quran does not document what is other than itself. It is not about the truth; it is the truth.

The divine message in the Quran was extended and elaborated (Denny, 1985) by exemplary teachings and the practices of the Prophet, who, as the final messenger of God, also was considered the most authentic interpreter of the Quran. Mohammed's exemplary words and deeds are known as Sunna and were recorded in collections called Hadith. Together with the Quran, they form the core of the Muslim law, the Sharia. Although Sharia has been extended and enlarged over time, Muslims still maintain that Allah alone is the ultimate source of Islamic law and of its authority. It follows that the teachings of Quran, the precedents preserved in the Sharia, and the practices traditionally prescribed for ritual performance continue to provide the basic framework for religious life and values.

Vision of Human Life   There are only a dozen passages in the Quran that make significant reference to elders, old age, and the process of aging. While they are few, they clearly and forcefully express the most characteristic features of the Islamic vision of human life (Watt, 1968). These features include the following: (a) Human life is relatively weak and limited in contrast to the absolute power and majesty of Allah; (b) as established by divine will, human life is limited and undergoes eventual destruction; (c) old age overtakes and destroys a person in the same way that even a flourishing and well-watered orchard will be burned up by a scorching whirlwind; (d) aging and the suffering associated with it provide one more sign and reminder of the overwhelming mercy, justice, and power of Allah; (e) those who have been blessed by sufficient resources should provide support to those who are less fortunate, less able, and weaker members of society, particularly orphans, elders, and women; (f) mature adult children should show kindness and respect to aged parents; and (g) the whole of human life is considered to be a trial, and at the precise time determined by Allah, death brings the trial to a close (Mir, 1987). In the hereafter, Allah will judge and punish or reward each soul.

Muslims in the United States   Muslim immigrants in the United States have come from countries such as Egypt, Iraq, Iran, Saudi Arabia, Kuwait, Jordan, Afghanistan, Pakistan, Bangladesh, Nigeria, Malaysia, and Indonesia.

Of the 6.5 to 7 million Muslims in the United States, about 44% are African American Muslim converts, many of whom indicate the Islamic faith as a part of their heritage. In addition, American Muslims also include about 8,000 recent White converts, 80% of whom are women who have converted to Islam after marrying Muslims (Goodwin, 1994).

In the United States, there are 1,200 mosques and 165 Islamic schools serving Muslim populations predominantly concentrated in California, New York, Illinois, New Jersey, Indiana, Michigan, Virginia, Texas, Ohio, and Maryland (Goodwin, 1994). Muslims in these and other states continue to participate in a variety of religious observances. Friday prayers represent one such observance. In addition to congregational prayers on Fridays, it is stipulated that all Muslims pray at home five times each day: on arising, when the sun reaches its zenith, when the sun reaches its mid-decline, sunset, and before retiring. Regardless of where they live, Muslims tend to read the Quran on a regular basis. They see monotheism as Islam's contribution not simply to the Arabs but to religion in its entirety. It is important to note that Islam stresses racial equality and has achieved a remarkable degree of interracial coexistence (Danner, 1988). The advances that Islam continues to make in Africa and among the Black population in the United States are not unrelated to the religion's principled record on this issue. It is this attitude toward interracial coexistence that has important implications for the daily lives of older Muslims in America. As indicated earlier, mature adult children are expected to show kindness and respect to aged parents. It is therefore common among American Muslims to provide informal care to their aging parents. This also allows older parents to share their wisdom, expertise, and cultural heritage with adult children and their families.

SUMMARY

This chapter has been devoted to an examination of religion and spirituality among Black Americans, Hispanics, American Indians, and Asian/Pacific Islanders. In the first section of the chapter, we distinguished between religion and spirituality, outlined procedures used to assess these constructs, and stressed the importance of including religion in the study of aging. In the next section, we focused on religious behaviors of elderly Blacks. While religious involvement is high among Black Americans of all ages, this is especially true for the oldest age cohorts. They participate in both organized and nonorganizational activities at a very high rate. In addition to attending church, a majority of them engage in daily prayer, read religious materials, watch or listen to religious programs, and request prayer. This involvement in organized and nonorganizational religious activities reduces the effects of stressors for them.

After reviewing the religious behaviors of Blacks, we examined the practices of Hispanics. We noted that, in the everyday life of older Hispanics, both Aztec and European influences are still in place today. Out of this mixture of Indian and European ideologies has evolved the unique concept of *fe*, which incorporates varying degrees of faith, spirituality, hope, cultural values, and beliefs. Attending religious services and engaging in private prayer are also common in this population. The next section focused on religious practices among American Indians. As noted for Hispanics, religion is not a "pure" concept for American Indians. They consider it essential that Christianity be rooted in Indian culture and practices. Traditionally, elders have had a special place in the culture and religions of the American Indian population. They are the wisdomkeepers, the repositories of the sacred ways and natural world philosophies that extend indefinitely back in time.

The concluding section of the chapter was devoted to an examination of Hindu, Buddhist, and Islamic conceptions of aging. Hinduism readily accepts other religions and views them as simply different languages through which God speaks to the human heart. It considers knowledge as the key ingredient for alleviating the pain and suffering of aging. Both Buddhism and Hinduism share the view that the fate of all beings is to suffer a ceaseless round of rebirths until they are able to discover and dedicate themselves to an effective method for attaining release. Islam views aging and the associated suffering as a reminder of the overwhelming mercy, justice, and power of Allah.

As a means of reviewing some significant concepts, complete the following quiz.

ACTIVE LEARNING EXPERIENCE: DIVERSITY IN RELIGION, SPIRITUALITY, AND AGING QUIZ

Purpose

The purpose of this activity is to assess your knowledge of variations in religion and spirituality among older Black Americans, Hispanics, American Indians, and Asian/Pacific Islanders. Upon completion of this activity, you will be able to:

1 Assess your knowledge of diversity issues in religion, spirituality, and aging.
2 Gain feedback regarding your knowledge of these issues.

Time Required

30 minutes (10 minutes to complete the quiz and 20 minutes to discuss your answers in class).

Procedure

1 Complete the quiz.
2 Your instructor leads a review of the answers to the quiz in class.

Diversity in Religion, Spirituality, and Aging Quiz

		True	False
1	Older White adults demonstrate significantly higher levels of religious participation than do older Black adults.	_____	_____
2	Participation in nonorganizational religious activities among elderly Blacks tends to be very low.	_____	_____
3	Black elders rely on their church for assistance more often than do elderly Whites.	_____	_____
4	Religious involvement of older Blacks has no effect in reducing the negative impact of life stressors.	_____	_____
5	The religious involvement of middle-aged and elderly Mexican American women is related to their life satisfaction.	_____	_____
6	For older persons of Mexican heritage, *fe* always implies an identification with a specific religious community.	_____	_____
7	The place of spiritual leaders in American Indian tribes is similar to that of religious leaders in the dominant society.	_____	_____
8	Older Black women are as active in religious organizations as are older Black men.	_____	_____
9	Among American Indians, orthodox religious beliefs and practices are often combined with indigenous ones.	_____	_____
10	According to Islam, aging is a sign of God's mercy, justice, and power.	_____	_____
11	Islam encourages an ascetic lifestyle and a detachment from family life.	_____	_____
12	For Asian Indian Hindus, old age is the time to obtain spiritual self-realization.	_____	_____
13	Buddhism promotes family life.	_____	_____
14	The majority of Asian refugees follow Islam.	_____	_____
15	For immigrant elders, the local church may play a unique role in resettlement and acculturation activities.	_____	_____

GLOSSARY

Aztecs   A pre-Colombian group that ruled much of what is now modern Mexico.

Bhagvad Gita   Refers to a very famous poem that is the spiritual textbook of almost all educated Hindus. Its first six chapters deal mainly with the psychology of the human spiritual life, the second six with devotion and the nature of God, and the third six with practical applications.

Fe   For older adults of Mexican heritage, the concept of *fe* incorporates varying degrees of faith, spirituality, hope, culture, values, and beliefs.

Karma   Associated with Hinduism, this term refers to action. The law of Karma says that you get what you make and nothing else. The binding effect of Karma lies not only in its nature of "what you make you have" but also in that it persists until you unmake it (or, in other words, "work it out").

Lakota   This is the second largest American Indian tribe. Whites often call this tribe by the name of Sioux.

Nirvana   A term usually associated with Buddhism. It refers to the extinction of all worldly desires and effects for a given person. Nirvana is also referred to as the "state of illumination."

Quran   The sacred text of Islam, considered by Muslims to contain the revelations of God through their prophet Mohammed. It is a manual of definitions and guarantees, and it provides Muslims a collection of maxims upon which to meditate.

SUGGESTED READINGS

Arden, H., & Wall, S. (1990). *Wisdomkeepers: Meetings with Native American spiritual elders*. Hillsboro, OR: Beyond Words.

This book describes interviews with 17 spiritual or political leaders representing a full range of American Indian communities. The authors learned a different way of thinking that affected their views about the earth, sovereignty, family, community, and the future. Included are a large number of excellent photographs.

Cole, T. R., Van Tassel, D.D., & Kastenbaum, R. (Eds.). (1992). *Handbook of the humanities and aging*. New York: Springer.

The authors cover aging through history, world religions, arts and literature, and contemporary topics in humanistic gerontology. The volume is composed of four sections: (a) aging, old age, and elders in history; (b) aging, spirituality, and world religions; (c) artistic expression, creativity, and representations of aging; and (d) humanistic gerontology: the state of the art. It includes Far Eastern cultures in the historical section; Jewish, Islamic, Hindu, and Buddhist perspectives in the section on religion and spirituality; and world history in the state-of-the-art section.

Koenig, H. G. (1995). *Research on religion and aging: An annotated bibliography*. Westport, CT: Greenwood Press.

The author provides a ready resource for identifying sound research in the field of religion and aging. Annotations are grouped primarily by subject content and secondarily by date of publication and specific author. The first section focuses on studies that explore patterns of religious beliefs, attitudes, experience, and private and public practice among older adults and examines how these factors change with aging. The second section includes studies that address the relationship between religion and health. The third section reviews studies that bring together and interpret research findings to make recommendations for those who work with older adults. The fourth section presents papers on the measurement of religiosity and spirituality. The conclusion provides a brief synthesis of the research on religion and aging.

Schachter-Shalomi, Z., & Miller, R. S. (1995). *From age-ing to sage-ing: A profound new vision of growing older*. New York: Warner Books.

This book proposes a new model of late-life development called sage-ing, a process that enables older people to become spiritually radiant, physically vital, and socially responsible "elders of the tribe." The three sections of the book focus on (a) the theory of spiritual "eldering," (b) spiritual eldering and personal transformation, and (c) spiritual eldering and social transformation. The appendix includes 11 exercises for sages in training.

Smith, H. (1991). *The world's religions* (2nd ed.). New York: Harper Collins.

This book provides an accessible introduction to the world's major religions. In addition to detailed chapters on Hinduism, Buddhism, Confucianism, Taoism, Islam, Judaism, and Christianity, this highly readable book also features valuable sections on the inner dimensions of these great religions. Included as well is a chapter on the primal religions, the native traditions of the Americas, Australia, Africa, and Oceania.

Thomas, L. E. (1994). The way of the religious renouncer: Power through nothingness. In L. E. Thomas & S. Eisenhandler (Eds.), *Aging and the religious dimension* (pp. 51–64). Westport, CT: Auburn House.

Thomas explores the issues of aging and religion by means of a case study of an elderly religious renunciate from India, along with a comparison of Gandhi's life in his later years. Using a cross-cultural perspective, the author examines these two instances in which aging has not led to a loss of prestige and personal authority. This analysis provides an in-depth look at the factors contributing to this phenomenon, and it explores the implications they might have for aging in Western society.

Tilak, S. (1989). *Religion and aging in the Indian tradition*. Albany: State University of New York Press.

This book interprets relevant material from Buddhist and Hindu texts helpful in understanding the meaning and significance attached to the process of aging in traditional India and posits aging as a process mediating between two structural polarities of life and death, discusses the mechanisms suggested in the classical Hindu medical texts to cope with and manage the stress of aging, and analyzes various Hindu myths that seek to interpret aging and its etiology in terms of deeds (Karma) and desire (Kama). The book is written at a level appropriate for professionals and advanced students.

KEY: DIVERSITY IN RELIGION, SPIRITUALITY, AND AGING QUIZ

1 **False.** Research by Levin, Taylor, and Chatters (1994) indicates that older Blacks report a higher degree of religious involvement than do older Whites. This includes religious instruction and volunteering in church.

2 **False.** Taylor and Chatters (1991) found that the prevalence of private religious activities among older Blacks tends to be very high. Examples of these activities include reading religious materials, working or listening to religious programs, engagement in prayer, and requests for prayer.

3 **True.** Research indicates that Black elders rely on their church for assistance more often than do elderly Whites, especially when community-based services are not available (Haber, 1984; Hirsch, Kent, & Silverman, 1972). The involvement of Black elders in the church supports Antonucci and Akiyama's (1987) concept of a ''convoy'' of social support, since these individuals' lifetime connection to the church generates a support network that provides help when needed.

4 **False.** Although life stressors tend to diminish feelings of self-worth and mastery, these negative effects are offset or counterbalanced by increased religious involvement among older Blacks (Krause & Tran, 1989).

5 **True.** Even after control for health, church attendance remains a predictor of a high level of life satisfaction in middle-aged and elderly Mexican American women (Levin & Markides, 1988).

6 **False.** *Fe* does not necessarily imply identification with a specific religious community. Instead, it incorporates varying degrees of faith, spirituality, hope, cultural values, and beliefs. It embodies a way of life as well as the culture in which it is lived.

7 **False.** Among American Indian tribes, spiritual elders are the wisdomkeepers, the repositories of the sacred ways, and natural world philosophies that extend indefinitely back in time (Arden & Wall, 1990). Their place is much more central than that of religious leaders in the dominant Western society. They share dreams and visions with members of their tribe, perform healing ceremonies, and may make apocalyptic prophecies.

8 **False.** Older Black women are more active in religious organizations than their male counterparts (Levin & Taylor, 1993; Ortega, Crutchfield, & Rushing, 1983). This involvement in church social events helps them maintain an informal support network that extends beyond family members (Hatch, 1992).

9 **True.** Many American Indians prefer to merge Christian and indigenous beliefs. They consider it essential that Indian Christianity be rooted in their culture and practices. It is not surprising to find the sacred pipe, the drum, sweat lodges, native prayers, and eagle feathers in Indian churches (Weaver, 1993).

10 **True**.   According to the Quran, aging is a sign of Allah's mercy, justice, and power (Thursby, 1992).

11 **False**.   Islam discourages ascetic lifestyles and emphasizes the family. It expects adult children to show kindness and respect to their aged parents (Smith, 1991).

12 **True**.   For the aging Hindu, the losses accompanying aging are accorded special status. Old age is the time to obtain spiritual self-realization through renunciation and contemplation (Christiansen, 1981). The signs of old age are not symbolic of physical and mental decline; rather, they are indications for beginning a new life task.

13 **False**.   Buddhism values giving up attachment to the seemingly enduring personal identity that is created by interaction with family, friends, and institutions. It values detachment from family life. Its determining orientation is toward the celibate, homeless, wandering world renouncer (Thursby, 1992).

14 **False**.   The vast majority of Asian refugees are Buddhists. They have come from Cambodia, Laos, and Vietnam, where more than 80% of the population follows Buddhism (Kitano & Daniels, 1995).

15 **True**.   For immigrant elders and their families, churches provide a place for meeting people, learning the language and culture of the United States, and obtaining social services (Kitano & Daniels, 1995).

Chapter 7

Death, Dying, and Grieving

OVERVIEW

Cultural Conceptions of Death and Bereavement
- To whom can current Western conceptions of death be traced?
- Describe Puritan beliefs about death and bereavement.
- Why does the larger American culture view mainstream Protestant and Catholic practices regarding death and grief as normative?

Kalish and Reynolds's Study
- Describe the methodology used by Kalish and Reynolds in their study of ethnicity and death.

African Americans
- What are some of the themes in African American views of death?
- Provide support for the following statement: African American funeral practices can be traced to West Africa and to the experience of slavery.
- What are some characteristics of many Black Baptist funerals?

Mexican Americans
- Why is Mexico sometimes referred to as a "death culture"?
- How is the Day of the Dead practiced in contemporary Mexico?
- What did Kalish and Reynolds find about Mexican Americans' death attitudes and behaviors?

Japanese Americans
- What are some generational differences in the death attitudes and customs of Japanese Americans?
- What did Kalish and Reynolds find regarding Japanese Americans' death attitudes and behaviors?
- What are some common characteristics of a traditional Japanese American funeral?

Islamic Americans

- What are some key Muslim beliefs regarding death?
- What are the duties that a Muslim relative must perform immediately following a family member's death?
- Describe Islamic mourning practices.

Jewish Americans

- Describe Jewish beliefs regarding life, death, and mourning.
- Describe some aspects of Jewish funerals.
- Discuss Jewish mourning practices.

Italian Americans

- Why does the death of family elders constitute an ongoing concern for Italian American adults?
- What part does food often play in response to the death of an Italian American elder?
- Describe several characteristics of many Italian American funerals.

Native Americans

- Provide examples of the great diversity in death attitudes and behaviors among different American Indian tribes.
- Describe common funeral practices among the Lakotas.
- What are some characteristic ways in which Lakotas mourn the death of a loved one?

Summary

Diversity in Death, Dying, and Grieving Quiz

Glossary

Suggested Readings

Key: Diversity in Death, Dying, and Grieving Quiz

In this concluding chapter, we examine some of the diverse ways Americans view their own death and the deaths of their loved ones. Emphasis is placed on Western conceptions of death, death anxiety, death customs, and grieving. Special attention is given to the death customs of Blacks, Mexican Americans, Japanese Americans, Muslims, Jews, Italian Americans, and American Indians.

The following vignettes illustrate some of the issues we address in this chapter.

Vignette 1: Benigno Bulosan is dead. Having suffered from emphysema for the last ten years, he died in his sleep at the age of 86. Benigno and his wife, Patria, did not discuss burial plans. Patria asks her oldest son, Ferdinand, to make the necessary arrangements with the cemetery. Ferdinand knows that his father would want to be grieved and buried as his father before him was in the Philippines. A big feast is planned. Patria serves as treasurer, collecting money from relatives so that there will be sufficient funds for the embalming, burial, and food. One of the Bulosan daughters is responsible for going to the store to select the food, and a cousin is assigned to be in charge of the cooking. Benigno's body is to stay in the home for three days. The bottom half of the coffin is wood, with the upper half having a glass cover. As relatives and friends view the body, they refrain from crying. Visitors bring flowers and light candles. A picture of Benigno has been placed on top of his coffin. Nobody touches his body. During the three days in which the body is at home, the family is to do no cleaning, and they do not leave the room to say goodbye to guests. Older friends and relatives strongly discourage pregnant women from participating in the three-day visitation or the funeral so as not to bring harm to their babies or complicate their deliveries. On the day of the funeral, the parish priest offers a Mass at the home. Family and friends accompany Benigno's coffin to church, where another Mass is given. Many participants cry at the loss of Benigno, but the older relatives take care not to allow any of their tears to get on the coffin's glass cover, for that could impede Benigno's entry into heaven.

Vignette 2: Thirty years ago, Samir Sabra emigrated to the United States from Lebanon. Now 78 years old and a widower, Samir isn't feeling well. He has lost a great deal of weight in the last few months. Whenever he has been sick, Samir has felt comfortable consulting his family physician, Dr. Azzam, also a Lebanese American. Dr. Azzam does not always tell his patients the "whole" truth. He judges what he thinks his patients can handle. Having worked with thousands of Arab Americans, he has found that many of his patients and their families find ways to psychologically deny the severity of their illnesses (Racy, 1969). He believes that many of his Arab patients do not want to hear the truth if they are seriously ill. Typically, Dr. Azzam does communicate a terminal prognosis to a stable member of the patient's family, but Samir Sabra lives alone and does not have a good relationship with either of his adult children. After running a series of tests, Dr. Azzam concludes that Samir has an advanced case of colon cancer. Samir is sure to rely on Dr. Azzam, but Azzam wants to be careful not to so upset Samir that Samir gives up hope, thus hastening the progression of the disease.

Discussion Questions

1 In the first vignette, which death customs did you find to be most different from the ones practiced by your family?

2 Do you believe that the practices described in the first vignette will help Benigno Bulosan's family and friends to grieve his loss? How will such practices help?

3 Isn't it a physician's responsibility to be truthful with patients? Do you agree with Dr. Azzam's inclination to be less than candid with Samir Sabra concerning the severity of his illness? Why or why not?

Through the following learning activity, you will explore your family's customs in regard to death and grieving.

ACTIVE LEARNING EXPERIENCE: FAMILY CUSTOMS REGARDING DEATH AND GRIEVING

Purpose

The goal of this activity is to provide you with an opportunity to examine your family's practices concerning death and grieving. Upon completion of this activity, you will be able to:

1 Describe practices common in your family.
2 Compare these practices with those of another student's family.

Time Required

60 minutes (40 minutes to prepare responses to the questions and 20 minutes for class discussion).

Procedure

1 Complete this activity as a homework assignment.
2 On the date the assignment is due, the instructor leads a class discussion regarding family customs and death.

Note: Instructors should be sensitive to students' feelings and experiences with dying and grieving. Some students who have suffered a recent loss may have difficulties with this activity. Instructors should provide a classroom climate in which students are comfortable in sharing experiences or free not to share.

Family Customs Regarding Death and Grieving

Prepare written answers to the following questions:

1 Suppose that an elderly relative dies. How would your family members grieve?
2 Would there be a proscribed period of mourning? If yes, how long would this period last, and what types of behaviors would the mourners practice?
3 What does your religion or spiritual system have to say about death?
4 Does your religion or spiritual system include a belief in an afterlife? Explain.
5 Describe what the "typical" funeral of an elderly family member would be like. Include a description of family, ethnic, or religious customs that the funeral would reflect.

CULTURAL CONCEPTIONS OF DEATH AND BEREAVEMENT

Attitudes and practices surrounding death and bereavement vary from culture to culture and from subculture to subculture. Philosophical and psychological issues concerning mortality, the meaning of life and death, and the losses associated with the death of a loved one appear to be universal concerns. As a means of coping with these concerns, ethnic and religious groups have developed beliefs, rituals, and norms for managing anxieties associated with death, the possibility of an afterlife, burials, and expectations regarding grieving practices (Markides & Mindel, 1987).

Current Western conceptions of death can be traced back to early Semitic people in what is now considered the Middle East; "their beliefs and practices evolved into the Judaic, Christian, and Islamic religions of today" (Spector, 1991, p. 120). These early Semitic people perceived evil spirits to surround the dying and the dead, and they developed rituals aimed at protecting those who were in the process of dying, the dead, and their families and communities. Numerous rites, including washing of the body, sending the dead off with food for the coming journey, and the development of prayers and incantations to protect survivors from the evil spirits, evolved into contemporary practices (Spector, 1991).

Many American death and bereavement attitudes are rooted in 17th- and 18th-century Puritan New England (Eisenbruch, 1984; Stannard, 1977). Believing in predestination, Puritans viewed the afterlife as already fixed, so there was no necessity for an elaborate funeral ceremony. The Puritan system of bereavement reflected the following elements: (a) no embalming, (b) a simple funeral, (c) no eulogy, and (d) a minimum of outward expression of grief. Apparently, the Puritans also attempted to get nearby Indians to engage in similar bereavement and funeral practices, which was contrary to their own religious practices (Eisenbruch, 1984).

David Stannard, a social historian, offers an explanation as to why many American funerals have become demonstrably more elaborate than those of Pilgrim forebears (Stannard, 1977). He contends that funerals in New England (the home of the Puritans) became much more extravagant during the middle of the 17th century with the death of many of the Puritan leaders and the growth of religious tolerance in England, their country of origin. These changes presented a threat to the Puritan community's survival, and perhaps more extravagant funerals and more open expressions of grief were efforts at maintaining the community's existence and importance (Eisenbruch, 1984; Stannard, 1977).

Kyriakos Markides and Charles Mindel (1987), in their review of aging and ethnicity, contend that modernization, having brought about increasing life expectancy and declining death rates, has contributed to a shift in the occurrence of death in Western societies from infancy and childhood to old age. These authors suggest that one consequence of the shift in mortality to the older years, is to make death more predictable, more controllable, and therefore less socially disruptive, leading, to a diminished importance of elaborate rituals. . . . While this "deritualization" of death may be viewed from one perspective as reflecting greater intellectual acceptance of the idea of death, it also means less emotional and psychological support for the bereaved. (Markides & Mindel, 1987, p. 149)

ETHNICITY, DEATH, AND GRIEVING

Interestingly, while many members of the dominant culture may make efforts to deny the reality of death, numerous American ethnic groups, through their religious and familial practices, continue to supply ritual and support for the dying and for those who grieve their death (Irish, Lundquist, & Nelsen, 1993). Since American society has been dominated by the mainstream Protestant and Catholic religions for the last 200 years or more, the larger culture views such Christian beliefs as normative and proper (Irish, 1993). While such practices do reflect the majority of the American population, they do not necessarily suggest the wide diversity of cultural conceptions of death, dying, and grieving found in contemporary society. Clearly, various ethnic groups view these matters in very diverse ways.

THE KALISH AND REYNOLDS STUDY

In an effort to understand the role of ethnicity in viewing death and bereavement, Richard Kalish and David Reynolds (1976) studied an ethnically diverse sample of Los Angeles residents. This research was multifaceted and contained the following elements: (a) a community survey, (b) an analysis of newspaper articles, (c) interviews with professionals representing four different ethnic groupings, and (c) observations made at funerals, hospital wards, cemeteries, long-term care facilities, and the coroner's office. While the staff members conducting this study reflected a diverse mix of ethnicity, religion, and gender, most were young.

The majority of resources included in the Kalish and Reynolds study went into the community survey. The survey included the following topical areas: (a) interviewees' views of their own death (expectations, thoughts, and fears), (b) deaths of others (frequency and talking to others about death), (c) survivors (acceptability of grieving and mourning behaviors), and (d) abstractions about death (the tragedy of various types of death and views concerning mass death and suicide). Prior to pilot testing the interview instrument, the research team constructed three major revisions; four staff members then piloted the fourth revision on eight to ten subjects each. These pilot subjects represented the groups (African Americans, Japanese Americans, Mexican Americans, and Anglo Americans) under consideration, both genders, and the range of socioeconomic classes. After completing another revision, bilingual individuals translated the questionnaires into Spanish and Japanese. Next, others fluent in each of these languages back-translated the instruments into English. At this point, research staff members piloted the current version of the questionnaire in English, Spanish, and Japanese. UCLA Survey Research Center staff modified the instrument and then field tested it in the three languages. Finally, the eighth version (with only very minor changes) was used in the actual study. Kalish and Reynolds "required that every interview be conducted by a person who was visibly of the same ethnicity as the interviewee" (1976, pp. 11–12). The researchers believed that respondents would be less open with interviewers from a different background than they would with interviewers from a similar cultural background. While the researchers considered the possibility that interviewers from similar backgrounds might overidentify with respondents from their cultural group and, perhaps, distort subject data, the researchers believed that this represented a lesser threat to the validity of the interview data.

The interview aspect of the study comprised 434 respondents, including 114 Mexican Americans, 110 Japanese Americans, 109 Blacks, and 101 Whites. Of the subjects, 219 were female, and the mean age was mid- to late 40s, with 28% over the age of 60. In sampling, the researchers made efforts to reduce educational and social class differences. To assess the reliability of the interview responses, the researchers conducted a telephone survey including 30% of the interview respondents, and, in addition, they ran "matched-pair comparisons of responses to English and non-English forms of the interview" (Kalish & Reynolds, 1976, p. 23). In matching the Japanese American and Mexican American samples by age, sex, education, and religion, Kalish and Reynolds found only one error in translation in the Spanish and Japanese versions of the interview instrument.

Kalish and Reynolds also content analyzed the four most widely read newspapers in the four ethnic communities under consideration. Specifically, the researchers were interested in how these papers reported deaths within the ethnic group categories. The services of bilingual research assistants were obtained for analyzing the non-English-language newspapers (Reynolds & Kalish, 1974). Kalish and Reynolds also conducted unstructured interviews with professionals from each of the four subject groups. They interviewed a wide assortment of persons whose work placed them in contact with dying and death, including police officers, clergy, nurses, physicians, funeral directors, nursing home administrators, cemetery workers, and coroners. This sample included 20 Japanese Americans, 17 Mexican Americans, 11 Anglo Americans, and 9 African Americans.

For the final aspect of this comprehensive study, research staff attended funerals representing each of the four ethnic categories and conducted observations in hospital wards, long-term care facilities, cemeteries, and a coroner's office.

Although the Kalish and Reynolds data were collected in 1970, this study still represents the most in-depth analysis of ethnicity, death, and dying conducted in the United States. In the following sections covering ethnicity, death, dying, and bereavement, we cite numerous findings from this classic example of social science research.

AFRICAN AMERICANS

African American death and grieving practices have been traced back to slavery, as well as to West African cultures (Genovese, 1976; Masamba & Kalish, 1976; Perry, 1993). Jean Masamba, an African pastoral psychologist, and Richard Kalish, an American social psychologist, have traced death themes in Black spirituals (Masamba & Kalish, 1976). The themes include death as (a) an underground symbol for liberation in the present; (b) an integral part of life; (c) the basis of fear; (d) the end of life, but not of all life; and (e) the fear of social extinction. African Americans may view death as a symbol for freedom from present injustice and misfortune, as a very real and important part of everyone's life, as something to be feared (especially a violent death), as an extension of life in heaven with God, or as the end of earthly social connections (when an individual is no longer remembered).

Black attitudes toward death as well as death customs should be seen in light of both slavery and African heritage. Millions of Africans were taken forcibly from their homes in chains and transported to the Western hemisphere (Takaki, 1993). Eugene Genovese (1976), in his eloquent social history of the world of the slave, includes a chapter titled "Let the Dead Bury the Dead." In describing slave funeral practices, Genovese reports that "the slaves' African inheritance, albeit adapted, modified, and transformed, showed through" (p. 197). For example, Genovese discusses the common practice among slaves of using broken earthenware to decorate graves, a practice that has been traced to the Bankongo tribe in northern Angola.

Slave funerals became an important element for maintaining a sense of community among the Black population (Perry, 1993). Such occasions were feared by some in the White population, who were concerned that a large gathering of Black slaves might lead to some form of insurrection, a slave revolt. Concerns were so great that, in some places, Black preachers were prohibited from presiding over funerals and Blacks were not allowed to have funerals at night. Frequently, slaves preferred evening funerals, since attendance would be much higher (Genovese, 1976; Perry, 1993).

In the late 20th century, death attitudes and practices continue to play a highly significant role in African American culture. As an important aspect of their larger study of ethnicity and death, David Reynolds and Richard Kalish (1974) addressed issues related to how long their respondents expected to live and how they wished to live. African American respondents expressed both an expectation and a desire to live longer than did Mexican American, Japanese American, and Anglo American subjects. Vern Bengtson and associates, in their study of attitudes toward death according to race, age, class, and gender, examined Blacks, Mexican Americans, and Anglo Americans in Los Angeles County (Bengtson, Cuellar, & Ragan, 1977). Their study demonstrated that fear of death decreased with age and that 26% of the oldest Blacks (those 70 to 74 years of age), as compared with 22% of older Mexican Americans and 27% of older Whites, indicated they were "very afraid" of death.

Black American subjects indicated that they experience more contact with death than other ethnic groups (Kalish & Reynolds, 1976). Kalish and Reynolds found that their African American subjects were significantly more likely to have been acquainted with someone who had died during the last two years than was the case with the other subject groups. However, Black respondents did not report thinking or dreaming about death any more than the other study subjects.

In addition, relative to Mexican and Japanese Americans, Black respondents indicated less dependence on family support in dealing with dying and grieving (Kalish & Reynolds, 1976). Apparently, while Blacks may be less dependent on family support, Black churches often serve to provide emotional support to parishioners struggling with death, dying, and grieving issues (Perry, 1993). As we indicated in Chapter 6, the church is a highly significant institution in the African American community, especially for Black elders. Churches have provided continuity, support, and hope during periods of great oppression (Genovese, 1976; Markides & Mindel, 1987).

Church funerals are a significant aspect of the African American community. Frequently, Black funerals function as social occasions as well as opportunities to express the worth and status of the deceased and that of the other members of the congregation (McDonald, 1973). Typically, these funeral services "encourage emotional expression and catharsis by incorporating religious songs into the ceremony and by providing for visual confrontation with the body" (Markides & Mindel, 1987, p. 156).

In the next learning activity, you will examine funeral customs practiced by many African American Baptists.

ACTIVE LEARNING EXPERIENCE: AN AFRICAN AMERICAN BAPTIST FUNERAL

Purpose

This activity provides an opportunity for you to analyze issues relevant to the funeral of an older adult who is an African American Baptist. Upon completion of this activity, you will be able to:

1   Discuss burial practices common to many African American Baptists.
2   Compare these customs with those practiced by your family or religion when an older adult dies.

Time Required

30 minutes (20 minutes to read the case and prepare group answers to the questions and 10 minutes for a general class discussion).

Procedure

    1   The instructor divides the class into groups of three to five.

    2   Each group selects a member who is to be responsible for writing down the group's answers and for reporting them to the class.

    3   Groups answer the questions following the case.

    4   Group recorders report their group's answers to the class.

    5   The instructor leads a discussion reflecting group responses.

An African American Baptist Funeral

Read the following case and answer the accompanying questions.

Etta Murray has died, and her entire church community mourns the loss. Etta, 85, was a very important person at the Second Avenue Baptist Church. For many years, she taught Sunday School, sang in the gospel choir, served as a deaconess, and was very active on the Mother Board. She was a devout Christian who not only went to church almost every Sunday and on Wednesday nights, but lived her religion as well. While Mrs. Murray never made much money (for a number of years, she worked as a housekeeper for a wealthy family), she was very "rich" in the warm relationships she had with family, friends, and neighbors. If most anyone in the neighborhood needed a "wise" person with whom to speak, Etta was often the one they chose. She was kind, yet practical.

Ten years earlier, Robert, Etta's husband, had died. Robert and Etta weren't able to have children, but they did wind up raising one of Robert's brother's sons. This young man, Stephen, was quite "spirited," and his wild ways got him into many difficulties. He's a grown man now, and he is flying from the West Coast to attend Etta's funeral and mourn the loss of his "mother."

Stephen knows that the funeral service will last a long time, at least an hour and a half. Since Etta had been a member of the church's gospel choir, the choir will sing several of her favorite hymns. Since she was active on the Mother Board, as a deaconess, and as a Sunday School teacher, there will be a representative from each of these groups addressing the mourners during the service. Telegrams from family and friends who live out of town and are not able to attend will be read. Reverend Thomas, who has known and been friends with Etta for many years, will give the eulogy. After the service, mourners will file by the open casket, and this will be their time to say goodbye. They trust that Etta is with God and Jesus in heaven. Mourners then proceed to the nearby cemetery for the burial.

Following Etta's burial, all of the mourners attend a dinner at the church. The dinner is prepared by Etta's dearest friends, the church ladies from the Mother Board. The ladies serve some of Etta's favorite foods. While they miss Etta's warmth and good humor, the mourners are confident that Etta's struggles are over and that she is at peace.

Discussion Questions

1 How does Etta Murray's funeral service compare with those that you have attended? Is it similar to or quite different from services with which you are familiar? In what ways?

2 The casket is open during the memorial service at church. How do you feel about that?

3 While Etta is mourned, the service, the burial, and the dinner are times for celebration. Etta's suffering has ended, and she is with God. How does that compare with the way in which an elder's death is handled in your cultural group?

MEXICAN AMERICANS

Mexican Americans have come from what has been described as a "death culture" or as a culture preoccupied with death (Moore, 1970; Younoszai, 1993). Contemporary Mexican death practices can be traced back to pre-Colombian groups such as the Aztecs and Mayas, as well as to the Spanish Catholics who participated in the conquest of ancient Mexico. The Aztecs practiced a form of ritual human sacrifice in which their

> priests would cut out a live victim's heart and sacrifice to the god of the sun. . . . The Aztecs were a warlike people and they made a ritual out of death, shedding blood in the act of killing, and then smearing it on the hair and on the faces of the priests. (Younoszai, 1993, p. 71)

During the pre-Colombian period, the Aztecs associated yellow-orange flowers (*zempasuchitl*) with death. Such flowers were used to adorn graves, frequently with designs. Mexicans continue to write names and draw figures on graves with these flowers (Younoszai, 1993).

The Spanish conquerers were appalled by the ritual human sacrifices of the native people, but they brought with them religious practices that also involved the symbolism of blood (Moore, 1970). In conjunction with certain Catholic holidays, the Spaniards would parade "statues of Christ through the streets with blood flowing freely from the thorn wounds on his head and the nails pounded into his hands and feet upon the cross" (Younoszai, 1993, p. 72).

In contemporary Mexico, there is widespread celebration of the Day of the Dead, which is a merging of the pre-Colombian Day of the Dead with the Catholic observances of All Hallows' Eve (Halloween), All Saints' Day, and All Souls' Day (Beimler & Greenleigh, 1991; Younoszai, 1993). These holidays are characterized by sweet treats and masks in the shape of skulls, skeletons, coffins, and ghosts. Kalish and Reynolds (1976) failed to find these practices among the Mexican American subjects in their Los Angeles study. Instead, they found Mexican Americans going to Mass, lighting candles for their dead relatives, and placing flowers at grave sites. These practices are consistent with those of other Catholics, not just Mexican Americans. It should be noted that while most Mexican Americans are Catholic, some are not.

Kalish and Reynolds (1976) also found that Mexican Americans expressed both a desire to live fewer years and an expectation to live the least amount of time of the four groups studied (Mexican and Japanese Americans, Blacks, and Anglos). Apparently, the expectations and wishes of the Mexican American sample are consistent with actuarial predictions (Markides & Mindel, 1987). Among the issues explored in the Kalish and Reynolds study was the decision to tell an individual that he or she was terminally ill. Among the four groups studied, Mexican Americans were the least likely to wish to be told if they were seriously ill, as well as the least likely to encourage communicating this information to others with such an affliction. A number of Mexican American respondents felt that communicating information of this nature would present additional difficulties for both the patient and the patient's family.

Mexican American families serve as "a protective network for helping the dying, and their survivors, handle the emotional problems associated with death" (Kalish & Reynolds, 1976, p. 166). Both the surveys with subjects and the interviews with Mexican American funeral directors pointed to the frequency with which families attempted to shield young children (less than ten years old) from visiting dying family members and from attending funeral services. Kalish and Reynolds found that frequently family members would visit their dying relative at the hospital in shifts, and in some cases they would "camp in." This observation is supported by Kalish and Reynolds' survey finding indicating that Mexican American respondents were the most likely of the four subject groups to encourage family members to visit them if they were dying, even if this presented an inconvenience for their relatives.

As we indicated in Chapter 6, the Mexican American family and the ways in which it copes with the various crises of life cannot be separated from religion, particularly Catholicism. Kalish and Reynolds found that their Mexican American interviewees would, if their spouse died, seek their family for support and comfort, but their second most important resource for support was God and their priest. In addition, interviewees who expressed a higher degree of religiosity desired a larger, more elaborate funeral. Tied to their religious orientation was a significant degree of fatalism. Thirty-eight percent of the Mexican American sample indicated that individuals are incapable of slowing down or hastening their own demise, since it is God who decides such matters.

JAPANESE AMERICANS

As we mentioned in Chapter 6, many Japanese and Japanese Americans use several religions in different aspects of their lives. Buddhism teaches its followers that, in order to comprehend the impermanence of life, they must contemplate and accept death. According to Buddhist teachings, a clear mind, characterized by "desirelessness," leads an individual to accept death both rationally and tranquilly. Death leads one to a different existence in a continual cycle of rebirths (Hamabata, 1990; Markides & Mindel, 1987; Truitner & Truitner, 1993).

While a large number of Japanese Americans are Christians, many Japanese Americans who are first-generation Americans (*issei*) identify with Buddhist traditions. Kalish and Reynolds (1976) found that different generations of Japanese American subjects demonstrated variations in attitudes and behaviors. For example, *issei* appeared more superstitious in that they maintained a virtual taboo concerning the discussion of death. Many *sisei* (second-generation Americans) appeared more uncomfortable in making public speeches at funerals and memorials than did most of the *issei* who were observed in this role. Kalish and Reynolds found that *sansei* (third-generation American) subjects had difficulties in comprehending the *issei* belief in the acceptance of death. Having been socialized in American culture, *sansei* have been educated to attempt to modify the external world, not just accept it. *Sansei* may avoid attending Buddhist funerals as a result of emotional discomfort and a lack of understanding of the Japanese language and Buddhist rituals.

Kalish and Reynolds attempted to assess a variety of attitudes about death, dying, and bereavement. For example, only 31% of Japanese American subjects indicated that they had felt they were close to dying, as compared with 48% of Blacks, 49% of Mexican Americans, and 37% of Anglos. Japanese American subjects were the most likely to want to be told if they were dying. Along with Mexican Americans, Japanese American subjects expressed the most restrictive behavioral norms concerning the mourning period following the death of a spouse. Seventeen percent of both Japanese and Mexican Americans, as compared with 30% of Blacks and 25% of Anglos, believed that it was appropriate to date other men or women at any interval following the death of one's spouse. Eighty-four percent of the Japanese American subjects had attended one or more funerals in the previous 2 years, in comparison with 67% of the Black, 60% of the Mexican American, and 56% of the Anglo subjects. Fifty-three percent of the Japanese Americans preferred cremation, while only 4% of Blacks, 5% of Mexican Americans, and 18% of Anglos preferred that their bodies be disposed of in this fashion.

The following activity addresses the funeral practices of many Japanese American Buddhists.

ACTIVE LEARNING EXPERIENCE: A JAPANESE AMERICAN BUDDHIST FUNERAL[1]

Purpose

This activity presents an opportunity for you to analyze a case regarding the Buddhist funeral of a Japanese American. Upon completion of this activity, you will be able to:

1 Describe Buddhist burial customs common to many Japanese Americans.
2 Compare these customs with those practiced by your family or religion.

Time Required

30 minutes (20 minutes to read the case and prepare group answers to the questions and 10 minutes for a general class discussion).

Procedure

1 The instructor divides the class into groups of three to five.
2 Each group selects a member who is to be responsible for writing down the group's answers and for reporting them to the class.
3 Groups answer the questions following the case.
4 Group recorders report their group's answers to the class.
5 The instructor leads a discussion reflecting group responses.

A Japanese American Buddhist Funeral

Read the following case and prepare answers to the accompanying questions.

> Kiyoshi Yamada has died of liver cancer. A 63-year-old, Mr. Yamada emigrated ten years ago from a small town on the main island of Japan to New York City to be with his eldest son and a number of other family members.
>
> After Kiyoshi's death at home, all of his New York relatives have come to his home to maintain a vigil over his dead body. A Buddhist priest comes and chants a sutra, and some of Kiyoshi's family members and friends join in the chanting. Kiyoshi's oldest son, Kazuo, notifies the head of the community of his father's death.
>
> Kazuo calls the crematorium to schedule the cremation. Kiyoshi's body is wrapped in a white kimono, with a white cloth for the forehead, white wrist wrap-

[1]Megumi Kondo designed this learning activity.

pers, and white leggings. These clothes indicate that the soul will travel into the next world. The clothed body is then placed in a coffin located on an altar with the head of the body facing north.

Female relatives and community members have cooked meals to give to those who come by the home to express their goodbyes to Kiyoshi. Only vegetarian meals are served. Family and friends are responsible for making sure that candles and incense are kept burning for 100 days following Kiyoshi's death. The light from the candles serves as a guide to the next world.

Usually, the funeral is held the day after an individual dies. At Kiyoshi's funeral, a black-and-white photograph of him, with black and white ribbon attached, is placed on the altar. His relatives provide white chrysanthemums and pale-colored flowers. A candle and incense are burned, and the priest chants the sutra with a wooden gong and a bell. The female relatives wear mourning dresses or kimonos, and the male family members wear black or other dark-colored suits with black mourning bands. Family members burn powdered incense and, using strings of beads, pray for Kiyoshi while the priest chants the sutra. Next, Kazuo, the head mourner and Kiyoshi's eldest son, gives a brief eulogy and thanks those present who have come to send his father off to the next world. Then family members place flowers, a few of Kiyoshi's favorite things, and some money into his coffin.

After the funeral service, Kazuo, as the head mourner, carries Kiyoshi's black-and-white photograph to the crematorium. Relatives follow the hearse to the crematorium, and they wait for Kiyoshi's body to be incinerated. After his bones and ashes come out of the incinerator, relatives pray with a string of beads. They pick up some of the remains with very long chopsticks and place them in an urn that is put into a wooden box and wrapped with a white cloth. The family takes it back to their home to be placed in front of the family Buddhist altar.

Discussion Questions

1   In what ways is Kiyoshi Yamada's funeral similar to ones that you have attended?

2   What are some ways in which this funeral differs from the ones with which you are familiar?

3   Cremation is a central element of Kiyoshi's funeral. Why is cremation a practical choice for disposing of the dead in Japan?

ISLAMIC AMERICANS

According to Donald Irish, Islam may well become "the second largest major religious faith in the United States" by the year 2000 (1993, pp. 192–193). America "is moving toward a Judeo-Christian-Muslim society" (p. 193). Through immigration and conversions, Islam is becoming a significant religious force in the United States.

In traditional Arab Muslim culture, the mention of death is generally avoided. When a patient is experiencing a terminal illness, physicians, family members, and patients themselves may deny the patient's actual prognosis.

While Muslims face death with the belief in life after death, they are not certain where their soul will be sent: heaven or hell. The soul's final destination depends on a person's actions and intentions during her or his lifetime (Racy, 1969; Smith & Haddad, 1981).

During their last dying moments, Muslims are to be in the company of a close relative. It is the relative's responsibility to perform several duties immediately following the family member's death: (a) turn the body to face in the direction of Mecca; (b) while sitting close to the body, read from the Quran; (c) close the body's eyes and mouth and cover the face; (d) straighten the legs and stretch the hands by the sides; (e) tell family and friends about the death as soon as possible; and (f) bathe the corpse and then cover it with white cotton (Gilanshah, 1993). Farah Gilanshah writes of the importance of ritual bathing of the recently deceased, indicating that

> before the bathing, the relatives should have an assurance from the doctor that the person is not alive. There are always two people who wash the dead body. Males always bathe a male and females always bathe a female. . . . Three kinds of water are used: water with leaves of the plum tree; camphorized water; and pure water. If only one kind of water is available, the caretakers are allowed to wash the body three times in the water that is available. (1993, p. 141)

The corpse is to be buried on the day of the death or on the day after the death, and the grave is to face toward Mecca. Mourners are encouraged to weep so that they can release their sadness. Afterward, a process of adjusting and reaching a sense of peace can begin. Islamic funerals are perceived as both expressive and depressing, and those who did not even know the deceased may find themselves weeping. After the funeral, there is a gathering at the home of the deceased. Friends and relatives share a meal, and the visitors may stay for an entire day. The family of the deceased is not left alone for a period of a week. A ceremony at the mosque is held three days after the burial, because "Muslims believe that the more prayers uttered for the deceased person at the time of death, and for days after that, the easier the departed one's life will be in the after world" (Gilanshah, 1993, p. 142).

JEWISH AMERICANS

Judaism teaches its followers to embrace life, to accept death's inevitability, to honor the deceased, and to bring comfort to the mourners. Specific rituals involving death and mourning vary among the major denominations of American Judaism: Orthodox, Conservative, and Reform (Cytron, 1993).

Many Jews believe that the corpse should be guarded between the time of death and the burial. The body is to be watched over until it goes to its final place of rest in the earth. Many Jews also believe that cremation is unnatural; as a result of this belief, and because contemporary Jews may associate cremation with the horrors of the Nazi Holocaust (Cytron, 1993), few choose cremation (Markides & Mindel, 1987).

Funerals are to be conducted with both simplicity and realism (Markides & Mindel, 1987). At the beginning of the funeral service, mourners are given a black ribbon to wear or a garment is cut, the latter symbolizing the deceased being "cut away" from family and friends. During the service, several Psalms are recited, a rabbi provides a eulogy, and sometimes family members offer a pleasant memory of the deceased. At the end of the service, those in attendance recite the Kaddish, a prayer for the dead that both accepts death and asks that mourners remember the dead through the acts of kindness they performed during their life (Cytron, 1993).

In Judaism, there are prescribed rituals varying in practice among the three denominations. In traditional families, an initial mourning period, termed "sitting Shiva," begins after the burial and lasts for 7 days (Herz & Rosen, 1982). On the anniversary of the death of a loved one, the family goes to the synagogue or temple and lights a special yarzheit candle, which is to burn for 24 hours (Cytron, 1993; Herz & Rosen, 1982). Also around this time, the family goes to the cemetery for the dedication of the tombstone. The prayer for the dead, the Kaddish, is to be said daily during the first year following the funeral and on every successive anniversary of the loved one's death (Herz & Rosen, 1982).

The next activity centers on generational differences and conflicts regarding burial customs in a particular Jewish American family.

ACTIVE LEARNING EXPERIENCE: A CASE OF BURIAL CUSTOMS AND INTERGENERATIONAL CONFLICT IN A JEWISH AMERICAN FAMILY

Purpose

The goal of this activity is to involve you in the analysis of a case devoted to issues surrounding burial rites, cultural experiences, and intergenerational conflicts in a Jewish American family. Upon completion of this activity, you will be able to:

    1   Describe the sensitivity of discussing issues surrounding extraordinary means, living wills, and so forth.

    2   Analyze conflicts arising from cohort and generational differences in death customs.

    3   Discuss the possible impact of the Holocaust on survivors and their American-born adult children.

Time Required

30 minutes (15 minutes to read the case and answer the accompanying questions and 15 minutes to discuss the case in class or with another person).

Procedure

1   The instructor divides the class into groups of three to five.
2   Each group selects a member who is to be responsible for writing down the group's answers and for reporting them to the class.
3   Groups answer the questions following the case.
4   Group recorders report their group's answers to the class.
5   The instructor leads a brief discussion reflecting group responses.

A Case of Burial Customs and Intergenerational Conflict

Read the following case and provide group answers to the accompanying questions.

Greta Sonnenberg is enduring liver cancer. While she dare not utter the word *terminal*, her three adult children have come to accept the idea that their mother is dying and that she may have only about six months more to live. Frederick, Harold, and Susan love their mother dearly. All three of them, although engaged in full-time professions and married with adolescent children of their own, have been devoted to their mother. Since Irving Sonnenberg, their father, died of a sudden heart attack four years ago, his widow has been very depressed. In her heart, she feels she is dying, but she is not able to verbalize her fears.

Although they are very uncomfortable in talking about it, the three children have decided to ask their mother if she has preferences in terms of a living will. Does she want the physicians to apply extraordinary means? Does she want a feeding tube if necessary? This discussion is very painful for Greta and for her children.

Greta doesn't respond to their questions and instead starts talking about what she wants for her funeral. Greta and her late husband purchased "drawers" at the Jewish cemetery in a nearby area of Philadelphia. Crying, she mentions that she assumes that all of the family will be buried near one another at the same Jewish cemetery. Harold states that he and his wife have decided to be cremated when they die. His mother cannot understand such a choice. She yells out: "How can you allow yourself to be cremated after what Hitler and his thugs did to our people? How can any Jew be cremated after Hitler's ovens?"

Greta storms out of the room. Her final wishes still are unclear. Harold cannot really understand his mother's point of view regarding cremation. After all, the Holocaust ended more than 50 years ago. Greta will never forget, since her father and two sisters died in the gas chambers of Auschwitz.

Frederick, Harold, and Susan are all visibly upset. Harold regrets bringing up his views on cremation. He's also worried that his mother might refuse to speak to him for weeks or months, and she might not have weeks or months left.

Discussion Questions

1   What can Harold do to ease the conflict with his mother?
2   Are Greta's children bound by tradition to themselves be buried in the same way as their parents? Explain.

3 The children still don't know what their mother desires regarding life supports, feeding tubes, and so forth. How and when should they bring up that subject?

ITALIAN AMERICANS

Family and relationships with family members are very important to many Italian Americans. Typically, adult children are devoted to their parents, so the eventual death of family elders constitutes an ongoing concern. Colleen Johnson, in her anthropological study of Italian American families, notes that "the idea prevails that one must do everything one can while the parents are still alive, for tomorrow they might not be here. . . . One must be kind and kiss parents, when they leave, for they might die in their sleep" (1985, p. 175).

Since home, family, and community are the focus of so much of Italian American life, the death of an elder brings an immediate response from many individuals. Often, food, flowers, and money are presented to the family. Much of Italian American family life revolves around food, and, in the case of death, a frequent reaction from extended family members and friends is to provide large amounts of food. In Colleen Johnson's study, one of the respondents exclaimed: "Italians feel food will solve any problem" (1985, p. 99).

It is customary to have a wake, during which mourners can view the open casket and, if they wish, kneel and say a prayer. The room in which the wake occurs, whether in a funeral parlor or the family home, is filled with flowers. Often, family friends give money and Mass cards (most Italian Americans are Catholics). Funerals may cost a great deal of money; thus, if a widow or widower lacks finances, the monetary assistance supplies a needed resource. Families may spend more money than they can really afford, but a lavish funeral signifies respect for the elder who has died. Italian Americans expect family and friends to attend the funeral, even if it is inconvenient or if they are not emotionally close to the deceased elder. Strong feelings and serious rifts may occur if family members or friends do not fulfill their social obligations in relation to the death and the funeral. In addition, the size of the funeral procession may symbolize the importance of the deceased and the family in the context of the community (Johnson, 1985).

Italian Americans are encouraged to express their grief at the death of their beloved elder. Family members may purchase advertisements in the community newspaper on the anniversary of the death. These ads may include a photograph of their loved one (Johnson, 1985).

NATIVE AMERICANS

Among American Indians, attitudes and behaviors related to death vary dramatically from tribe to tribe (Brokenleg & Middleton, 1993; Markides & Mindel, 1987). While the Chiricahua, Lipan, Mescalero, and Jicarilla Apache tribes express little anxiety concerning their own death, many Navajos and Pueblos demonstrate a great deal of fear regarding death. Fearing ghosts, traditional Navajos are quick to bury the dead, since they believe the dead may have negative effects on the living. Such fears also extend to the terminally ill, who may spend the final few days of their lives in hospitals or shelters away from home. Pueblo Indians demonstrate a fear of dying, death, and the dead as well, but not to the extent of Navajos (Markides & Mindel, 1987). Specific taboos may be associated with death. For example, a number of tribes associate the sound or sight of an owl with the impending death of someone close (Brokenleg & Middleton, 1993; Craven, 1973).

Of the approximately 350 American Indian tribes, the Lakota are the second largest. The Lakota view death as a natural aspect of the human experience, part of the cycle of nature. For all who die, there is a guaranteed afterlife. When death appears imminent, terminally ill Lakota will distribute valuables to family members and friends to show acceptance of upcoming death and to demonstrate appreciation to those with whom they have had a significant relationship. Upon the death of a loved one, the extended Lakota family will gather for the wake and funeral. Perhaps 500 to 1,000 mourners will attend ceremonies, and the family is responsible for feeding those in attendance. Ceremonies take place at the home reservation, even if the family of the departed has lived away for several generations (Brokenleg & Middleton, 1993).

Brokenleg and Middleton (1993) describe several Lakota grieving customs in the following passage:

> As each person greets the family mourners, the mourners' expression of grief is renewed in intensity. Cutting the hair, cutting or scratching the forearms and face, tearing clothing, and wearing black are common and appropriate outward displays of grief. These are no empty displays, but rather the ritualized expressions of deep grief. (p. 108)

Christian clergy are more likely than medicine men to be involved substantially in various death rituals, with most Lakota families practicing a blend of tribal and Christian beliefs. Tribal customs do not allow for cremation, since the body is sacred and the home of the deceased (Brokenleg & Middleton, 1993).

Traditionally, there is a three-day-long wake. It is common for friends to donate money to help the family with the various costs (e.g., feeding community members). Tribal songs and Christian hymns are sung. Prayers and reminiscences of the deceased are given. A meal is served, along with cigarettes (giving cigarettes is a centuries-old tradition). This cycle of activities is repeated. In order to feed the spirits of dead family members who may be in attendance, portions of the food are placed outside. Mourners view the body and are permitted to touch, kiss, and embrace it. Important objects such as jewelry or locks of a mourner's hair may be placed in the casket.

Except for the final hymn, most outward expression of grief is curtailed during the funeral. Friends and relatives assist at the grave site by helping to fill in the grave. If the weather is bad, friends will dig the grave prior to the family's arrival. Following grave site rituals, it is customary for male and female mourners to cry (Brokenleg & Middleton, 1993).

SUMMARY

This chapter has been devoted to a discussion of culture and death, dying, and grieving, including a section on cultural conceptions of death and bereavement in which we described the roots of contemporary American death customs. In this section, particular attention was paid to the death practices of the Puritans of the 17th and 18th centuries. Most of the chapter has been concerned with death, dying, and grieving among several American cultural groups. A special section described the Kalish and Reynolds study of ethnicity and death, which is the most comprehensive of its type to date. Kalish and Reynolds (1976) interviewed 434 Los Angeles residents: 114 Mexican Americans, 110 Japanese Americans, 109 African Americans, and 101 Anglo Americans. Data collection methods included interviews with professionals who regularly come in contact with death (e.g., funeral directors), content analyses of ethnic community newspapers, and observations at funerals, hospital wards, cemeteries, and so forth. Much of the chapter concerned itself with the death and grieving practices of African Americans, Mexican Americans, Japanese Americans, Islamic Americans, Jewish Americans, Italian Americans, and Native Americans (with an emphasis on the Lakota tribe). Detailed case studies covering African American Baptist, Japanese American Buddhist, and Jewish American death customs were included.

In order to review some important chapter concepts, complete the following quiz.

ACTIVE LEARNING EXPERIENCE: DIVERSITY IN DEATH, DYING, AND GRIEVING QUIZ

Purpose

The purpose of this activity is to assess your knowledge of issues of diversity in death, dying, and grieving. Upon completion of this activity, you will be able to:

1 Assess your knowledge of diversity issues in death, dying, and grieving.

2 Receive feedback regarding your knowledge of these issues.

Time Required

30 minutes (10 minutes to complete the quiz and 20 minutes to discuss your answers in class).

Procedure

1 Complete the quiz.
2 Your instructor leads a review of the answers to the quiz in class.

Diversity in Death, Dying, and Grieving Quiz

Indicate whether each of the following items is true or false.

		True	False
1	The majority American culture views Christian beliefs about death as normative and proper.	_____	_____
2	Early American Puritan funerals were quite elaborate affairs.	_____	_____
3	African American burial customs reflect both West African beliefs and the experience of slavery.	_____	_____
4	Some outsiders view Mexican culture as preoccupied with death and dying.	_____	_____
5	According to the Islamic faith, the dead are to be turned to face in the direction of Mecca immediately after death occurs.	_____	_____
6	Death anxiety is usually highest in old age.	_____	_____
7	In the Lakota spiritual system, death is viewed as unnatural and profane.	_____	_____
8	The Kaddish, the Jewish prayer for the dead, affirms life and rejects death.	_____	_____
9	Following cremation, Japanese Buddhists pick up bone fragments of their loved one with long chopsticks and place them in an urn.	_____	_____

	True	False
10 Fear of death varies among tribes of American Indians.	_____	_____

GLOSSARY

Issei   Refers to the name given for first-generation Japanese Americans.

Kaddish   The name of the Jewish prayer for the dead.

Living Will   A document that indicates what medical services a person wants or does not want in specified circumstances. For example, an individual may stipulate that ''no extraordinary means'' be used in order to keep him or her alive. Living wills reflect the idea of ''death with dignity,'' a concept included in ongoing eithical and theological debates.

Puritans   A Protestant sect that migrated to America from England in the 17th and 18th centuries to escape religious persecution. Settling in New England, Puritans had strict codes regarding many aspects of life, including death customs.

Sansei   Refers to third-generation Japanese Americans.

Semites   Ancient peoples of the Middle East from whom were developed Judaism, Christianity, and Islam.

Sisei   Refers to second-generation Japanese Americans.

Sitting Shiva   This initial Jewish mourning period starts after burial and ends 7 days later.

The Day of the Dead   A holiday, celebrated in Mexico, that combines pre-Colombian traditions with the Catholic observances of All Hallows' Eve, All Saints' Day, and All Soul's Day. Celebrants don masks portraying skeletons and ghosts and eat sweet treats of similar designs.

Yarzheit   Refers to a special candle that Jews burn on anniversaries of the death of a loved one. It is to burn for 24 hours.

SUGGESTED READINGS

Genovese, E. D. (1976). *Roll, Jordan, roll: The world the slaves made*. New York: Vintage Books.

Eugene Genovese, a social historian, has written a fascinating account of the lives of America's slaves. This beautifully written book includes a chapter on African American funerals in which the author traces some burial customs to their West African origins.

Hamabata, M. M. (1990). *Crested kimono: Power and love in the Japanese business family*. Ithaca, NY: Cornell University Press.

The author, a third-generation Japanese American, writes about the everyday life of wealthy Japanese families. An entire chapter is devoted to death and funeral practices. The book is well researched and written in an engaging style.

Irish, D. P., Lundquist, K. F., & Nelsen, V. J. (1993). *Ethnic variations in dying, death, and grief: Diversity in universality*. Washington, DC: Taylor & Francis.

An excellent resource on diversity, death, and grief, this book includes a chapter on cross-cultural variation in grief as well as separate chapters on African American, Mexican American, Hmong, Native American, Jewish, Buddhist, Islamic, and Quaker and Unitarian death customs. A chapter on personal reflections on grief, death, and diversity includes a variety of learning activities. An appendix includes questions that readers might have concerning each of the groups covered in the text.

Johnson, C. L. (1985). *Growing up and growing old in Italian-American families*. New Brunswick, NJ: Rutgers University Press.

This anthropological study of Italian American family life includes several chapters devoted specifically to elders and to relationships between elders and their adult children. Sections of chapters cover death and Italian American funerals.

Kalish, R. A., & Reynolds, D. K. (1981). *Death and ethnicity: A psychocultural study*. Farmingdale, NY: Baywood.

Originally published in 1976 by the Andrus Gerontology Center at the University of Southern California, this classic study focuses on the topic of death and ethnicity. Kalish and Reynolds completed an exhaustive analysis of African American, Japanese American, Mexican American, and Anglo subjects on numerous death-related topics. They also included observations, interviews with professionals in death-related fields, and content analyses of newspapers.

Smith, J. I., & Haddad, Y. Y. (1981). *The Islamic understanding of death and resurrection*. Albany: State University of New York Press.

This authoritative text familiarizes Westerners with Islamic teachings on death and resurrection through the use of religious and philosophical sources. The book is written in a such a way that the reader does not need to have prior knowledge of Islam and Islamic cultures.

KEY: DIVERSITY IN DEATH, DYING, AND GRIEVING QUIZ

1 **True**. Since the majority of Americans identify with either Catholicism or one of a variety of Protestant denominations, Christian beliefs concerning death and death customs dominate in contemporary America (Irish, 1993).

2 **False**. Believing in predestination, early Puritans did not see a need for elaborate funerals (Eisenbruch, 1984; Stannard, 1977).

3 **True**. Some African American funeral practices have been traced to West African beliefs and to slavery. Slave funerals served to solidify the Black community, and many Black slaves viewed death as a symbol of freedom (Masamba & Kalish, 1976). One practice common among slaves was to decorate graves with broken earthenware, a practice traced back to a West African tribe (Genovese, 1976).

4 **True**. Some outsiders view Mexico as a "death culture." This preoccupation with death is viewed by foreigners as reflected in Aztec human sacrifice, contemporary Mexican art, and celebrations connected with the Day of the Dead (Beimler & Greenleigh, 1991; Moore, 1970).

5 **True**. It is imperative that a close relative turn the body to face Mecca immediately after death occurs (Gilanshah, 1993).

6 **False**. In their comprehensive study of death and ethnicity, Kalish and Reynolds (1976) found that death anxiety decreased with age.

7 **False**. The Lakota spiritual system views death as a natural aspect of the human experience and as part of the cycle of nature. There is a guaranteed afterlife for all who die (Brokenleg & Middleton, 1993).

8 **False**. The Jewish prayer for the dead, the Kaddish, affirms life and accepts death (Cytron, 1993).

9 **True**. Following cremation of the body, Japanese Buddhists may pick up some bones and ashes of their loved one with long chopsticks and place them in an urn (Hamabata, 1990).

10 **True**. Attitudes concerning death vary dramatically from tribe to tribe. Many Pueblos and Navajos express intense anxiety concerning death, while Chiricahua, Lipan, Mescalero, and Jicarilla Apache demonstrate little fear of their own demise (Brokenleg & Middleton, 1993; Markides & Mindel, 1987).

References

AARP Minority Affairs Initiative. (1987). *A portrait of older minorities*. Washington, DC: American Association of Retired Persons.

Abbott, J. (1980). Work experience and earnings of middle-aged Black and White men, 1965–1971. *Social Security Bulletin, 43*, 16–34.

Aldwin, C. M. (1990). The elders' stress life inventory: Egocentric and nonegocentric stress. In M. A. Stephens, S. E. Hobfall, J. H. Crowther, & D. L. Tennenbaum (Eds.), *Stress and coping in later life families* (pp. 49–69). New York: Hemisphere.

Aldwin, C. M. (1991). Does age affect the stress and coping process? Implications of age differences in perceived control. *Journal of Gerontology: Psychological Sciences, 46*, 174–180.

Aldwin, C. M. (1992). Aging, coping, and efficacy: Theoretical framework for examining coping in life-span developmental context. In M. Wykle, E. Kahana, & J. Kowal (Eds.), *Stress and health among the elderly* (pp. 96–113). New York: Springer.

Allen, K. R., & Chin-Sang, V. (1990). A lifetime of work: The context and meanings of leisure for aging Black women. *The Gerontologist, 30*, 734–740.

American Association of Retired Persons. (1988). *Attitudes of Americans over 45 years of age on volunteerism*. Washington, DC: Author.

American Association of Retired Persons. (1993). *A profile of older Americans: 1993*. Washington, DC: Author.

American Association of Retired Persons. (1994). *A profile of older Americans*. Washington, DC: Author.

Anderson, R. H., & Burkhauser, R. V. (1985). The retirement-health nexus: A new measure of an old puzzle. *Journal of Human Resources, 20*, 315–330.

Andrews, J. W., Lyons, B., & Rowland, D. (1992). Life satisfaction and peace of mind: A comparative analysis of elderly Hispanic and other elderly Americans. In T. L. Brink (Ed.), *Hispanic aged mental health* (pp. 21–42). New York: Haworth Press.

Aneshensel, C. S., Rutter, C. M., & Lackenbruch, P. A. (1991). Social structure, stress, and mental health. *American Sociological Review, 56*, 167–178.

Angel, J. L., & Hogan, D. P. (1994). The demography of aging populations. In *Minority elders: Five goals toward building a public policy base* (2nd ed., pp. 9–21). Washington, DC: Gerontological Society of America.

Angelou, M. (1969). *I know why the caged bird sings*. New York: Random House.

Antonucci, T. C. (1985). Social support: Theoretical advances, recent findings and pressing issues. In I. G. Sarason & B. R. Sarason (Eds.), *Social support: Theory, research, and applications* (pp. 21–57). Dordrecht, The Netherlands: Martinus Nijhoff.

Antonucci, T. C., & Akiyama, H. (1987). Social support networks in adult life and a preliminary examination of the convoy model. *Journal of Gerontology, 42*, 519–527.

Arden, H., & Wall, S. (1990). *Wisdomkeepers: Meetings with Native American spiritual elders*. Hillsboro, OR: Beyond Words.

Arluke, A., Levin, J., & Suchwalko, J. (1984). Sexuality and romance in advice books for the elderly. *The Gerontologist, 24*, 415–418.

Arroyo, R. & Lopez, S. A. (1984). Being responsive to the Chicano community: A model for service delivery. In B. W. White (Ed.), *Color in White society* (pp. 63–73). Silver Spring, MD: National Association of Social Workers.

Aschenbrenner, J. (1975). *Lifelines: Black families in Chicago*. New York: Holt, Rinehart & Winston.

Asian American Health Forum. (1990). *Asian and Pacific Islander American California proportionate mortality rates* (Monograph Series 2). San Francisco: Author.

Atchley, R. C. (1975). Adjustment to loss of job at retirement. *International Journal of Aging and Human Development, 6*, 17–27.

Atchley, R. C. (1976). *The sociology of retirement*. New York: Schenkman.

Atchley, R. C. (1982). The process of retirement: Comparing women and men. In M. Szinovacz (Ed.), *Women's retirement* (pp. 153–168). Beverly Hills, CA: Sage.

Atchley, R. C. (1989). A continuity theory of normal aging. *The Gerontologist, 29*, 183–190.

Atchley, R. C. (1991). *Social theories in aging*. Belmont, CA: Wadsworth.

Baker, N. G. (1981). Social work through an interpreter. *Social Work, 26*, 391–397.

Bane, S. D. (1992). Rural minority populations. In E. P. Stanford & F. M. Torres-Gil (Eds.), *Diversity: New approaches to ethnic minority aging* (pp. 123–128). Amityville, NY: Baywood.

Baquet, C. R. (1988). Cancer prevention and control in the Black population: Epidemiology and aging implications. In J. S. Jackson, P. Newton, A. Ostfield, D. Savage, & E. Schneider (Eds.), *The Black American elderly: Research on physical and psychosocial health* (pp. 50–68). New York: Springer.

Barresi, C. M. (1987). Ethnic aging and the life course. In D. E. Gelfand & C. M. Barresi (Eds.), *Ethnic dimensions of aging* (pp. 18–34). New York: Springer.

Barresi, C. M. (1990). Ethnogerontology: Social aging in national, racial, and cultural groups. In K. Ferraro (Ed.), *Gerontology: Perspectives and issues* (pp. 247–265). New York: Springer.

Barrow, G. M. (1992). *Aging, the individual, and society* (5th ed.). St. Paul, MN: West.

Barusch, A. S., & Spaid, W. M. (1989). Gender differences in caregiving: Why do wives report greater burden? *The Gerontologist, 29*, 667–676.

Bazargan, M., Barbre, A. R., & Torres-Gil, F. M. (1992). Voting behavior among low-income Black elderly: A multi-election perspective. *The Gerontologist, 12*, 584–591.

Beimler, R. R., & Greenleigh, J. (1991). *The days of the dead*. San Francisco: Collins.

Belgrave, L. L. (1988). The effects of race differences in work history, work attitudes, economic resources and health on women's retirement. *Research on Aging, 10*, 383–398.

Belgrave, L. L. (1989). Understanding women's retirement: Progress and pitfalls. *Generations, 13*, 99–152.

Belgrave, L. L., Haug, M. R., & Gomez-Bellenge, F. (1987). Gender and race differences in effects of health and pension on retirement before 65. *Comprehensive Gerontology, 1*, 109–117.

Bell, D., Kasschau, P., & Zellman, G. (1976). *Delivering services to elderly members of minority groups: A critical review of the literature.* Santa Monica, CA: Rand.

Bellantoni, M. F., & Blackman, M. R. (1996). Menopause and its consequences. In E. L. Schneider & J. W. Rowe (Eds.), *Handbook of the biology of aging* (pp. 415–430). San Diego, CA: Academic Press.

Belsky, J. K. (1990). *The psychology of aging: Theory, research and interventions* (2nd ed.). Pacific Grove, CA: Brooks/Cole.

Bengtson, V. L. (1979). Ethnicity and aging: Problems and issues in current social science inquiry. In D. E. Gelfand & A. J. Kutzik (Eds.), *Ethnicity and aging* (pp. 9–30). New York: Springer.

Bengtson, V. L., Cuellar, J. B., & Ragan, P. K. (1977). Stratum contrasts and similarities in attitudes toward death. *Journal of Gerontology, 32*, 76–88.

Bengtson, V. L., Grigsby, E. D., Corry, E. M., & Hruby, M. (1977). Relating academic research to community concerns: A case study in collaborative effort. *Journal of Social Issues, 33*, 75–92.

Billingsley, A. (1968). *Black families in White America.* Englewood Cliffs, NJ: Prentice Hall.

Binstock, R. H., & George, L. K. (Eds.). (1996). *Handbook of aging and the social sciences* (4th ed.). San Diego, CA: Academic Press.

Birren, J. E. (1988). A contribution to the theory of the psychology of aging: As counterparts of development. In J. E. Birren & V. L. Bengtson (Eds.), *Emergent theories of aging* (pp. 153–176). New York: Springer.

Birren, J. E., & Schaie, K. W. (Eds.). (1996). *Handbook of the psychology of aging* (4th ed.). San Diego, CA: Academic Press.

Block, M. R. (1984). Retirement preparation needs of women. In H. Dennis (Ed.), *Retirement preparation* (pp. 129–140). Lexington, MA: Lexington Books.

Block, M. R., Davidson, J. L., & Grambs, J. D. (1981). *Women over forty.* New York: Springer.

Bonwell, C. C., & Eison, J. A. (1991). *Active learning creating excitement in the classroom* (ASHE-ERIC Higher Education Report 91, No. 1). Washington, DC: ERIC Clearinghouse on Higher Education.

Bossé, R., Aldwin, C. M., Levinson, M. R., & Ekerdt, D. J. (1987). Mental health differences among retirees and workers: Findings from the Normative Aging Study. *Psychology and Aging, 2*, 383–389.

Bound, J., Schuenbann, M., & Waidmann, T. (1996). Race differences in labor force attachment and disability status. *The Gerontologist, 36*, 311–321.

Braun, K. L., Takamura, J. C., Forman, S. M., Sasaki, P. A., & Meininger, L. (1995). Developing and testing outreach materials on Alzheimer's disease for Asian and Pacific Island Americans. *The Gerontologist, 35*, 122–126.

Briggs, V. M., Fogel, W., & Schmidt, F. H. (1977). *The Chicano worker.* Austin: University of Texas Press.

Brink, T. L. (Ed.). (1992). *Hispanic aged mental health.* New York: Haworth Press.

Brody, E. M. (1981). Parent care as a normative family stress. *The Gerontologist, 25*, 19–28.

Brokenleg, M., & Middleton, D. (1993). Native Americans: Adapting, yet retaining. In D. P. Irish, K. F. Lundquist, & V. J. Nelsen (Eds.), *Ethnic variations in dying, death, and grief: Diversity in universality* (pp. 101–112). Washington, DC: Taylor & Francis.

Bryant, S., & Rakowski, W. (1992). Predictors of mortality among elderly African-Americans. *Research on Aging, 14*, 50–67.

Bull, C. N. (Ed.). (1993). *Aging in rural America*. Newbury Park, CA: Sage.

Burtless, G. T. (1987). Occupational effects on the health and work capacity of older men. In G. T. Burtless (Ed.), *Work, health and income among the elderly* (pp. 103–150). Washington, DC: Brookings Institution.

Burton, L. M., Dilworth-Anderson, P., & Bengtson, V. L. (1992). Creating culturally relevant ways of thinking about diversity and aging. In E. P. Stanford & F. M. Torres-Gil (Eds.), *Diversity: New approaches to ethnic minority aging* (pp. 129–140). Amityville, NY: Baywood.

Butler, R. N., Lewis, M. I., & Sunderland, T. (1991). *Aging and mental health: Positive psychosocial and biomedical approaches* (4th ed.). New York: Merrill.

Byer, C. O., & Shainberg, L. W. (1991). *Dimensions of human sexuality* (3rd ed.). Dubuque, IA: William C. Brown.

Byer, C. O., & Shainberg, L. W. (1995). *Dimensions of human sexuality* (4th ed.). Dubuque, IA: William C. Brown.

Caldwell, C. H., Chatters, L. M., Billingsley, A., & Taylor, R. J. (1995). Church-based support programs for elderly Black adults: Congregational and clergy characteristics. In M. Kimble, S. H. McFadden, J. W. Ellor, & J. J. Seeber (Eds.), *Aging, spirituality, and religion: A handbook* (pp. 306–324). Minneapolis, MN: Fortress Press.

Cantor, M. H. (1979). The informal support system of New York's inner city elderly: Is ethnicity a factor? In D. E. Gelfand & A. J. Kutzik (Eds.), *Ethnicity and aging* (pp. 153–174). New York: Springer.

Caro, F. G., & Bass, S. A. (1995). Increasing volunteering among older people. In S. A. Bass (Ed.), *Older and active: How Americans over 55 are contributing to society* (pp. 71–96). New Haven, CT: Yale University Press.

Carr, J., & Vitaliano, P. (1985). The theoretical implications of converging research on depression and the culture-bound syndromes. In A. Kleinman & B. Good (Eds.), *Culture and depression: Studies in the anthropology and cross-cultural psychiatry of affect and disorder* (pp. 244–266). Berkeley: University of California Press.

Carson, V. B. (Ed.). (1989). *Spiritual dimensions of nursing practice*. Philadelphia: W. B. Saunders.

Cassidy, M. L. (1985). Role conflict in the postparental period. *Research on Aging, 7*, 433–454.

Cavanaugh, J. C. (1993). *Adult development and aging* (2nd ed.). Pacific Grove, CA: Brooks/Cole.

Chan, S. (1992). Families with Filipino roots. In E. W. Lynch & M. J. Hanson (Eds.), *Developing cross-cultural competence* (pp. 259–300). Baltimore: Paul H. Brookes.

Chatters, L. M., & Taylor, R. J. (1989). Age differences in religious participation among Black adults. *Journal of Gerontology: Social Sciences, 44*, S183–S189.

Chatters, L. M., Taylor, R. J., & Jackson, J. S. (1985). Size and composition of the informal helper networks of elderly Blacks. *Journal of Gerontology, 40*, 605–614.

Chen, J. N., & Soto, D. (1979). *Service delivery to aged minorities: Techniques of successful programs.* Sacramento, CA: Sacramento State University, School of Social Work.

Chen, Y. P. (1994). Improving the economic security of minority persons as they enter old age. In *Minority elders: Five goals toward building a public policy base* (2nd ed., pp. 22–31). Washington, DC: Gerontological Society of America.

Chirikos, T. N., & Nestel, G. (1983). *Economic aspects of self-reported work disability.* Columbus: Center for Human Resource Research, Ohio State University.

Christiansen, D. (1981). Dignity in aging. In C. LeFevre & P. D. LeFevre (Eds.), *Aging and the human spirit: A reader in religion and gerontology* (pp. 297–309). Chicago: Exploration Press.

Clark, D. O., Maddox, G. L., & Steinhauser, K. (1993). Race, aging and functional health. *Journal of Aging and Health, 5*, 536–553.

Clipp, E. C., & George, L. K. (1990). Psychotropic drug use among caregivers of patients with dementia. *Journal of the American Geriatrics Society, 38*, 227–235.

Collins, R., & Coltrane, S. (1991). *Sociology of marriage and the family: Gender, love, and property.* Chicago: Nelson-Hall.

Colon, I. (1992). Race, belief in destiny, and seat belt usage: A pilot study. *American Journal of Public Health, 82*, 875–877.

Cone, J. H. (1985). Black theology in American religion. *Journal of the American Academy of Religion, 53*, 755–771.

Cool, L. E. (1990). The effects of social class and ethnicity on the aging process. In P. Silverman (Ed.), *The elderly as modern pioneers* (pp. 263–282). Bloomington: Indiana University Press.

Corcoran, M., & Duncan, G. J. (1978). A summary of Part 1 findings. In G. J. Duncan & J. N. Morgan (Eds.), *Five thousand American families* (Vol. 6, pp. 3–46). Ann Arbor: Institute for Social Research, University of Michigan.

Cormican, J. D. (1976). Linguistic subcultures and social work practice. *Social Casework, 57*, 589–592.

Cormican, J. D. (1978). Linguistic issues in interviewing. *Social Casework, 59*, 145–151.

Costa, P. T., McCrae, R. R., Zonderman, A. B., Barbarno, H. E., Lebowitz, B., & Larson, D. M. (1986). Cross-sectional studies of personality in a national sample: Stability in neuroticism, extroversion, and openness. *Psychology and Aging, 1*, 144–150.

Covey, H. C. (1988). Historical terminology used to represent older people. *The Gerontologist, 28*, 291–297.

Coward, R. T., McLaughlin, D. K., Duncan, R., & Bull, C. N. (1994). An overview of health and aging in rural America. In R. T. Coward, D. K. McLaughlin, R. Duncan, & C. N. Bull (Eds.), *Health services for rural elders* (pp. 1–32). New York: Springer.

Cox, C., & Gelfand, D. E. (1987). Patterns of family assistance, exchange and satisfaction among Hispanic, Portuguese, and Vietnamese elderly. *Journal of Cross-Cultural Gerontology, 2*, 241–255.

Cox, C., & Monk, A. (1993). Black and Hispanic caregivers of dementia victims: Their needs and implications for services. In C. M. Barresi & D. E. Stull (Eds.), *Ethnic elderly & long-term care* (pp. 57–67). New York: Springer.

Cozby, P. C. (1993). *Methods in behavioral research* (5th ed.). Mountain View, CA: Mayfield.

Cragg, K. (1988). *Readings in the Qur'an*. London: Collins.

Crandall, R. C. (1980). *Gerontology: A behavioral science approach*. Reading, MA: Addison-Wesley.

Craven, M. (1973). *I heard the owl call my name*. New York: Dell.

Cronin, C. A. (1988). Resources for managers of an aging work force. In H. Dennis (Ed.), *Fourteen steps in managing an aging work force* (pp. 157–169). Lexington, MA: D. C. Heath.

Cuellar, J. B., Harris, L. C., & Jasso, R. (1980). An acculturation scale for Mexican American normals and clinical populations. *Hispanic Journal of Behavioral Sciences, 3*, 199–217.

Curley, L. (1978). Retirement: An Indian perspective. In E. P. Stanford (Ed.), *Retirement: Concepts and realities of minority elders* (pp. 43–47). San Diego, CA: San Diego State University.

Cutler, S. J., & Hendricks, J. (1990). Leisure time use across the life course. In R. H. Binstock & L. K. George (Eds.), *Handbook of aging and social sciences* (3rd ed., pp. 169–185). New York: Academic Press.

Cytron, B. D. (1993). To honor the dead and comfort the mourners: Traditions in Judaism. In D. P. Irish, K. F. Lundquist, & V. J. Nelsen (Eds.), *Ethnic variations in dying, death, and grief: Diversity in universality* (pp. 113–124). Washington, DC: Taylor & Francis.

Danigelis, N. C., & McIntosh, B. R. (1993). Resources and the productive activity of elders: Race and gender as contexts. *Journals of Gerontology, 48*, S192–S203.

Dannefer, D. (1988). The neglect of variability in the study of aging. In J. E. Birren & V. L. Bengtson (Eds.), *Emergent theories of aging* (pp. 356–384). New York: Springer.

Danner, V. (1988). *The Islamic tradition*. Amity, NY: Amity House.

Davies, H., Priddy, J. M., & Tinklenberg, J. R. (1986). Support groups for male caregivers of Alzheimer's patients. *Clinical Gerontologist, 5*, 385–395.

Denny, F. M. (1985). *An introduction to Islam*. New York: Macmillan.

DeRenzo, E., & Malley, J. (1992). Increasing use of ageist language in skin-care product advertising: 1969 through 1988. *Journal of Women & Aging, 4*, 105–126.

Devore, W. (1983). Ethnic reality: The life model and work with Black families. *Social Casework, 63*, 525–531.

Dieppa, M. D. (1978). *Retirement: A differential experience of Mexican Americans and Anglos*. Unpublished doctoral dissertation, University of Denver.

Dillon, K. M., & Jones, B. S. (1981). Attitudes toward aging portrayed by birthday cards. *International Journal of Aging and Human Development, 13*, 79–84.

Dowd, J. J. (1975). Aging as exchange: A preface to theory. *Journal of Gerontology, 30*, 584–594.

Dowd, J. J. (1978). Aging as exchange: A test of the distributive justice proposition. *Pacific Sociological Review, 21*, 351–375.

Dowd, J. J., & Bengtson, V. L. (1978). Aging in minority populations: An examination of the double jeopardy hypothesis. *Journal of Gerontology, 33*, 427–436.

Edmonds, M. M. (1993). Physical health. In J. S. Jackson, L. M. Chatters, & R. J. Taylor (Eds.), *Aging in Black America* (pp. 151–166). Newbury Park, CA: Sage.

Eglit, H. C. (1992). *Age discrimination*. Colorado Springs, CO: Shepard's/McGraw Hill.

Eisenbruch, M. (1984). Cross-cultural aspects of bereavement. II: Ethnic and cultural variations in the development of bereavement practices. *Culture, Medicine and Psychiatry, 8,* 315–347.

Ellor, J. W., & Bracki, M. A. (1995). Assessment, referral and networking. In M. Kimble, S. H. McFadden, J. W. Ellor, & J. J. Seeber (Eds.), *Aging, spirituality, and religion: A handbook* (pp. 148–160). Minneapolis, MN: Fortress Press.

Eng, E., Hatch, J., & Callan, A. (1985). Institutionalizing social support through the church and the community. *Health Education Quarterly, 12,* 81–92.

Engler, J., & Goleman, D. (1992). *The consumer's guide to psychotherapy*. New York: Simon & Schuster.

Erikson, E. H. (1958). *Young man Luther: A study in psychoanalysis and history*. New York: Norton.

Erikson, E. H. (1963). *Childhood and society* (2nd ed.). New York: Norton.

Erikson, E. H.(1969). *Gandhi's truth: On the origins of militant nonviolence*. New York: Norton.

Erikson, E. H. (1982). *The life cycle completed: A review*. New York: Norton.

Fandetti, D. V., & Gelfand, D. E. (1976). Care of the aged: Attitudes of White ethnic families. *The Gerontologist, 16,* 544–549.

Feinson, M. J. (1991). Re-examining some common beliefs about mental health and aging. In B. B. Hess & E. W. Markson (Eds.), *Growing old in America* (4th ed., pp. 125–135). New Brunswick, NJ: Transaction.

Ferraro, G., Trevathan, W., & Levy, J. (1994). *Anthropology: An applied perspective*. Minneapolis, MN: West.

Ferraro, K. F. (1987). Double jeopardy to health for Black older adults. *Journal of Gerontology, 42,* 528–533.

Ferraro, K. F. (1990). Cohort analysis of retirement preparation, 1974–1981. *Journal of Gerontology: Social Science, 45,* S21–S31.

Ferraro, K. F. (1993). Are Black older adults health pessimistic? *Journal of Health and Social Behavior, 34,* 201–214.

Fiti, J. E., & Kovar, M. G. (1987). The supplement on aging to the 1984 National Health Interview Survey. *Vital and Health Statistics, 1*(21).

Flaim, P. O. (1973). Discouraged workers and changes in unemployment. *Monthly Labor Review, 96,* 8–16.

Ford, C. V., & Sbordone, R. J. (1980). Attitudes of psychiatrists toward elderly patients. *American Journal of Psychiatry, 137,* 571–575.

Frankfort-Nachmias, C. F., & Nachmias, D. (1992). *Research methods in the social sciences* (4th ed.). New York: St. Martin's Press.

Fried, S. B. (1988). Learning activities for understanding aging. *Teaching of Psychology, 15,* 160–162.

Fried, S. B., & Mehrotra, C. M. (1994, November). *Active learning strategies for diversity and aging*. Poster session presented at the annual meeting of the Gerontological Society of America, Atlanta, GA.

Fried, S. B., Van Booven, D., & MacQuarrie, C. (1993). *Older adulthood: Learning activities for understanding aging*. Baltimore: Health Professions Press.

Fry, C. L. (1988). Theories of age and culture. In J. E. Birren & V. L. Bengtson (Eds.), *Emergent theories of aging* (pp. 447–481). New York: Springer.

Fullmer, E. S. (1995). Challenging biases against families of older gays and lesbians. In G. C. Smith, S. S. Tobin, E. A. Roberterson-Tchabo, & P. W. Power (Eds.), *Strengthening aging families: Diversity in practice and policy* (pp. 99–119). Thousand Oaks, CA: Sage.

Gafner, G., & Duckett, S. (1992). Treating the sequelae of a curse in elderly Mexican Americans. In T. L. Brink (Ed.), *Hispanic aged mental health* (pp. 145–153). New York: Haworth Press.

Gallego, D. T. (1988). Religiosity as a coping mechanism among Hispanic elderly. In M. Sotomayor & H. Curiel (Eds.), *Hispanic elderly: A cultural signature*. Edinburg: University of Texas, Pan American Press.

Gallup Report. (1984). *Religion in America*. Princeton, NJ: Princeton Religion Research Center.

Garcia, A. (1993). Income security and elderly Latinos. In M. Sotomayor & A. Garcia (Eds.), *Elderly Latinos: Issues and solutions for the 21st century* (pp. 17–28). Washington, DC: National Hispanic Council on Aging.

Garcia, J. (1985). A needs assessment of elderly Hispanics in an inner-city senior citizen complex: Implications for practice. *Journal of Applied Gerontology, 4*, 72–85.

Garcia, J., Kosberg, J., Mangum, W., Henderson, J., & Henderson, C. (1992, November). *Caregiving for and by Hispanic elders: Perceptions of four generations of women*. Paper presented at the annual meeting of the Gerontological Society of America, Washington, DC.

Gardner, R. (1994). Mortality. In N. W. Zane, D. T. Takeuchi, & K. N. J. Young (Eds.), *Confronting critical health issues of Asian and Pacific Islander Americans* (pp. 53–104). Thousand Oaks, CA: Sage.

Gelfand, D. E. (1982). *Aging: The ethnic factor*. Boston: Little, Brown.

Gelfand, D. E. (1994). *Aging and ethnicity: Knowledge and services*. New York: Springer.

Gelfand, D. E., & Barresi, C. M. (1987). Current perspectives in ethnicity and aging. In D. E. Gelfand & C. M. Barresi (Eds.), *Ethnic dimensions of aging* (pp. 5–17). New York: Springer.

Gelles, R. (1995). *Contemporary families: A sociological view*. Thousand Oaks, CA: Sage.

Genovese, E. D. (1976). *Roll, Jordan, roll: The world the slaves made*. New York: Vintage Books.

George, L. K. (1981). Subjective well-being: Conceptual and methodological issues. In C. Eisdorfer (Ed.), *Annual review of gerontology and geriatrics* (pp. 345–384). New York: Springer.

George, L. K. (1984). The burden of caregiving: How much? What kinds? For whom? *Center Reports on Advances in Caregiving, 8*, 1–8.

George, L. K. (1990). Social structure, social processes and social-psychological states. In R. H. Binstock & L. K. George (Eds.), *Handbook of aging and the social sciences* (3rd ed., pp. 186–204). San Diego, CA: Academic Press.

George, L. K., Fillenbaum, G. G., & Palmore, E. B. (1984). Sex differences in the antecedents and consequences of retirement. *Journal of Gerontology, 39*, 364–371.

George, L. K., & Gwyther, L. P. (1986). Caregiver well-being: A multidimensional examination of family caregivers of demented adults. *The Gerontologist, 26*, 253–259.

German, P. S., Shapiro, S., Skinner, E. A., VonKorff, M., Klein, L. E., Turner, R. W., Teitelbaum, M. T., Burka, J. B., & Burns, B. J. (1987). Detection and management of mental health problems of older adults by primary care providers. *Journal of the American Medical Association, 257,* 489–493.

Gibbs, T. (1988). Health-seeking behavior of elderly Blacks. In J. S. Jackson (Ed.), *The Black American elderly* (pp. 282–291). New York: Springer.

Gibson, R. C. (1982). Blacks at middle and late life: Resources and coping. Annals of the American Academy of Political and Social Science, 464, 79–90.

Gibson, R. C. (1986a). Blacks in an aging society. *Proceedings of the American Academy of Arts and Sciences, 115,* 349–371.

Gibson, R. C. (1986b). Outlook for the Black family. In A. Pifer & L. Bronte (Eds.), *Our aging society* (pp. 181–197). New York: Norton.

Gibson, R. C. (1987). Reconceptualizing retirement for Black Americans. *The Gerontologist, 27,* 691–698.

Gibson, R. C. (1991a). Age-by-race differences in the health and functioning of elderly persons. *Journal of Aging and Health, 3,* 335–351.

Gibson, R. C. (1991b). The subjective retirement of Black Americans. *Journal of Gerontology: Social Sciences, 46,* S204–S209.

Gibson, R. C. (1994). The age-by-race gap in health and mortality in the older population: A social science research agenda. *The Gerontologist, 34,* 454–462.

Gibson, R. C., & Jackson, J. S. (1992). The Black oldest old: Health, functioning, and informal support. In R. M. Suzman, D. P. Willis, & K. G. Manton (Eds.), *The oldest old* (pp. 321–340). New York: Oxford University Press.

Gibson, R. C., & Stoller, E. P. (1994). *Worlds of difference: Inequality in the aging experience.* Thousand Oaks, CA: Pine Forge Press.

Gilanshah, F. (1993). Islamic customs regarding death. In D. P. Irish, K. F. Lundquist, & V. J. Nelsen (Eds.), *Ethnic variations in dying, death, and grief: Diversity in universality* (pp. 137–145). Washington, DC: Taylor & Francis.

Gilhooly, M. L. M. (1984). The impact of care-giving on care-givers: Factors associated with the psychological well-being of people supporting a demented relative in the community. *British Journal of Medical Psychology, 57,* 35–44.

Giordano, J. (1992). Ethnicity and aging. *Journal of Gerontological Social Work, 6,* 23–37.

Goodwin, J. (1994). *Price of honor.* Boston: Little, Brown.

Gordon, C., Gaitz, C. M., & Scott, J. (1976). Leisure and lives: Personal expressivity across the life span. In R. H. Binstock & E. Shanas (Eds.), *Handbook of aging and the social sciences* (2nd ed., pp. 310–341). New York: Van Nostrand Reinhold.

Greene, R. L., Jackson, J. S., & Neighbors, H. W. (1993). Mental health and help-seeking behavior. In J. S. Jackson, L. M. Chatters, & R. J. Taylor (Eds.), *Aging in Black America* (pp. 185–200). Newbury Park, CA: Sage.

Gustman, A. L., & Steinmeier, T. L. (1994). *Retirement in a family context: A structural model for husbands and wives* (NBER Working Paper No. 4629). Cambridge, MA: National Bureau of Economic Research.

Gutmann, D. L. (1966). Mayan aging—A comparative TAT study. *Psychiatry, 29,* 246–259.

Gutmann, D. L. (1968). Aging among the highland Maya: A comparative study. In B. Neugarten (Ed.), *Middle age and aging* (pp. 444–452). Chicago: University of Chicago Press.

Gutmann, D. L. (1974). Alternatives to disengagement: The old men of the Highland Druze. In R. A. LeVine (Ed.), *Culture and personality: Contemporary readings* (pp. 232–245). Chicago: Aldine.

Gutmann, D. L. (1987). *Reclaimed powers: Toward a new psychology of men and women in later life*. New York: Basic Books.

Gutmann, D. L (1992). Culture and mental health in later life revisited. In J. E. Birren, R. B. Sloane, & G. D. Cohen (Eds.), *Handbook of mental health and aging* (2nd ed., pp. 75–97). San Diego, CA: Academic Press.

Haber, D. (1984). Church-based programs for Black caregivers of noninstitutionalized elders. *Journal of Gerontological Social Work, 7,* 43–49.

Hagestad, G. O., & Neugarten, B. L. (1985). Age and the life course. In E. Shanas & R. H. Binstock (Eds.), *Handbook of aging and the social sciences* (2nd ed., pp. 36–61). New York: Van Nostrand Reinhold.

Hall, D. K. (1988). *The border: Life on the line*. New York: Abbeville.

Hamabata, M. M. (1990). *Crested kimono: Power and love in the Japanese business family*. Ithaca, NY: Cornell University Press.

Harbert, A. S., & Ginsberg, L. H. (1979). *Human services for older adults*. Belmont, CA: Wadsworth.

Harel, Z., Erlich, P., & Hubbard, R. (Eds.). (1990). *The vulnerable aged: People, services, and policies*. New York: Springer.

Hatch, L. R. (1992). Gender differences in orientation toward retirement from paid labor. *Gender and Society, 6*(1), 66.

Haug, M. H., Belgrave, L. L., & Jones, S. (1992). Partner's health and retirement adaptation of women and their husbands. *Journal of Women and Aging, 43*(3), 5–29.

Hayes, C. L., & Guttmann, D. L. (1986). The need for collaboration among religious, ethnic, and public-service institutions. In C. L. Hayes, R. A. Kalish, & D. L. Guttmann (Eds.), *European-American elderly* (pp. 198–211). New York: Springer.

Hayward, M. D. (1986). The influence of occupational characteristics on men's early retirement. *Social Forces, 64,* 1032–1045.

Height, D., Toya, J., Kamekawa, L., & Maldonaldo, D. (1981). Senior volunteering in minority communities. *Generations, 5,* 14–18.

Helson, R., & McCabe, L. (1994). The social clock project in middle age. In B. F. Turner & L. E. Troll (Eds.), *Women growing older: Psychological perspectives* (pp. 68–93). Thousand Oaks, CA: Sage.

Helson, R., Mitchell, V., & Moane, G. (1984). Personality and patterns of adherence and nonadherence to the social clock. *Journal of Personality and Social Psychology, 46,* 1079–1096.

Helson, R., & Moane, G. (1987). Personality change in women from college to mid-life. *Journal of Personality and Social Psychology, 52,* 1176–1186.

Helson, R., & Wink, P. (1992). Personality changes in women from the early 40's to the early 50's. *Psychology and Aging, 7,* 46–55.

Henderson, J. N. (1994). Ethnic and racial issues. In J. F. Gubrium & A. Sankar (Eds.), *Qualitative methods in aging research* (pp. 33–50). Thousand Oaks, CA: Sage.

Henderson, K. A. (1990). The meaning of leisure for women: An integrative review of the research. *Journal of Leisure Research, 22,* 228–243.

Herz, D. E. (1988). Employment characteristics of older women, 1987. *Monthly Labor Review, 111*(9), 3–12.

Herz, F. M., & Rosen, E. J. (1982). Jewish families. In M. McGoldrick, J. W. Pearce, & J. Giordano (Eds.), *Ethnicity and family therapy* (pp. 364–392). New York: Guilford Press.

Herzog, A. R. (1989). Physical and mental health in older women: Selected research issues and data sources. In A. R. Herzog, K. C. Holden, & M. M. Seltzer (Eds.), *Health and economic status of older women* (pp. 35–91). Amityville, NY: Baywood.

Hill, R. (1972). *The strengths of Black families.* New York: Emerson-Hall.

Hing, E., & Bloom, B. (1990). Long-term care for the functionally dependent elderly. *Vital and Health Statistics, 13,* 28.

Hirsch, C., Kent, D. P., & Silverman, S. L. (1972). Homogeneity and heterogeneity among low-income Negro and White aged. In D. P. Kent, R. J. Kastenbaum, & S. Sherwood (Eds.), *Research planning and action for the elderly: The power and potential of social science* (pp. 400–500). New York: Behavioral Publishers.

Hlavaty, J. P. (1986, April). *Alzheimer's disease and the male spouse caregiver.* Paper presented at the 10th Annual Ohio Conference on Aging, Columbus.

Hollis, F., & Woods, M. E. (1981). *Casework: A psychosocial therapy* (3rd ed.). New York: Random House.

Holtzman, J. M., Berman, H., & Ham, R. (1980). Health and early retirement decisions. *Journal of the American Geriatrics Society, 28,* 23–28.

Hooyman, N. R., & Kiyak, H. A. (1996). *Social gerontology: A multidisciplinary perspective* (4th ed.). Needham Heights, MA: Allyn & Bacon.

Horn, J. C., & Meer, J. (1987). The vintage years. *Psychology Today, 21,* 76–84.

Hornstein, G. A., & Wapner, S. (1984). The experience of the retiree's social network during the transition to retirement. In C. M. Aanstoos (Ed.), *Exploring the lived world: Readings in phenomenological psychology* (pp. 119–136). Carrollton: West Georgia College Press.

Hornstein, G. A., & Wapner, S. (1985). Modes of experiencing and adapting to retirement. *International Journal of Aging and Human Development, 21,* 548–571.

Horowitz, A. (1985). Sons and daughters as caregivers to older parents: Differences in role performance and consequences. *The Gerontologist, 25,* 612–617.

House, J. S., Kessler, R. C., Herzog, A. R., Mero, R. P., Kinney, A. M., & Breslow, M. J. (1992). Social stratification, age, and health. In K. W. Schaie, D. G. Blazer, & J. S. House (Eds.), *Aging, health behaviors, and health outcomes* (pp. 1–32). Hillsdale, NJ: Erlbaum.

Husaini, B., Moore, S., & Cain, V. (1991, January). *Psychiatric symptoms and help-seeking behavior among the elderly: Black-White comparisons.* Paper presented at the Historic Black Colleges and Universities Gerontological Association meeting, Norfolk, VA.

Huyck, M. H. (1990). Gender differences in aging. In J. E. Birren & K. W. Schaie (Eds.), *Handbook of the psychology of aging* (3rd ed., pp. 124–132). San Diego, CA: Academic Press.

Huyck, M. H., & Duchon, J. (1986). Over the miles: Coping, communicating and commiserating through age-theme greeting cards. In L. Nahemow, K. A. McClusky-

Fawcett, & P. E. McGee (Eds.), *Humor and aging* (pp. 139–159). Orlando, FL: Academic Press.

Iams, H. M. (1986, March). Employment of retired-worker women. *Social Security Bulletin*, pp. 5–13.

Idler, E. L. (1987). Religious involvement and the health of the elderly: Some hypotheses and an initial test. *Social Forces, 66,* 226–238.

Irish, D. P. (1993). Introduction—Multiculturalism and the majority population. In D. P. Irish, K. F. Lundquist, & V. J. Nelsen (Eds.), *Ethnic variations in dying, death, and grief: Diversity in universality* (pp. 1–10). Washington, DC: Taylor & Francis.

Irish, D. P., Lundquist, K. F., & Nelsen, V. J. (Eds.). (1993). *Ethnic variations in dying, death, and grief: Diversity in universality.* Washington, DC: Taylor & Francis.

Jackson, J. J. (1971). The blacklands of gerontology. *Aging and Human Development, 2,* 156–171.

Jackson, J. J. (1980). *Minorities and aging.* Belmont, CA: Wadsworth.

Jackson, J. S. (1988). *The Black American elderly: Research on physical and psychological health.* New York: Springer.

Jackson, J. S., Antonucci, T. C., & Gibson, R. C. (1990). Cultural, racial, and ethnic minority influences on aging. In J. E. Birren, & K. W. Schaie (Eds.), *Handbook of the psychology of aging* (3rd ed., pp. 103–123). San Diego, CA: Academic Press.

Jackson, J. S., & Gibson, R. C. (1985). Work and retirement among the Black elderly. In Z. S. Blau (Ed.), *Current perspectives on aging the life cycle* (pp. 193–222). Greenwich, CT: JAI Press.

Jackson, M. (1972). The Black experience with death: A brief analysis through Black writings. *Omega, 3,* 203–209.

Jaffe, A. J., Cullen, R. M., & Boswell, T. D. (1980). *The changing demography of Spanish Americans.* New York: Academic Press.

Jennings, G. (1980). *Aztec: A novel.* New York: Atheneum.

Jette, A. M., (1996). Disability trends and transitions. In R. H. Binstock & L. K. George (Eds.), *Handbook of aging and the social sciences* (pp. 94–116). San Diego, CA: Academic Press.

John, R. (1991). The state of research on American Indian elders' health, income security, and social support networks. In *Minority elders: Longevity, economics, and health, building a public policy base* (pp. 38–50). Washington, DC: Gerontological Society of America.

John, R. (1994). The state of research on American Indian elders' health, income security, and social support networks. In *Minority elders: Five goals toward building a public policy base* (pp. 46–58). Washington, DC: Gerontological Society of America.

Johnson, C. L. (1985). *Growing up and growing old in Italian-American families.* New Brunswick, NJ: Rutgers University Press.

Johnson, H. R., Gibson, R. C., & Luckey, I. (1990). Health and social characteristics: Implications for services. In Z. Harel, E. A. McKinney, & M. Williams (Eds.), *Black aged: Understanding diversity and service needs* (pp. 69–81). Newbury Park, CA: Sage.

Johnson, T. W. (1995). Utilizing culture in work with aging families. In G. C. Smith, S. S. Tobin, E. A. Robertson-Tchabo, & P. W. Power (Eds.), *Strengthening aging families: Diversity in practice and policy* (pp. 175–201). Thousand Oaks, CA: Sage.

Kahana, E., Kahana, B., & Kinney, J. (1990). Coping among vulnerable elders. In Z. Harel, P. Erlich, & R. Hubbard (Eds.), *The vulnerable aged: People, services, and programs* (pp. 64–85). New York: Springer.

Kalish, R. A., & Reynolds, D. K. (1981). *Death and ethnicity: A psychocultural study.* Farmingdale, NY: Baywood. (Original work published 1976)

Kavanaugh, K. H., & Kennedy, P. H. (1992). *Promoting cultural diversity: Strategies for health care professionals.* Newbury Park, CA: Sage.

Kaye, L. W., & Applegate, J. S. (1990). *Men as caregivers to the elderly: Understanding and aiding unrecognized family support.* Lexington, MA: Lexington Books.

Keith, J. (1988). Participant observation: A modest little method whose presumption may amuse you. In K.W. Schaie, R. Campbell, W. Meredith, & J. Nesselrode (Eds.), Methodological issues in aging research (pp. 211–230). New York: Springer.

Kelly, J. R. (1994). African American caregivers: Perceptions of the caregiving situation and factors influencing the delay of the institutionalization of elders with dementia. *The ABNF Journal, 5*(4), 106–109.

Kent, D. P. (1971). The elderly in minority groups: Variant patterns of aging. *The Gerontologist, 11*, 26–29.

Kessler, R. C., Price, R. H., & Wortman, C. B. (1985). Social factors in psychopathology: Stress, social support, and coping processes. *Annual Review of Psychology, 36*, 531–572.

Kimmel, D. C. (1992). The families of older gay men and lesbians. *Generations, 16*, 37–38.

Kitano, H. H., & Daniels, R. (1995). *Asian Americans: Emerging minorities* (2nd ed.). Englewood Cliffs, NJ: Prentice Hall.

Kleinman, A. (1980). *Patients and healers in the context of culture.* Berkeley: University of California Press.

Koenig, H. G., George, L. K., & Siegler, I. C. (1988). The use of religion and other emotion-regulation coping strategies among older adults. *The Gerontologist, 28*, 303–310.

Koenig, H. G., Smiley, M., & Gonzales, J. A. P. (1988). *Religion, health, and aging.* New York: Greenwood Press.

Korte, A. O., & Villa, R. F. (1988). Life satisfaction among older Hispanics. In M. Sotomayor & H. Curiel (Eds.), *Hispanic elderly: A cultural signature* (pp. 65–94). Edinburg, TX: Pan American University Press.

Krause, N. (1988). Gender and ethnicity differences in psychological well-being. In G. L. Maddox & M. P. Lawton (Eds.), *Annual review of gerontology and geriatrics* (Vol. 8, pp. 156–186). New York: Springer.

Krause, N. (1992). Stress, religiosity, and psychological well-being among older Blacks. *Journal of Aging and Health, 4*, 412–439.

Krause, N. (1993). Race differences in life satisfaction among aged men and women. *Journal of Gerontology: Social Sciences, 48*, 235–244.

Krause, N., & Goldenhar, L. M. (1992). Acculturation and psychological distress in three groups of elderly Hispanics. *Journal of Gerontology: Social Sciences, 47*, 279–288.

Krause, N., & Tran, T. V. (1989). Stress and religious involvement among older Blacks. *Journal of Gerontology: Social Sciences, 44*, S4–S13.

Kroeger, N. (1982). Preretirement preparation: Sex differences in access, sources, and use. In M. Szinovacz (Ed.), *Women's retirement* (pp. 95–111). Beverly Hills, CA: Sage.

Krout, J., Cutler, S. J., & Coward, R. T. (1990). Correlates of senior center participation: A national analysis. *The Gerontologist, 30,* 72–79.

Krout, J. A. (1983). Knowledge and use of services by the elderly: A critical review of the literature. *International Journal of Aging and Human Development, 17,* 153–167.

Kunitz, S. J., & Levy, J. E. (1989). Aging and health among Navajo Indians. In K. Markides (Ed.), *Aging and health: Perspectives on gender, race, ethnicity, and class* (pp. 211–245). Newbury Park, CA: Sage.

Kunitz, S. J., & Levy, J. E. (1991). *Navajo aging.* Tucson: University of Arizona Press.

Lacayo, C. G. (1982). Triple jeopardy: Under-served Hispanic elders. *Generations, 6,* 25–28.

Larson, E. B., & Imai, Y. (1996). An overview of dementia and ethnicity with special emphasis on the epidemiology of dementia. In G. Yeo & D. Gallagher-Thompson (Eds.), *Ethnicity and the dementias* (pp. 9–20). Bristol, PA: Taylor & Francis.

Larson, R., Zuzanek, J., & Mannel, R. (1985). Being alone versus being with people: Disengagement in the daily experience of older adults. *Journal of Gerontology, 40,* 375–381.

Leedy, P. D. (1993). *Practical research: Planning and design* (5th ed.). New York: Macmillan.

Levin, J. S., & Markides, K. S. (1988). Religious attendance and psychological well-being in middle-aged and older Mexican Americans. *Sociological Analysis, 49,* 66–72.

Levin, J. S., & Taylor, R. J. (1993). Gender and age differences in religiosity among Black Americans. *Gerontologist, 33*(1), 16–23.

Levin, J. S., Taylor, R. J., & Chatters, L. M. (1994). Race and gender differences in religiosity among older adults: Findings from four national surveys. *Journal of Gerontology, 49,* S137–S145.

Levine, M. L. (1980). 'Age discrimination' as a legal concept for analyzing age-work issues. In P. K. Ragan (Ed.), *Work and retirement: Policy issues* (pp. 45–67). Los Angeles: University of Southern California Press.

Levy, J. E. (1967). The older American Indian. In E. G. Youmans (Ed.), *Older rural Americans* (pp. 221–238). Lexington: University of Kentucky Press.

Lichtenberg, P. A., & Strzepek, D. M. (1990). Assessment of institutionalized dementia patients' competencies to participate in intimate relationships. *The Gerontologist, 30,* 117–120.

Liebig, P. S. (1988). The work force of tomorrow: Its challenge to management. In H. Dennis (Ed.), *Fourteen steps in managing an aging work force* (pp. 3–21). Lexington, MA: Heath.

Lin-Fu, J. S. (1988). Population characteristics and health care needs of Asian Pacific Americans. *Public Health Reports, 103,* 18–27.

Liu, W. T. (1986). Health services for Asian elderly. *Research on Aging, 8,* 156–175.

Lockery, S. (1991). Family and social supports: Caregiving among racial and ethnic minority elders. *Generations, 15*(4), 58–62.

Logue, B. J. (1991). Women at risk: Predictors of financial stress for retired women workers. *The Gerontologist, 31,* 657–665.

Longino, C. F., Jr., Warheit, G. J., & Green, J. A. (1989). Class, aging, and health. In K. C. Markides (Ed.), *Aging and health: Perspectives on gender, race, ethnicity, and class* (pp. 79–109). Newbury Park, CA: Sage.

Lopez, M., & Pearson, R. E. (1985). The support needs of Puerto Rican elderly. *The Gerontologist, 25*, 483–487.

Lorig, K., & Fries, J. F. (1986). *The arthritis helpbook: A tested self-management program for coping with your arthritis.* Reading, MA: Addison-Wesley.

Lubben, J. E., & Becerra, R. M. (1987). Social support among Black, Mexican, and Chinese elderly. In D. E. Gelfand & C. M. Barresi (Eds.), *Ethnic dimensions of aging* (pp. 130–144). New York: Springer.

Luborsky, M., & Rubinstein, R. L. (1987). Ethnicity and lifetimes: Self-concepts and situational contexts of ethnic identity in late life. In D. E. Gelfand & C. M. Barresi (Eds.), *Ethnic dimensions of aging* (pp. 35–50). New York: Springer.

Maldonado, D. (1975). The Chicano aged. *Social Work, 20*, 213–216.

Maldonado, D. (1995). Religion and persons of color. In M. A. Kimble, S. H. McFadden, J. W. Ellor, & J. J. Seeber (Eds.), *Aging, spirituality, and religion: A handbook* (pp. 119–128). Minneapolis, MN: Fortress Press.

Malveaux, J. M. (1987). Comparable worth and its impact on Black women. In M. C. Simms & J. Malveaux (Eds.), *Slipping through the cracks: The status of Black women* (pp. 47–62). New Brunswick, NJ: Transaction.

Malveaux, J., & Wallace, P. (1987). Minority women in the workplace. In K. S. Koziara, M. H. Moskow, & L. D. Tanner (Eds.), *Working women: Past, present, future* (pp. 265–298). Washington, DC: Bureau of National Affairs.

Manns, W. (1981). Support systems of significant others in Black families. In H. P. McAdoo (Ed.), *Black families* (pp. 238–251). Beverly Hills, CA: Sage.

Manson, S. M. (1989). Long-term care in American Indian communities: Issues for planning and research. *The Gerontologist, 29*, 38–44.

Manson, S. M. (1993). Long-term care of older American Indians: Challenges in the development of institutional services. In C. M. Barrresi & D. E. Stull (Eds.), *Ethnic elderly & long-term care* (pp. 130–143). New York: Springer.

Manton, K. G., & Johnson, K. W. (1987). Health differentials between Blacks and Whites: Recent trends in mortality and morbidity. *Milbank Quarterly, 65*(Suppl. 1), 129–199.

Marcos, L. R., & Alpert, M. (1976). Strategies and risks in psychotherapy with bilingual patients: The phenomenon of language independence. *American Journal of Psychiatry, 133*, 1275–1278.

Markides, K. S. (1978). Reasons for retirement and adaptation to retirement by elderly Mexican Americans. In E. P. Stanford (Ed.), *Retirement: Concepts and realities of minority elders* (pp. 83–90). San Diego, CA: San Diego State University.

Markides, K. S. (Ed.). (1989). *Aging and health: Perspectives on gender, race, ethnicity, and class.* Newbury Park, CA: Sage.

Markides, K. S., & Black, S. A. (1996). Race, ethnicity, and aging: The impact of inequality. In R. H. Binstock & L. K. George (Eds.), *Handbook of aging and the social sciences* (pp. 153–170). San Diego, CA: Academic Press.

Markides, K. S., Coreil, J., & Rogers, L. P. (1989). Aging and health among Southwestern Hispanics. In K. S. Markides (Ed.), *Aging and health: Perspectives on gender, race, ethnicity, and class* (pp. 177–210). Newbury Park, CA: Sage.

Markides, K. S., Levin, J. S., & Ray, L. A. (1987). Religion, aging and life satisfaction: An eight-year, three-wave longitudinal study. *The Gerontologist, 27*, 660–665.

Markides, K. S., Liang, J., & Jackson, J. S. (1990). Race, ethnicity, and aging: Conceptual and methodological issues. In R. H. Binstock & L. K. George (Eds.), *Handbook of aging and the social sciences* (3rd ed., pp. 112–129). San Diego, CA: Academic Press.

Markides, K. S., & Martin, H. W. (1983). *Older Mexican Americans.* Austin, TX: Center for Mexican American Studies.

Markides, K. S., & Mindel, C. H. (1987). *Aging & ethnicity.* Newbury Park, CA: Sage.

Marsh, W., & Hentges, K. (1988). Mexican folk remedies and conventional medical care. *American Family Physician, 37,* 257–262.

Martin, E., & Martin, J. (1978). *The Black extended family.* Chicago: University of Chicago Press.

Masamba, J., & Kalish, R. A. (1976). Death and bereavement: The role of the Black church. *Omega, 7,* 23–34.

Masters, W. H., & Johnson, V. E. (1966). *Human sexual response.* Boston: Little, Brown.

Matsumoto, D. (1996). *Culture and psychology.* Pacific Grove, CA: Brooks/Cole.

McCartney, J. R., Izeman, H., Roger, D., & Cohen, N. (1987). Sexuality and the institutionalized elderly. *Journal of the American Geriatrics Society, 35,* 331–333.

McCrae, R. R., & Costa, P. T. (1984). *Emerging lives and enduring dispositions: Personality in adulthood.* Boston: Little, Brown.

McCrae, R. R., & Costa, P. T. (1988). Age, personality and the spontaneous self-concept. *Journal of Gerontology: Social Sciences, 43,* 177–185.

McDonald, M. (1973). The management of grief: A study of Black funeral practices. *Omega, 4,* 139–148.

McGoldrick, M. (1982). Ethnicity and family therapy: An overview. In M. McGoldrick, J. W. Pearce, & J. Giordano (Eds.), *Ethnicity and family therapy* (pp. 3–30). New York: Guilford Press.

McGuire, F. A., Dottavio, D., & O'Leary, J. T. (1986). Constraints to participation in outdoor recreation across the life span: A nationwide study of limitors and prohibitors. *The Gerontologist, 26,* 538–544.

McSherry, E. (1983). The spiritual dimension of elder health care. *Generations, 8,* 13–21.

Mehrotra, C. M. (1984). Appraising the performance of older workers. In P. K. Robinson, J. Livingston, & J. E. Birren (Eds.), *Aging and technological advances* (pp. 353–355). New York: Plenum.

Meyers, C., & Jones, T. B. (1993). *Promoting active learning.* San Francisco: Jossey-Bass.

Mindel, C. H. (1980). Extended familism among urban Mexican Americans, Anglos, and Blacks. *Hispanic Journal of Behavioral Sciences, 2,* 21–34.

Mir, M. (1987). *Dictionary of Qur'anic terms and concepts.* New York: Garland.

Mitchell, O. S., Levine, P. B., & Pozzebon, S. (1988). Retirement differences by industry and occupation. *The Gerontologist, 28,* 545–551.

Mitchell, V., & Helson, R. (1990). Women's prime of life: Is it the 50's? *Psychology of Women Quarterly, 14,* 451–470.

Moberg, D. O. (1971). *Spiritual well-being: Background and issues.* Washington, DC: White House Conference on Aging.

Moberg, D. O. (1984). Subjective measures of spiritual well-being. *Review of Religious Research, 25,* 351–365.

Moen, P. (1996). Gender, age and the life course. In R. H. Binstock & L. K. George (Eds.), *Handbook of aging and the social sciences* (4th ed., pp. 171–187). San Diego, CA: Academic Press.

Moore, J. (1970). The death culture of Mexico and Mexican Americans. *Omega, 1*, 271–291.

Morioka-Douglas, N., & Yeo, G. (1990). *Aging and health: Asian/Pacific Island American elders* (Working Paper Series No. 3). Stanford, CA: Stanford Geriatric Education Center.

Morris, A. (1984). *The origins of the civil rights movement: Black communities organizing for change.* New York: Free Press.

Morycz, R. R., Malloy, J., Bozich, M., & Martz, P. (1987). Racial differences in family burden: Clinical implications for social work. *Journal of Gerontological Social Work, 10*, 133–154.

Moss, F. E., & Halamandaris, V. J. (1977). *Too old, too sick, too bad.* Germantown, MD: Aspen Systems.

Moss, M. S., & Lawton, M. P. (1982). Time budgets of older people: A window on four life-styles. *Journal of Gerontology, 37*, 115–123.

Mutram, E. (1985). Intergenerational family support among Blacks and Whites: A response to culture or to socioeconomic difference? *Journal of Gerontology, 40*, 382–398.

Myerhoff, B. G. (1979). *Number our days.* New York: Dutton.

National Indian Council on Aging. (1981). *American Indian elderly: A national profile.* Albuquerque, NM: National Indian Council on Aging.

National Institute on Adult Daycare. (1984). *Standards for adult day care.* Washington, DC: National Council on Aging.

National Pacific/Asian Resource Center on Aging. (1989). *Demographic and socioeconomic characteristics of the Pacific/Asian elderly* (Working draft). Seattle, WA: Author.

Negstad, J., & Arnholt, R. (1986). Day centers for older adults: Parish and agency partnership. *Journal of Religion and Aging, 2*(4), 25–31.

Neugarten, B. L., & Hagestad, G. O. (1976). Age and the life course. In R. H. Binstock & E. Shanas (Eds.), *Handbook of aging and the social sciences* (pp. 35–55). New York: Van Nostrand Reinhold.

Newman, E. S., Sherman, S. R., & Higgins, C. E. (1982). Retirement expectations and plans: A comparison of professional men and women. In M. Szinovacz (Ed.), *Women's retirement* (pp. 113–122). Beverly Hills, CA: Sage.

O'Hare, W. P. (1992). America's minorities—The demographics of diversity. *Population Bulletin, 47*(4).

O'Hare, W. P., & Felt, J. (1991). *Asian Americans: America's fastest growing minority group.* Washington, DC: Population Reference Bureau.

Ortega, S. T., Crutchfield, R. D., & Rushing, W. A. (1983). Race differences in elderly personal well-being. *Research on Aging, 5*, 101–118.

Palmore, E. B. (1981). Attitudes toward aging shown by humor: A review. In L. Nahemow, K. A. McClusky-Fawcett, & P. E. McGee (Eds.), *Humor and aging* (pp. 101–119). Orlando, FL: Academic Press.

Palmore, E. B., Burchett, B. M., Fillenbaum, G. G., George, L. K., & Wallman, L. M. (1985). *Retirement: Causes and consequences.* New York: Springer.

228   REFERENCES

Pargament, K. I. (1992). Of means and ends: Religion and the search for significance. *International Journal for the Psychology of Religion, 2,* 201–299.

Peplau, L. A. (1991). Lesbian and gay relationships. In J. C. Gonsiorek & J. D. Weinrich (Eds.), *Homosexuality: Research implications for public policy* (pp. 177–196). Thousand Oaks, CA: Sage.

Pepper, L. G. (1976). Patterns of leisure and adjustment to retirement. *The Gerontologist, 16,* 441–446.

Perry, H. L. (1993). Mourning and funeral customs of African Americans. In D. P. Irish, K. F. Lundquist, & V. J. Nelsen (Eds.), *Ethnic variations in dying, death, and grief: Diversity in universality* (pp. 51–65). Washington, DC: Taylor & Francis.

Poston, D. L., & Alvirez, D. (1973). On the cost of being a Mexican American worker. *Social Science Quarterly, 53,* 697–709.

Price, M. (1994). African American daughters' attitudes about caregiving to frail, elderly parents. *The ABNF Journal, 5*(4), 112–116.

Quinn, J. F., & Kozy, M. (1996). The role of bridge jobs in retirement transition: Gender, race, and ethnicity. *The Gerontologist, 36,* 363–372.

Rabins, P. V., Lucas, M., Teitelbaum, M. L., Mark, S. R., & Folstein, M. F. (1983). Utilization of psychiatric consultation for elderly patients. *Journal of the American Geriatrics Society, 31,* 581–585.

Racy, J. (1969). Death in an Arab culture. *Annals of the New York Academy of Sciences, 64,* 871–880.

Raskind, M. A., & Peskind, E. R. (1992). Alzheimer's disease and other dementing disorders. In J. E. Birren, R. B. Sloane, & G. D. Cohen (Eds.), *Handbook of mental health and aging* (2nd ed., pp. 477–513). San Diego, CA: Academic Press.

Rathbone-McCuan, E., & Coward, R. T. (1985, November). *Male helpers: Unrecognized informal supports.* Paper presented at the 38th Annual Scientific Meeting of the Gerontological Society of America, New Orleans, LA.

Reynolds, D. K., & Kalish, R. A. (1974). Anticipation of futurity as a function of ethnicity and age. *Journal of Gerontology, 29,* 224–231.

Rhodes, L. (1982). Retirement, economics and the minority aged. In R. C. Manuel (Ed.), *Minority aging* (pp. 123–131). Westport, CT: Greenwood Press.

Richardson, V., & Kilty, K. M. (1989). Retirement financial planning among Black professionals. *The Gerontologist, 29,* 32–37.

Riddick, C. C. (1985). Life satisfaction for older female homemakers, retirees, and workers. *Research on Aging, 7,* 383–393.

Riddick, C. C., & Stewart, D. G. (1994). An examination of the life satisfaction and importance of leisure in the lives of older female retirees: A comparison of Blacks to Whites. *Journal of Leisure Research, 26,* 75–87.

Ries, P., & Brown, S. (1991). *Disability and health: Characteristics of persons by limitation of activity and assessed health status, 1984–88.* Washington, DC: National Center for Health Statistics.

Rix, S. E. (1990). *Older workers.* Santa Barbara, CA: ABC-CLIO.

Roger, C. J., & Galleon, T. E. (1978). Characteristics of elderly Pueblo Indians in New Mexico. *The Gerontologist, 18,* 482–487.

Rosen, R. C., & Leiblum, S. R. (Eds.). (1991). *Erectile disorders: Diagnosis and treatment.* New York: Guilford Press.

Rosenblatt, P. C. (1988). Grief: The social context of private feelings. *Journal of Social Issues, 44,* 67–78.

Rothstein, F. R. (1988). *Commitment to an aging workforce: Strategies and models for helping older workers achieve full potential.* Washington, DC: National Council on Aging.

Rybarczyk, B. D. (1994). Diversity among American men: The impact of aging, ethnicity, and race. In C. T. Kilmartin (Ed.), *The masculine self* (pp. 113–131). New York: Macmillan.

Rybash, J. M., Roodin, P. A., & Santrock, J. W. (1991). *Adult development and aging* (2nd ed.). Dubuque, IA: William C. Brown.

Ryckman, R. M. (1996). *Theories of personality* (6th ed.). Pacific Grove, CA: Brooks/ Cole.

Saluter, A. (1991). *Marital status and living arrangements: March 1990* (Current Population Reports, U.S. Bureau of the Census Publication No. P-20-450). Washington, DC: U.S. Government Printing Office.

Sayles-Cross, S. (1990). Perspectives on the status of elder Blacks in America. *The ABNF Journal, 1*(1), 10–13.

Schaefer, R. T. (1990). *Racial and ethnic groups* (4th ed.). Glenview, IL: Scott, Foresman.

Seligman, M. E. P. (1994). *What you can change and what you can't: The complete guide to successful self-improvement.* New York: Alfred A. Knopf.

Senate Select Committee on Aging, U.S. House of Representatives. (1988). *Exploding the myths: Caregiving in America.* Washington, DC: U.S. Government Printing Office.

Shea, G. F. (1991). *Managing older employees.* San Francisco: Jossey-Bass.

Shomaker, D. (1981). Navajo nursing homes: Conflicts of philosophies. *Journal of Gerontological Nursing, 7,* 531–536.

Shomaker, D. (1990). Health care, cultural expectations, and frail elderly Navajo grandmothers. *Journal of Cross-Cultural Gerontology, 5,* 21–34.

Shuster, M. H., & Miller, C. S. (1981). Performance evaluations as evidence in ADEA cases. *Employee Relations Law Journal, 6,* 561–583.

Smith, H. (1991). *The world's religions* (2nd ed.). New York: Harper Collins.

Smith, J. I., & Haddad, Y. Y. (1981). *The Islamic understanding of death and resurrection.* Albany: State University of New York Press.

Snyder, B., & Keefe, K. (1985). The unmet needs of family caregivers for frail and disabled adults. *Social Work in Health Care, 10,* 1–14.

Social Security Administration. (1982). *Private pension coverage and vesting by race and Hispanic descent* (DHHS Staff Report No. 42). Washington, DC: U.S. Government Printing Office.

Soldo, B. J,. & Agree, E. M. (1988). America's elderly. *Population Bulletin, 43*(3).

Sorlie, P. D., Backlund, M. S., Johnson, N. J., & Rogat, F. (1993). Mortality by Hispanic status in the United States. *Journal of the American Medical Association, 270,* 2646–2668.

Sotomayer, M. (1971). Mexican American interaction with social systems. *Social Casework, 52,* 316–324.

Soumerai, S. B., & Avon, J. (1983). Perceived health, life satisfaction, and activity in urban elderly: A controlled study of the impact of part-time work. *Journal of Gerontology, 38,* 356–362.

Spector, R. E. (1991). *Cultural diversity in health and illness* (3rd ed.). Norwalk, CT: Appleton & Lange.

Spector, R. E. (1996). *Cultural diversity in health and illness* (4th ed.). Stamford, CT: Appleton & Lange.

Stanford, E. P. (1977). *Comprehensive service delivery systems for the minority aged.* San Diego, CA: University Center on Aging, San Diego State University.

Stanford, E. P., Happersett, C. J., Morton, D. J., Molgaard, C. A., & Peddecord, K. M. (1991). Early retirement and functional impairment from a multi-ethnic perspective. *Research on Aging, 13*, 5–38.

Stannard, D. E. (1977). *The Puritan way of death: A study in religion, culture, and social change.* New York: Oxford University Press.

Stoller, E. P., & Gibson, R. C. (1994). Introduction: Different worlds in aging: Gender, race, and class. In E. P. Stoller & R. C. Gibson (Eds.), *Worlds of difference: Inequality in the aging experience* (pp. xvii–xxviii). Thousand Oaks, CA: Pine Forge Press.

Stoller, E. P., & Gibson, R. C. (Eds.). (1994). *Worlds of difference: Inequality in the aging experience.* Thousand Oaks, CA: Pine Forge Press.

Stone, R., Cafferata, G. L., & Sangl, J. (1987). Caregivers of the frail elderly: A national profile. *The Gerontologist, 27*, 617–626.

Sue, D. W., & Sue, D. (1990). *Counseling the culturally different: Theory and practice* (2nd ed.). New York: Wiley.

Sue, S., McKinney, H., Allen, D., & Hall, J. (1974). Delivery of community mental health services to Black and White clients. *Journal of Consulting and Clinical Psychology, 42*, 794–801.

Sung, K. (1990). A new look at filial piety. *The Gerontologist, 30*, 610–617.

Szinovacz, M. (1989). Retirement, couples and household work. In S. J. Bahi & E. T. Peterson (Eds.), *Aging the family.* Lexington, MA: Lexington Books.

Taeuber, C. M. (1990). Diversity: The dramatic reality. In S. A. Bass, E. A. Kutza, & F. M. Torres-Gil (Eds.), *Diversity in aging* (pp. 1–45). Glenview, IL: Scott, Foresman.

Takaki, R. (1993). *A different mirror: A history of multicultural America.* Boston: Little, Brown.

Takeuchi, D. T., & Young, K. N. J. (1994). Overview of Asian and Pacific Islander Americans. In N. W. Zane, D. T. Takeuchi, & K. N. Y. Young (Eds.), *Confronting critical issues of Asian and Pacific Islander Americans* (pp. 3–21). Thousand Oaks, CA: Sage.

Tanjasiri, S. P., Wallace, S. P., & Shibata, K. (1995). Picture imperfect: Hidden problems among Asian Pacific Islander elderly. *The Gerontologist, 35*, 753–760.

Taussig, I. M., Henderson, V. W., & Mack, W. (1992). Spanish translation and validation of a neurophysical battery: Performance of Spanish- and English-speaking Alzheimer's disease patients and normal comparison subjects. In T. L. Brink (Ed.) *Hispanic aged mental health* (pp. 95–108). New York: Haworth Press.

Taylor, R. J. (1985). The extended family as a source of support to elderly Blacks. *The Gerontologist, 25*, 488–495.

Taylor, R. J. (1986). Religious participation among elderly Blacks. *The Gerontologist, 26*, 630–636.

Taylor, R. J. (1993). Religion and religious observances. In J. S. Jackson, L. M. Chatters, & R. J. Taylor (Eds.), *Aging in Black America* (pp. 101–123). Newbury Park, CA: Sage.

Taylor, R. J., & Chatters, L. M. (1986a). Church-based informal support among elderly Blacks. *The Gerontologist, 26,* 637–642.

Taylor, R. J., & Chatters, L. M. (1986b). Patterns of informal support to elderly Black adults: Family, friends, and church members. *Social Work, 31,* 432–438.

Taylor, R. J., & Chatters, L. M. (1991). Nonorganizational religious participation among elderly Black adults. *Journal of Gerontology, 46,* S103–S111.

Tennstedt, S. L., McKinlay, J. B., & Sullivan, L. M. (1989). Informal care for frail elders: The role of secondary caregivers. *The Gerontologist, 29,* 677–683.

Thibault, J. M., Ellor, J. W., & Netting, F. W. (1991). A conceptual framework for assessing the spiritual functioning and fulfillment of older adults in long-term care settings. *Journal of Religious Gerontology, 7,* 29–45.

Thomas, C., & Kelman, H. R. (1990). Gender and the use of health services among elderly persons. In M. G. Ory & H. R. Warner (Eds.), *Gender, health, and longevity: Multidisciplinary perspectives* (pp. 137–156). New York: Springer.

Thorson, J. A., & Powell, F. C. (1993). The rural aged, social value, and health care. In C. N. Bull (Ed.), *Aging in rural America* (pp. 134–145). Newbury Park, CA: Sage.

Thursby, G. R. (1992). Islamic, Hindu, and Buddhist conceptions of aging. In T. R. Cole, D. D. Van Tassel, & R. J. Kastenbaum (Eds.), *Handbook of the humanities and aging* (pp. 175–196). New York: Springer.

Tilak, S. (1989). *Religion and aging in the Indian tradition.* Albany: State University of New York Press.

Tobin, S. S., Ellor, J. W., & Anderson-Ray, S. M. (1986). *Enabling the elderly: Religious institutions within the community service system.* Albany: State University of New York Press.

Torres-Gil, F. M. (1984). Preretirement issues that affect minorities. In H. Dennis (Ed.), *Retirement preparation* (pp. 109–128). Lexington, MA: Lexington Books.

Torres-Gil, F. M., & Negm, M. (1980, March–April). Policy issues concerning the Hispanic elderly. *Aging,* pp. 2–5.

Tran, T. V. (1990). Language acculturation among older Vietnamese refugee adults. *The Gerontologist, 30,* 94–99.

Triandis, H. C. (1994). *Culture and social behavior.* New York: McGraw-Hill.

Trotter, R. (1985). Folk medicine in the Southwest. *Postgraduate Medicine, 78,* 167–179.

Truitner, K., & Truitner, N. (1993). Death and dying in Buddhism. In D. P. Irish, K. F. Lundquist, & V. J. Nelsen (Eds.), *Ethnic variations in dying, death, and grief: Diversity in universality* (pp. 125–136). Washington, DC: Taylor & Francis.

U.S. Bureau of the Census. (1992). *Current population survey.* Washington, DC: U.S. Department of Commerce, Bureau of the Census.

U.S. Bureau of the Census. (1993). *Census of the population, 1990: Social and economic characteristics* (CP-2-1). Washington, DC: U.S. Department of Commerce, Bureau of the Census.

U.S. Bureau of the Census. (1996). *Statistical abstract of the United States: 1996* (116th ed.). Washington, DC: Author.

U.S. Department of Labor. (1989, January). *Labor workers' problems of older women.* Washington, DC: U.S. Department of Labor.

U.S. Senate Special Committee on Aging. (1991). *Aging America: Trends and projections.* Washington, DC: Author.

Valle, R. (1989). Cultural and ethnic issues in Alzheimer's disease research. In L. Light & B. D. Lebowitz (Eds.), *Alzheimer's disease treatment and family stress: Directions for research* (pp. 122–154). Rockville, MD: National Institute of Mental Health.

Van Steenberg, C., Ansak, M. L., & Chin-Hansen, J. (1993). On Lok's model: Managed long-term care. In C. M. Barresi & D. E. Stull (Eds.), *Ethnic elderly & long-term care* (pp. 178–190). New York: Springer.

Verbrugge, L. M. (1983). Women and men: Mortality and health of older people. In M. W. Riley, B. B. Hess, & K. Bond (Eds.), *Aging in society: Selected reviews of recent research* (pp. 139–174). Hillsdale, NJ: Erlbaum.

Verbrugge, L. M. (1989). Gender, aging, and health. In K. S. Markides (Ed.), *Aging and health: Perspectives on gender, race, ethnicity, and class* (pp. 23–78). Newbury Park, CA: Sage.

Verbrugge, L. M. (1990). The twain meet: Empirical explanations of sex differences in health and morality. In M. G. Ory & H. R. Warner (Eds.), *Gender, health, and longevity: Multidisciplinary perspectives* (pp. 159–199). New York: Springer.

Verbrugge, L. M., & Wingard, D. (1986). Sex differentials in health and mortality. In A. Stromberg (Ed.), *Women, health, and medicine* (pp. 60–82). Palo Alto, CA: Mayfield.

Villa, R. F., & Jaime, A. (1993). La fe de la gente. In M. Sotomayor & A. Garcia (Eds.), *Elderly Latinos: Issues and solutions for the 21st century* (pp. 129–142). Washington, DC: National Hispanic Council on Aging.

Vissing, Y. M., Salloway, J. C., & Siress, D. L.(1994). Organization of Alzheimer's services for rural areas. *Educational Gerontology, 20*, 303–318.

Wallace, S. P., Snyder, J. L., Walker, G. K., & Ingman, S. R. (1992). Racial differences among users of long-term care: The case of adult day care. *Research on Aging, 14*, 471–495.

Walmsley, S. A., & Allington, R. L. (1982). Reading abilities of elderly persons in relation to the difficulty of essential documents. *The Gerontologist, 22*, 36–38.

Wang, C. (1988). Lear's magazine "For the woman who wasn't born yesterday": A critical review. *The Gerontologist, 28*, 600–601.

Watt, W. M. (1968). *What is Islam?* London: Longmans, Green.

Waugh, E. H., Abu-Laban, B., & Qureshi, R. B. (Eds.). (1983). *The Muslim community in North America.* Edmonton: University of Alberta Press.

Waxman, H. M., & Carner, E. A. (1984). Physician's recognition, diagnosis, and treatment of mental disorders in elderly medical patients. *The Gerontologist, 24*, 593–597.

Weaver, J. (1993). Native reformation in Indian country: Forging a relevant spiritual identity among Indian Christians. *Christianity and Crisis, 53*(2), 39–41.

Weeks, J. R., & Cuellar, J. B. (1981). The role of family members in the helping networks of older people. *The Gerontologist, 21*, 388–394.

Westermeyer, J. (1987). Clinical considerations in cross-cultural diagnosis. *Hospital and Community Psychiatry, 38*, 160–164.

Wiley, F. M. (1971). Attitudes towards aging and the aged among Black Americans: Some historical perspectives. *Aging and Human Development, 2*, 66–70.

Williams, G. C. (1980). Warrior no more. In C. L. Fry (Ed.), *Aging in culture and society* (pp. 101–111). New York: Bergen.

Williams, J. A. (Ed.). (1963). *Islam.* New York: Washington Square Press.

Williams, R. B. (1988). *Religions of immigrants from India and Pakistan: New threads in the American tapestry*. Cambridge, England: Cambridge University Press.

Woehrer, C. E. (1978). Cultural pluralism in American families: The influence of ethnicity on social aspects of aging. *The Family Coordinator, 27,* 329–339.

Wood, J. B., & Parham, I. A. (1990). Coping with perceived burden: Ethnic and cultural issues in Alzheimer's family caregiving. *Journal of Applied Gerontology, 9,* 325–339.

Wykle, M. L., & Kaskel, B. (1994). Increasing the longevity of minority older adults through improved health status. In *Minority elders: Five goals toward building a public policy base* (2nd ed., pp. 32–39). Washington, DC: Gerontological Society of America.

Yee, B. W. K.(1990). Gender and family issues in minority groups. *Generations, 14,* 30–42.

Yee, B. W. K. (1992). Elders in Southeast Asian refugee families. *Generations, 16*(3), 24–27.

Yee, B. W. K., & Nguyen, D. (1987). Correlates of drug abuse among Indochinese refugees: Mental health implications. *Journal of Psychoactive Drugs, 19,* 77–83.

Yeo, G. (1991). Ethnogeriatric education: Need and content. *Journal of Cross-Cultural Gerontology, 6,* 229–241.

Yeo, G. (1996). Background. In G. Yeo & D. Gallagher-Thompson (Eds.), *Ethnicity and the dementias* (pp. 3–7). Bristol, PA: Taylor & Francis.

Yeo, G., & Gallagher-Thompson, D. (Eds.). (1986). *Ethnicity and the dementias.* Washington, DC: Taylor & Francis.

Young, R. F., & Kahana, E. (1989). Specifying caregiver outcomes: Gender and relationship aspects of caregiving strain. *The Gerontologist, 29,* 660–666.

Younoszai, B. (1993). Mexican American perspectives related to death. In D. P. Irish, K. F. Lundquist, & V. J. Nelsen (Eds.), *Ethnic variations in dying, death, and grief: Diversity in universality* (pp. 67–78). Washington, DC: Taylor & Francis.

Yu, E. S. H. (1986). Health of the Chinese elderly in America. *Research on Aging, 8,* 84–109.

Yu, E. S. H., Kim, K., Liu, W. T., & Wong, S. C. (1993). Functional abilities of Chinese and Korean elders in congregate housing. In C. M. Barresi & D. E. Stull (Eds.), *Ethnic elderly and long-term care* (pp. 87–100). New York: Springer.

Yu, E. S. H., & Liu, W. T. (1992). US national health data on Asian Americans and Pacific Islanders. *American Journal of Public Health, 82,* 1645–1652.

Yu, E. S. H., & Liu, W. T. (1994). Methodological issues. In N. W. Zane, D. T. Takeuchi, & K. N. J. Young (Eds.), *Confronting critical health issues of Asian and Pacific Islander Americans* (pp. 22–50). Thousand Oaks, CA: Sage.

Zamanian, K., Thackery, M., Starrett, R. A., Brown, L. G., Lassman, D. K., & Banchard, A. (1992). Acculturation and depression in Mexican American elderly. In T. L. Brink (Ed.), *Hispanic aged mental health* (pp. 109–121). New York: Haworth Press.

Zarit, S. H., Todd, P. A., & Zarit, J. M. (1986). Subjective burden of husbands and wives as caregivers: A longitudinal study. *The Gerontologist, 26,* 260–266.

Zawadski, R., & Stuart, M. (1990). ADC growth uneven, but impressive. *NCOA Networks, 2*(9).

Zborowski, M. (1969). *People in pain.* San Francisco: Jossey-Bass.

Zsembik, B. A., & Singer, A. (1990). The problem of defining retirement among minorities: The Mexican Americans. *The Gerontologist, 30,* 749–757.

Appendix

LEARNING ACTIVITY EVALUATION FORM[1]

Please complete this evaluation form. Information received from your evaluation will assist in planning future learning activities. Your cooperation is appreciated.

Name of Activity:_____

1. To what extent do you feel that the learning increased your knowledge of diversity and aging? (Circle your response.)

A lot		Some		Not at all
5	4	3	2	1

2. How much time did it take you to complete the activity?

_____ hours   _____ minutes

3. How well did this activity meet the stated objectives?

All objectives were met		Fair		No objectives were met
5	4	3	2	1

4. Evaluate this activity as a learning experience.

Excellent		Fair		Poor
5	4	3	2	1

5. Please make any additional comments regarding the learning activity.

---

[1]Adapted from Fried, Van Booven, & MacQuarrie, 1993, p. 198.

Index